PENGUIN BO

OBSCURE KIN

Edward Fox was born in New York in 1958. He studied English at Cambridge and Middle Eastern Languages and Cultures at Columbia. He now lives in London, where he works as a freelance journalist. *Obscure Kingdoms* is his first book.

EDWARD FOX

OBSCURE KINGDOMS

JOURNEYS TO DISTANT ROYAL COURTS

PENGUIN BOOKS

PENGUIN BOOKS

Published by the Penguin Group
Penguin Books Ltd, 27 Wrights Lane, London W8 5TZ, England
Penguin Books USA Inc., 375 Hudson Street, New York, New York 10014, USA
Penguin Books Australia Ltd, Ringwood, Victoria, Australia
Penguin Books Canada Ltd, 10 Alcorn Avenue, Toronto, Ontario, Canada M4V 3B2
Penguin Books (NZ) Ltd, 182–190 Wairau Road, Auckland 10, New Zealand

Penguin Books Ltd, Registered Offices: Harmondsworth, Middlesex, England

First published by Hamish Hamilton 1993
Published in Penguin Books 1995
1 3 5 7 9 10 8 6 4 2

Printed in England by Clays Ltd, St Ives plc

To Phyllis

Contents

Illustrations

All the photographs were taken by the author with the exception of no. 10 which is © Lindley Wilson.

Acknowledgements

I HAVE MADE nothing up, except to change some names and some identifying details. For the chapter on Tonga I am grateful to Pilimilose, Alisi and Sione; and to Maggie Simmons, then at *Condé Nast's Traveler*, for an assignment which began the series of journeys that resulted in this book.

I would like to thank the following for their help in connection with the other chapters:

Oman: Brian Pridham, University of Exeter; Salim Tabook; John Peterson; Khalfan al-Barwani, Jumah al-Shidi and Saleh al-'Alawi at the Oman Centre for Traditional Music; Ken Brazier at the Oman Embassy in London; and the Omani Ministry of Information.

Nigeria: Dr John Peel and Akin Oyetade, School of Oriental and African Studies, London; Lucy Duran; Muraina Oyelami; Dr Karin Barber, University of Birmingham; Dr Peter Morton-Williams; John Lavers, Kano University; Dr Akin Euba, University of Bayreuth; Nasir Ado Bayero for an introduction to his father, the Emir; the late Susanne Cronjé; Lindley Wilson; Bade Ajuwon, and Bayo Ogundijo, Obafemi Awolowo University, Ifẹ̀.

Swaziland: James Dlamini; Vincent Sithole and R. L. Mamba of the University of Swaziland.

Java: Dr Ignatius Suharno, cultural attaché at the Embassy of the Republic of Indonesia, London; Dr Ben Arps, SOAS; Dr Damarjati Suparjar of Gadjah Madah University, Yogyakarta; Agustina Ismurjilah; and Ric Suhardi, the Sultan's private secretary.

I would also like to thank the literary agents who were involved in the selling of this book – Susan Schorr, Deborah Karl, Gillon Aitken and Anthony Harwood – and above all my editor and publisher Andrew Franklin at Hamish Hamilton for his confidence and patience in this project. Thanks also to Alan Ross, editor of *London Magazine*, and to the London Library. I would like to convey particular thanks to the numerous members of staff at SOAS whom I approached for advice on the cultures dealt with here. They were always generous with their time and knowledge.

Special love and blessings go to Gian Douglas Home and Tahar al-Haddadi, Phyllis Fox, James Fox, Genevieve Fox, Mrs Elisabeth Furse, Adam Gorb, Mike Hutchinson, Charlotte and Muir Mackean, Sally Mould, and Joanna Wade, particularly for their support during the prolonged final stages of the writing of this book.

I have quoted from the following: on p. 16, Samuel Beckett, *Imagination Dead Imagine*, London: Calder, 1966; on p. 19, John Martin, *Tonga Islands: Wil Mariner's Account*, London, 1817; on pp. 22 and 23, the *Tonga Government Gazette*; p. 35, verses from the Stuart court masque *Salmacida Spolia* (1640) by Sir William Davenant; on p. 53, Roy Strong, *Theatre of the Stuart Court*; throughout Chapter 2, official correspondence on Oman to be found in the India Office Library; on pp. 63 and 146–7, al-Maghili, *The Obligations of Princes*, tr. T. H. Baldwin, Beirut, 1932; on pp. 62 and 67, Nizam al-Mulk, *The Book of Government*, tr. Hubert Darke, London: Routledge, 1960; on p. 63, Fred Halliday, *Arabia without Sultans*, Harmondsworth: Penguin, 1979; on pp. 68 and 88, Kai Ka'us ibn Iskandar, *A Mirror for Princes, the Qabusnamah*, tr. Reuben Levy, London: Cresset, 1951; on p. 69, Ferdowsi, *The Epic of the Kings: The Shahnamah*, tr. Reuben Levy, London: Arcana, 1990; on p. 69, *Wisdom of Royal Glory ('Kutadqu Biliq'), A Turko-Islamic Mirror for Princes*, tr. Robert Dankoff, Chicago: University of Chicago Press, 1983; on pp. 69, 70 and 81, al-Ghazali, *Book of Counsel for Kings ('Nasihat al-Muluk')*, tr. F. R. C. Bagley, Oxford: Oxford University Press, 1964; on p. 75, the interview with Qaboos that appeared in *Leaders* magazine, Vol. 13, no. 4, Oct.–Dec. 1990; on p. 77, Carl Jung, *Mysterium Coniunctionis*, tr. R. F. C. Hull, London: Routledge, 1963; on p. 86, *Poems of al-Mutanabbi*, tr. A. J. Arberry, Cambridge: Cambridge University Press, 1967; on p. 89, Susanne Wenger,

The Sacred Groves of Oshogbo, Vienna: Kontrapunkt, 1990; on p. 88, Brian Masters, *Dreams about HM the Queen and Other Members of the Royal Family*, London: Blond & Briggs, 1972; on pp. 100 and 118, verses from Ulli Beier and Bakare Gbadamosi, *Yoruba Poetry*, Ibadan: Ministry of Education, 1959; on p. 104, R. L. Lander, *Records of Captain Clapperton's Last Expedition to Africa*, 2 vols., London, 1830, and Sir Alan Burns, *History of Nigeria*, London: George Allen & Unwin, 1972; on p. 131, Norbert Elias, *The Court Society*, New York: Pantheon, 1983; on pp. 131–2, Akin Euba, 'Music fit for kings: the traditional concept of kingship music in Africa', in *Essays on Music in Africa*, Vol. 1, Bayreuth: Iwalewahaus, 1988; on p. 142, Hugh Clapperton, *Journal of a Second Expedition into the Heart of Africa*, London, 1829; on p. 144, Heinrich Barth, *Barth's Travels in Nigeria*, ed. A. H. M. Kirk-Greene, London: Oxford University Press, 1962; on p. 158, J. S. M. Matsebula, *The King's Eye*, Cape Town: Maskew Miller Longman, 1983; on p. 202, Sir Thomas Stamford Raffles, *History of Java*, 1817, Vol. 2; on p. 210, K. P. H. Brongtodiningrat, *The Royal Palace (Karaton) of Yogyakarta, Its Architecture and Its Meaning*, Yogyakarta: Karaton Museum, 1975; on p. 214, Karlheinz Stockhausen, *Towards a Cosmic Music*, London: Element Books, 1989; and on p. 223, *The Glass Palace Chronicle of the Kings of Burma*, tr. Pe Maung Tin and G. H. Luce, Oxford: Oxford University Press, 1923.

INTRODUCTION:

A Lantern in the Palace Gate

AS FAR AS I am able to remember now, so long after I started working on it, the idea for this book came to me in a dream. It was the kind of dream the truly deluded would take for a vision: a message from God via one of His angels, or one of the other local deities to whom He franchises His divinity around the globe. Or rather the subject of the book that resulted from it is so tangled up in religious ideas that this is how it seems now, with corrupted hindsight.

In 1984 I was working as a reporter for a newspaper in Charleston, West Virginia, covering holy-roller churches and suburban municipalities. I had been there for two years and was by that time going crazy with boredom, and plotting means of escape. One night after work, while waiting for a colleague in the Windows on the River bar on the top floor of the Holiday Inn, with a large Irish whiskey already inside me, the two words of the title floated up into my conscious mind like soda-water bubbles rising upwards to the surface from an invisible point in the ice-cold, amber, spiritous depths of a highball glass. I would like to say that the Yoruba deity Eshu delivered them to me on a brass disc in letters of fire, giving me no other explanation or instruction other than to get on with it, for that is how it seems now. It was a miraculous gift: my way out of middle America, my ticket, my highway.

So I got on with it, even though at first I had nothing more than a title. What would appear between the covers of a book called *Obscure Kingdoms*? Why had I been summoned, so to speak, to write it? I was an American, middle-class, a political agnostic. What did I know, or care, about kings, or kingdoms, or kingship? The idea itself was a joke; it was a book that someone in a comic novel would be writing but never be able to finish. There was something impudent in yoking together beings who consider themselves solitary and splendid and incomparable, particularly under the epithet 'obscure'. It would also be impossible to write: I could never get access to my subjects.

I realize now that part of the reason for this strange commission lay in the fact that I had grown up in a country officially called the United Kingdom, although few people called it that. As an American, I found it a puzzling country. How could a Protestant, nominally democratic country be a monarchy whose head of state was also supreme religious leader? Until recently, public discussion about the monarchy amounted to the vulgar gossip of the tabloid newspapers, and a repertoire of saloon-bar clichés. For a central institution of English culture, there was something mute and dysfunctional about it: the paradoxes were all covered up. The Queen remained personally anonymous and absolutely remote, assiduously protected from the public gaze by a cordon of frosty courtiers. Her political and religious roles had withered in all but name. The meaning of kingship seemed to have been lost sight of. But what was that? What did kingship really mean? What were the assumptions the English seemed unable to articulate? Since kings existed everywhere, at all times in history, there must be some universal model or archetype to which one could look for an answer. This book is an attempt to report fleeting glimpses of that universal model, in a few of its infinite variety of forms.

I sought these forms in a diverse selection of places, countries not usually considered together, to witness kingship in a variety of guises. The approach I adopted was to aim to demolish all my familiar cultural reference points, to disorient myself completely in the world. I would stay long enough in a place for me to begin to feel that I would never leave (although my sojourns lasted only from six to ten weeks). I would not be a traveller, observing the landscape from the perspective of someone moving through it; I wanted to see how kingship looked from the perspective of the people who lived there. This programme of cultural disorientation involved avoiding reference to European kingdoms, though the presence of Louis XIV – whose reign, because of the wealth and talent at its disposal, seems to have employed every conceivable device in the elaboration of the idea of kingship – proved irresistible. In each place I visited, I would attempt to meet the king. In this I had varying degrees of success. In general, the more powerful a ruler was, the harder he was to meet. I had no special advantages for this undertaking. I would use the means of access available to ordinary subjects. I went both to places that were monarchies – where the institution of kingship formed the government of the state (Tonga, Oman and Swaziland) – and to republics (Nigeria and Indonesia) which contained living traditions of kingship.

Three related issues interested me. First, the relationship between power and display. Kingship depends on spectacle: royal power is guaranteed by ceremonial. Was this just mesmerizing propaganda, like Oz hiding behind a curtain of manipulative fakery, or dramatic ritual with real significance for its audience? Under this heading I also put traditions of remoteness and access, how a king hides and shows himself. On the one hand, a king must be distant from people to create a mystique around himself, to become personally invisible behind an awesome, marvellous, ubiquitous and all-powerful royal image (and to protect himself physically from his subjects). On the other hand, his subjects must have physical access to him, to establish a bond of trust between ruler and ruled, and to allow them to feast their eyes on him. Second, there was the religious dimension. The relationship between the ruler and the divine is always present in traditions of kingship, but is elaborated in a variety of ways. Somehow, the marvellous power of an individual has a link with the awesome power of God, or of the gods. Finally, I was interested in the literature of instruction for kings on the techniques of statecraft, the 'mirrors for princes', a genre of writing that many different cultures have produced, each in its own way. In these 'mirrors' are to be found the political concepts and terminology on which the kingdom is based.

I was so naïve! I thought I would explore kingdoms that were completely independent of European influence, historically and culturally. I knew nothing about indirect rule, the British imperial policy of governing through local traditional rulers – propping them up, even inventing them where necessary, and deploying the mystique of kingship as a strategy of imperial conquest. Again and again I found myself face to face with what I was fleeing: the hand of the British, recreating the empire in their own image. If it were not for British patronage, there would be no monarchies in Tonga, Oman or Swaziland, and the landscape of traditional rulers in Nigeria would be completely different. Even Java, which belonged to the Dutch empire until Indonesia's independence in 1945, was in the hands of the British long enough (1811–16) for them to leave their mark. Indeed, no sooner had I finished writing the first chapter than I was living in Britain again, the obvious base camp, and where all the imperial records were kept. It had drawn me back.

I was also interested in the historical question of how the world's remaining monarchies have managed to survive. Certainly, they are sinking beneath the topsoil of history. Either they are fortunate backwaters, and have survived because of their geographical remoteness and geopolitical insignificance, like Tonga and Bhutan, isolated, living relics of the British empire, or else, as in the case of oil-producing monarchies, prominently those in Arabia, they are being used as guarantors of political stability in a policy of indirect rule practised by the United States, the British empire's successor.

Kings have always depended for their political acceptance on an assumed link between temporal and divine power: that the king is God's junior cousin, with a strong family resemblance, and rules by His authority. The many complex myths and arguments that establish this relationship in most cultures are effective because of the link that already exists in the human mind. Kings and gods emanate from a common source: the sphere of power and fear.

This link with the divine, with its profound psychological resonance, lies at the centre of the cluster of cultural forms associated with kingship. In the first place, it causes kings to be associated with ideas of sacredness. Kings are either explicitly or implicitly sacred – meaning that they are venerated and set apart from the ordinary by virtue of a divine attribute. Sacredness comes to be attached to phenomena that we would call either marvellous or frightening, or that defy understanding, like lightning, meteorites, the sun, the moon, certain texts and numbers, works of visual art, mountains, groves, or people possessing extraordinary qualities, like lunatics, seers, twins, female hysterics, prophets and, because of their symbolic significance and because of the power they wield, kings.

But the difference between kings and gods is that a king is a living reflection of human preoccupations and a god is not. Kings represent the human self in an exalted state, in a state of the highest possible fulfilment, visibly triumphing over all the major mortal considerations: wealth, sex, power, beauty, esteem and the mystery of one's place in the cosmos. The archetype is an anthropomorphic deity. This aspect of the self lies potentially in everyone, but it is never given outward expression except by kings and manic psychotics. Even without state power, kings survive because they are actors playing this role for our benefit.

Originally, a king was an individual possessing supreme power in a society, gained by force of arms. The projection of the symbolism of kingship on to him by everyone else, the particular sacredness called charisma, came later: for power is the most sacred thing of all – it is frightening, marvellous, and defies understanding. Once given cultural expression, this aura of superhuman sacredness is then used by kings to legitimize their temporal power, and to subdue their subjects. It doesn't matter whether kings believe in it themselves.

The aesthetic effulgences of kingship – the diverse traditions of art, architecture, coinage, ceremonial, theatre, dance, panegyric, codes of speech and behaviour, and now television that cultures of kingship have devised – work in two ways: as expressions of profound psychological meaning for popular consumption and, consequently, as instruments of rule. The king's aura of sacredness is both reflected and created by these forms. Through them the sacredness of the king is formalized and institutionalized. They express and reinforce the king's sacredness, support his political position, and assert his power, by creating awe, wonder and ultimately acceptance in the minds of his subjects. All states guarantee their own power by sacralizing it in this way, through spectacle, pageantry and display.

As for 'obscure', this is intended in the *OED*'s sense 'of a place, not readily seen or discovered; hidden, retired, secret; remote from observation', or more precisely in the sense suggested in his book *Local Knowledge* by the anthropologist Clifford Geertz, who sought to show 'how the deeply different can be deeply known without becoming any less different; the enormously distant enormously close without becoming any less far away'. It is implicit in the title, I now see, that I acknowledge my position as a stranger in a lightweight suit, a professional white man, looking in at non-Western societies from the outside, immersing himself in them as deeply as possible, but always with a return air ticket in his pocket.

Each chapter is distinct in tone not only because of the intervals of time that separated the journeys (I visited Tonga in 1987, Oman once in 1989 and twice in 1990, Nigeria also in 1990, Swaziland and Java in 1991), but because each of these cultures is, in its own way, its own separate universe, with the king its radiant nucleus.

CHAPTER I

Distant Kingdom – Tonga

I HAD ONLY been in Tonga five days when I caught my first glimpse of the King. Tongatapu, the kingdom's main island, where the capital, Nuku'alofa, is located, is only thirty-five kilometres across. On an island this small, you would be bound to see him eventually. That's why I came: I wanted to start with a king I could *see*. It was Saturday, 26 September 1987, about eleven o'clock in the morning. The clouds described a rococo vision of infinity on the bright austral sky. The King's name was Taufa'ahau Tupou IV. His fame blazed like the sun.

I was riding a bicycle along the airport road into the town, through the flat, tame Tongan landscape of coconut palms and pawpaw trees, when I heard behind me a siren announcing the royal motorcade. A blue Toyota four-wheel-drive police car was moving slowly down the middle of the road, with its headlights shining. The traffic parted like the Red Sea before Moses. This vehicle was followed by two police motorcycles moving side by side, and a large red Jeep with the King inside. I saw him through the smoked-glass window: the King was alone in the back seat, sitting squarely in the middle, leaning forward attentively, willing the motorcade onward. He wore a dark-blue nylon jacket and a huge pair of ski goggles that covered half his face. Physically, he looked like a giant panda: cute, but formidable; benign, but frightening. Another police car brought up the rear.

The people stood still at the side of the road as the motorcade passed. I had read that it is customary to sit cross-legged on the ground when the King passes; I was surprised that no one was doing this. I dismounted my bicycle instead. A little flag, the royal standard, flew on the Jeep's prow. Nobody said anything. No one waved or saluted, but then no one minded either. They were used to him. After the motorcade had passed, normal traffic resumed.

Tonga is the last Polynesian monarchy. That's also why I came: to find out how it had survived, when all the historical odds were against it. The other monarchs of the South Seas all fell or were pushed from their perches at around the turn of the century. The reign of Queen Lili'uokalani of Hawaii was ended by American gunboats in 1893. The last king of Tahiti, Pomare V, a drunk, died in 1891. His tomb at Papeete is topped by a large Benedictine bottle carved in stone. Niue's last king fell off the branch in 1903. Only the Tongan throne has endured, in a kind of sleepy stability.

The Kingdom of Tonga demonstrates one of the first principles of survival for a non-European monarchy: it must be geographically remote. Where Bhutan, for instance, has its Himalayas to protect it, Tonga has its miles of ocean. The Tonga Islands are as far away from anywhere else as it is possible to be. Nuku'alofa is 1,800 kilometres north-east of New Zealand, 500 kilometres south of Apia, Western Samoa, 700 kilometres east of the main island of Fiji and 400 kilometres west of Niue.

It is also very small. Most of the kingdom's 153 islands are specks on the map one could walk across in a few hours. Only thirty-six of them are inhabited. The islands were created in a volcanic spurt, and lie within their vast rectangle of territorial ocean like paint thrown from a bucket, trembling on a seismic ridge, shaken by daily tremors. These three geographical factors have shaped Tongan culture and kingship: Tonga's remoteness, its compact land area, and its rich volcanic soil which makes possible an abundance of food. They have produced the precarious political micro-ecology in which this rarest of endangered species has survived.

That night we had clams for dinner. By 'we' I mean myself and Sione and Alisi Soakai, the parents of a university friend named Pilimilose. After years of fitful correspondence with Pilimilose, and transferring her address from one address book to the next, I finally was able to take up her invitation to visit her in Tonga. But by the time I got there she was in Fiji, studying still.

Pilimilose was the first Tongan to attend the University of Cambridge. It was generally and incorrectly believed that she was a princess of some sort, and Pilimilose herself did her best to live up to this reputation. She a flair for grand gestures, and would receive male callers in her bath, regal behaviour which recalled the royal levee. Her size, and her erect, dignified bearing, focused attention on her; when she walked down King's Parade it was like a royal progress. Once she invited me to a lunch party at her lodgings in a small terraced house in a grey, drizzly Cambridge street. She had created a Polynesian feast for about a dozen people in surroundings normally associated with baked beans and sausages. 'I'm sorry about the raw-fish salad,' she said. 'It's not usually made with salmon, but that's all they had in the market.' Rumour had it that she was engaged to the Crown Prince of Tonga, who had given her a Hermès scarf, and she would eventually become Queen. She says she rejected him. She never did any work and did rather badly in her exams, I recall.

I ended up staying with her parents for two months, sleeping in Pilimilose's bedroom. It was a sunny, white room with a pointed ceiling and windows on three sides, one of them facing the glittering blue void of the Pacific. Every day, when I awoke, my eye would alight on a postcard of the Statue of Liberty I had sent her from New York a year earlier, wedged into the frame of a mirror. Pilimilose never appeared the whole time I was there. The magazine that had given me a plane ticket and a contract to write about my reunion with an old friend in a distant kingdom never got its piece.

The household consisted of Sione, Alisi, Alisi's elderly mother, and a teenage boy named Kiosi. Kiosi was an example of the Tongan way of 'adopting' children, which as far as I could discern involved passing them between families in the most informal way, like long-term babysitting or an extended loan. Kiosi came from a large family in a village outside of town. Here he slept in a palm-branch *fale*, an impromptu thatched house, beside the main house. He spent a good proportion of his time helping Alisi with domestic chores. No one was sure how old he was, but he must have been about seventeen. He would go around the house hollering like an elephant or slurpily eating a mango, or leave the cassette-player in the kitchen blaring reggae all day, to the annoyance of Alisi's mother, who would scold him loudly in Tongan. One night Kiosi went to a dance, and on his return backed the Toyota pick-up into a fence. The next morning I heard violent slapping sounds outside, alternating with reproachful noises coming from Alisi. She was telling him off for his misdemeanour, and emphasizing her points by rhythmically slapping the large dollop of dough she was kneading, as if she would like to do the same to Kiosi.

The Soakai household was the ideal vantage point from which to view Tongan culture and kingship. From here – indeed from any household in Tonga – a thread of hierarchical relationships led to the king. It was a society of commoner, noble and king, in which everyone had a rank in relation to everyone else. Sione Soakai had been the head of the Tonga Copra Board; in his retirement he tended a bush farm. In the traditional order of Tongan society, Sione was a *matapule*, an attendant of a chief or king. The original Soakai had come from Fiji and had been appointed *matapule* to the ancient Tongan king, the Tui Tonga. No Tongan was (or indeed is) allowed to eat in the presence of the King, but Soakai was a foreigner (because he was from Fiji), so Soakai had the ancient, singular privilege of being allowed to eat with the Tui Tonga. Every night I ate dinner with the descendant of this original Soakai. His status in the Tongan hierarchy was defined in terms of his relationship to food and drink. Food was the Tongan sacrament and social cement.

And I have never eaten so well in my life. My diary records a fantasia of Polynesian plenty. At dinner on 22 September 1987, for example, 'The three of us polished off chicken in coconut cream, leftover roast suckling pig, a fish stew, mashed potato, bread, green salad.'

23 September: 'Dinner of octopus cooked in coconut, suckling pig, corned beef in something rather like spinach, yams, potatoes, taro, salad.'

25 September: 'Dinner consisted of mussels steamed in coconut, chicken, cassava and various other roots, passion fruit juice and Sara Lee frozen cake (!).'

Sunday, 27 September: 'Huge Tongan feast for lunch, including a suckling pig two feet long, yams, taro, chicken and potatoes, octopus, clams, corned beef, salad. Dessert was breadfruit in caramel sauce.'

In the *Tonga Chronicle* there was a picture of a yam that had won first prize at the Vava'u agricultural show. It was seven feet long and about a foot in diameter. Sione said, 'That yam would feed a whole *palangi* [European] battalion, or about ten Tongans.'

While Alisi was in the kitchen, Sione and I would sit at the table and every night we would take turns saying grace. The only one I knew was the Latin grace I had heard as an undergraduate, and imperfectly remembered: '*Oculi omnium aespiciunt et inte sperant Domine, quae ex laga liberalitate tua per Dominum nostrum Jesum Christum amen.*' I think Sione liked it. He said once, 'I recognized "Christum".' He would say grace in Tongan on the other nights, a pious murmur of airy syllables. We would lower our heads.

On the night we had clams – the night of the day I had had my first glimpse of the King – he said that the clams used to be bigger when he was a boy. They are dug from the beach on the Nuku'alofa seafront, and sold in the market. I took his remark as ruing the way Tonga's swelling population was burdening the natural plenty that had always made life in Tonga so easy, so Tongan. After dinner he took a nap in his recliner chair, which occupied the centre of the sitting-room. He prided himself on the fact that, like Churchill at the height of hostilities during the Second World War, he could take a nap anywhere, at any time – go to sleep instantly and sleep deeply for five minutes, and awake fully refreshed. I recall that he was wearing an orange knitted hat that evening.

It was an odd-shaped house, built by Sione himself, with a gabled corrugated-metal roof. Gutters led from the roof into round cement tanks to collect rainwater. Whenever I opened the screen door, or as I passed through the garden gate when I came in from outside, the sound would wake the three or four only partly domesticated dogs which were part of the household. They would run towards me, barking furiously and biting my ankles when they spotted a good chance. They obeyed Alisi, but no one else, because she would wave a stick at them.

The house was surrounded by brilliantly coloured flowering bushes, and was set in a garden with ducks and geese running about. Green and orange pawpaws hung in voluptuous drops from the trees. Nobody planted them, but there was always a ripe pawpaw when you wanted one. Behind the house, shaggy black pigs snuffled about in pens, and squealed away for shelter when approached. The garden gave way to bush at its fringes. There was a small cow in a patch of long grass, tethered to a stake. Lunch was everywhere. One of the problems the missionaries of the last century had in Tonga was convincing the Tongans of the value of the Protestant work ethic. Food was so abundant here, in the rich black soil of these volcanic islands, that little effort was needed to obtain it.

The King himself was a walking advertisement for the importance of food in Tongan culture. He was said to weigh somewhere in the region of three hundred pounds. Everybody knows this. But why does he weigh so much? The King weighs so much because he has eaten more than anyone else. He has eaten more than anyone else because he is King. It is a token of power. E. W. Gifford wrote in *Tongan Society* (Honolulu, 1929), 'The idea prevails that a chief is normally a large, portly person. On one occasion my interpreter remarked, "Can't you see he is a chief? See how big he is."'

The King would regularly display his kingly size by publicly trying to lose weight. Three afternoons a week he would put on his shorts and a T-shirt and ride a bicycle with a custom-made extra-wide seat several laps up and down the road between the palace and the royal burial-ground, a distance of about a kilometre. The police would close the roads that run across it, and as the traffic built up behind the traffic cones, and the crowd gathered, and the bare-legged tourists squinted into their cameras, an atmosphere of public gaiety and anticipation built up. A score of big lads from the armed forces would perform limbering-up exercises at the palace gate. Then the King would emerge on his bicycle down the royal driveway and on to the street. The King's escort would fall into place on either side of him, in a wing formation, and run alongside him while the King pedalled, demonstrating the continued vigour of the royal person.

There were easier ways to get exercise, of course, but that's not the point. Every time the King completed a lap, a soldier would ring a large brass bell on the palace wall, pealing a celebration of the triumph of fitness. By cycling between the palace and the royal burial-ground, the King was showing that he was that day's number of laps away from his last ride to the burial-ground himself. This lesson was all the more fruitful for the fact that the King is now over seventy-five and for many years after his accession was thought to be too overweight to last long in office. Sione told me that when the present King was Crown Prince and Agriculture Minister, and overeating, and his mother, Queen Salote, was trying to make him lose weight, he would summon Sione to the palace at around lunch-time on the pretext of urgent agricultural business, and the two of them would secretly polish off huge lunches of yam and suckling pig. (Once, later, when a doctor asked the King if he ate potatoes, he said, 'No, only yams.' 'How many per day?' 'Just two.' The doctor was surprised by this show of moderation. 'Well, stick to just two yams – no more.' He didn't know how big Tongan yams were.)

The royal exercising had become as famous a worldwide media spectacle as Queen Salote's choosing to ride in an open-topped carriage in the rain during Queen Elizabeth II's coronation in 1953 – on the grounds that Tongan etiquette required one to keep one's head uncovered in the presence of a superior.

This modern ritual of royalty is indirectly related to the taboo of the King's food. Tongan kingship developed out of chieftainship, warlordship: one didn't eat in front of the chief, presumably because one was afraid of him. If he wanted your food, he could take it. The King is the one who has visibly eaten the most. The taboo (a Tongan word) of the King's food arose as a formalization of that expression of fear.

Under the Tui Tonga, the ancient Tongan kings, all land and the food it produced belonged to the King. Through religious sanction, the King also received the 'first fruits': the first of any harvest of fish, pigs or fruit. People gave these things to the King because they were afraid of him and because of the bigger, invisible power he claimed as his ally. Any fish or pig over a certain size was also his as of right. There was even, in the lexicon of polite terms for anything pertaining to the royal person, a word for the Tui Tonga's hunger: *fietaumafa*.

It was believed that anyone who violated the taboo of the food of a king or a chief would come down with a sore throat, which could be cured only by the king or chief whose food-taboo had been violated stroking the violator's neck.

The same taboo can be seen behind Louis XIV's custom of eating alone at a raised table while his nobles stood below him, watching him eat. Louis XIV's *fietaumafa* was not like his subjects' hunger: it was an exalted, awesome, formalized devouring.

Captain Cook, who made three visits to the Tonga islands, in 1773, 1774 and 1777, saw this taboo as a kind of economic policy, as it meant that the King could control commerce in food. In July 1777 he wrote in his journal,

> Taboo as I have before observed is a word of an extensive signification; Human Sacrifices are called Tangata Taboo, and when any thing is forbid to be eaten, or made use of they say such a thing is Taboo; they tell us that if the King should happen to go into a house belonging to a subject, that house would be Taboo and never more be inhabited by the owner; so that where ever he travels there are houses for his reception; indeed none of them at no time make free with each others habitations. Old Toobough [a chief] was at this time over [in charge of] the Taboo . . . [He] and his deputies inspected into all the produce of the earth, saw that every man cultivated and planted his quota; ordered what should be eat and what should not. By this wise regulation, they effectually guard against a famine, in seeing that a sufficient quantity of ground is planted, ordering such articles for food as are in the greatest plenty, and prohibiting such as are scarce or not arrived at their full grouth.

Sione arranged for me to meet the Princess Pilolevu, the King's daughter. He said I should bring her a present of some sort. He suggested chocolate, then apples. I went to the market with Alisi and bought a crate of Australian apples for T$47.50. One hundred and ten large red apples, to satisfy the Princess's *fietaumafa*.

The appointment was for two o'clock. Sione came back from the farm at noon, and by half past one was dressed in formal Tongan attire (a *vala*, or skirt, with a *taovala*, a mat tied over it with bright rope). We rehearsed how he would introduce me, and he said he would leave after that. Everything had to be done correctly: Sione was very anxious about that.

The Princess's house was on the road that stretched the length of the Nuku'alofa waterfront. When we reached the house (like something you would find at St Leonard's-on-Sea, with plastic planters shaped like swans on the lawn) we drove in the back way, and Sione and I entered the back door and left the apples on the kitchen table. He said it was the custom to give presents very humbly, but you must bring a present when you visit a royal. Then we walked in through the front door, across a terrace covered in green Astroturf.

Pilolevu was sitting on a long sofa. She was tall, fair-skinned, quite big, and wore a black-and-white patterned dress and a red necklace and earrings. Sione introduced me to the Princess in Tongan in a clenched and self-abasing way, in a choked, cringing voice, and then took our picture: me sitting leaning tensely forward on a chair, Pilolevu on a sofa, beside a bright yellow cushion shaped like a banana. Both of the shoes I was wearing had been chewed by the Soakais' half-wild dogs.

After Sione had left, I asked the Princess for her views on tourism in Tonga. She thought it was Tonga's great hope for the future. She was organizing the cleaning-up of the beer cans on the seafront, and raising money to build a sports stadium. She did a lot of speech-making and ribbon-cutting: she was an active royal, after the British pattern.

I quickly ran out of things to say. There was a silence.

'What are you interested in, actually?' she said. I stammered out something about how I was hoping to interview the King. She gave me a puzzled look.

As I was leaving, she said, 'If you need any help getting to see my father, let me know.' The interview was not exactly a success, but at least I had received a sign of royal favour.

That night, after dinner, Sione asked me to give him an account of my interview with Pilolevu. Robed in his dressing-gown, he retired to his recliner, invited me to pour myself a whisky, and cut his toenails with a pair of clippers while I spoke.

At the conclusion of my summary, I asked him what the name Pilolevu meant.

'Big Pillow, I think,' he said.

'Why is she called that?'

'You'd better ask her husband.'

Sione was making a transcultural joke. In fact, Pilolevu means Big Cup.

The days passed. Tonga made only the gentlest imprint on the senses: just 'islands, waters, azure, verdure', and little work. In the mornings I would lie in bed and listen to the dawn chorus. As I lay half-asleep, it assumed colours and shapes: blue squeaks and mauve corkscrews and brown honks and fluttering yellow tweets and sawtoothed arpeggios. After lunch, I would take a siesta. Sometimes I would listen to the local radio station, A3Z:

Exports of bananas from Vava'u have declined for the third year running, according to the Department of Agriculture. Speaking in Vava'u Friday, the Director of Agriculture said farmers there should increase banana production.

Tonga's Minister of Education is attending a workshop seminar in Sydney. He is expected to return to Tonga early next week.

International news: In the Solomon Islands, a gift of 200 bicycles and 100 tricycles has been received from the People's Republic of China. The bicycles arrived in kit form. Assembly of the shipment is expected to be completed at the end of this week.

One of my first tasks on arrival in Tonga had been to buy a bicycle. There was an Indian shop in the town centre that sold them. The shop had a creaky wooden floor and was very dark inside, crammed with goods and crowded with people. The only type of bicycle available was the 'Phoenix' brand, made in the People's Republic of China to a design that looked as if it predated the Long March. The Phoenix came in two indistinguishable colours: black and dark green. It had no gears, old-fashioned brakes involving a precarious system of articulated rods and clamps, a wide leather saddle stuffed with horsehair, with springs like a Victorian sofa, decals depicting fierce dragons of undulating serpentine form and stylized floral motifs, and a huge bell that could have woken up a whole rural cooperative. It weighed a ton and cost 160 pa'anga. After it was assembled, I did as the law required and took it to the police station to be registered. A three-digit number was applied to the rear mudguard by a police officer using a pot of red paint and a matchstick that he took from a box in his pocket.

It was about 3 per cent faster than walking. The next day, some distance from Nuku'alofa, the left pedal drooped and I had to push it home. Within a few days the seat began to come loose, and to wobble on two axes, and later the right-hand brake failed, and had to be repaired with a paper-clip. Pedalling was a Sisyphean labour. In this way I passed through all the villages of Tongatapu.

Most of the time I was travelling along a straight, flat road through bush: dense palm forest intercropped with yams, pawpaws, and banana and mango trees. There are no wild animals in Tonga, apart from bats, birds and small creeping things. Land that isn't used for agriculture has a village on it: there is no wilderness. Tonga is a bonsai kingdom on a table-top. Land is scarce and population dense; the government used to give a plot of land to young men on reaching the age of sixteen, but there's no more land to give away now, and too many young men. Crimson blooms blazed in small plots outside small, neat houses. Children would stand in the doorways and stare in curiosity as I passed and shout, 'Where are you going?' Every village had a kiosk-sized general store and a church of some sort. The older churches, of white weatherboard with red corrugated roofs, were Church of Tonga or one of its Methodist offshoots; the new ones, uniformly built of brown blocks, with a basketball court at the side, were Mormon. The Mormons had spent millions of dollars building a church in nearly every village in Tonga – nearly sixty, often to serve a population of no more than a dozen people.

Going downhill (and there were precious few hills on this very flat island), the Chinese bicycle barely coasted. It was on one of these strenuous tours I caught my first sight of the King.

In other cultures, kingship depends for its effectiveness on a strict and parsimonious economy in the doling out of glimpses of the royal person. We are allowed – indeed encouraged – to feast our eyes on the king from time to time, but not too often. Louis XIV wrote in his memoirs, 'The majesty of kings largely consists in not allowing themselves to be seen.' This was impossible in Tonga. The islands were too small for the King to hold himself aloof and apart. Versailles, with its long vistas and symmetries focusing on the King's chambers, symbolizing and demonstrating royal power, would cover the whole of Nuku'alofa. Tongatapu was so small and densely populated that, according to tradition, one could communicate from one end of the island to the other by calling from one farm to the next, a practice called *fanongonongo tokoto* ('making proclamation while reclining').

Yet the King was still King, and had to be treated as such. His majesty had to be constructed by means other than triumphal art and architecture or regulated, idealized glimpses of the royal person. In modern Tonga, pictures and statues of the King are rarely seen. There is a large bronze statue of the King at the airport at Tongatapu, in military uniform, but it was a gift from the Mormons. Early Tongan kingship was constructed through religion, cosmology, language and the customs of taboo, not through visual art or literature. Taboo was both the ideology and the protocol of establishing distance between the King and his subjects. It established him as a kind of supernatural being, different from everyone else.

Taboo seems to arise out of a fear of assassination. If you have won power by force, you are always afraid of its being used against you. So spatial relations involving the King and his subjects are strictly regulated. The Tui Tonga had a custom of striking the knees of *matapules* who came too close. A curse would fall on anyone who touched the King. Nothing could be above the King's head, where he couldn't see it.

These social relations were guaranteed and reflected by language. The Tongan language reflects Tongan society's strict sense of social hierarchy in the use of different words for things pertaining to people of different status: the King's hunger, for example, as opposed to a chief's or a commoner's. Taboo includes the language of respect, and what we would call manners. (There was no such ritual distance between the ancient Vietnamese kings and the people, it seems: the latter could search themselves for body lice in his presence.)

Tongan kingship was also constructed through religion. Pre-Christian Tonga was, like Christian Tonga, a social order cemented by religion. The pre-Christian Tongan religion kept the King and his chiefs on top by means of an eschatology that offered them a kind of Polynesian paradise, and commoners the prospect of rotting like tree-trunks into the earth, body and soul. (The Tongan historian Sione Latukefu adds the qualification, 'though some commoners doubted this'.) The head of this spiritual hierarchy (which by the dawn of Christianity had split from the hierarchy of temporal power) was the Tui Tonga, a chief descended from the gods who created the world.

The chiefs' spirits went to an island west of Tongatapu called Polutu, where all beings were immortal.

> This island is supposed to be much larger than all their own islands put together, to be well stocked with all kinds of useful and ornamental plants, always in a state of high perfection, and always bearing the richest fruits and the most beautiful flowers . . . [When] these fruits or flowers are plucked, others immediately occupy their place, and . . . the whole atmosphere is filled with the most delightful fragrance that the imagination can conceive. The island is also well stocked with beautiful birds of all imaginable kinds, as well as with abundance of hogs, all of which are immortal, unless they are killed to provide food for the hotooas or gods; but the moment a hog or bird is killed, another living hog or bird immediately comes into existence to supply its place . . .

This is according to Wil Mariner, an English seaman who was captured by Tongan warriors on Vava'u in 1806 and for four years lived in Tonga as the military adviser to the Chief of Vava'u, Finau. His experiences were compiled by Dr John Martin in a book which was a best-seller in England when it appeared in 1817. Mariner witnessed the twilight of the gods in Tonga, the last days before the islands were Christianized by Wesleyan missionaries of the London Missionary Society.

The Christianization of Tonga coincided with its unification under the rule of one chief, Taufa'ahau, who eventually became the first King in the western sense. The slow and dogged progress of little groups of Wesleyan missionaries, who at first were scarcely literate enthusiasts, took place at a time when war among the islands was a way of life for young men. It was a destructive social problem that had got out of control, like duelling in eighteenth-century Europe, or drug gangs in American cities. It began when Tongan youths started travelling to Fiji by canoe for excitement. Inspired by the example of Fiji's warring tribes, they came back with an appetite for violence, and practised cannibalism in the flush of victory. From their point of view, the missionaries were only of interest for the manufactured goods they traded for food.

Perhaps because of this unstable situation, Christianity was accepted voluntarily. It represented a social and supernatural order that wasn't stacked against everyone except the chiefs. It promised more than a life that was cheap (if mercifully short), followed by the prospect of a meaningless void as one's reward for a lifetime of suffering. Tongans accepted Christianity out of a real spiritual taste for it. The missionaries also introduced effective medical care and the miracle of written language.

The great leap forward happened when Taufa'ahau, the Chief of Ha'apai, the island group immediately north of Tongatapu, transferred his backing from the old gods to God. It was obvious the old gods were out of their depth when literacy and steel weapons were needed. To Taufa'ahau, Christianity was a source of superior power. In a climate of endless warfare, it was a force he could use to fulfil his kingly ambition to prevail over everyone else. Like Taufa'ahau himself, Christianity challenged, and sought to overthrow, the status quo. The people Taufa'ahau conquered were not only required to acknowledge his sovereignty, they had also to adopt Christianity. He burned down the huts in which the old gods were kept. He desecrated a sacred hut on Vava'u by showing the people that what they had worshipped as a god up to then, protected behind a veil of mystery and taboo, was just a sea shell wrapped in layers of cloth. To test the Christian God's effectiveness, he threw the Tongan missionary who was instructing him overboard to retrieve a lost spear while on a canoe voyage, reasoning that if God were real He would save both the missionary's life and the spear. Unable to resist a rare, humorous wink at history, God saw to it that the missionary made it ashore alive, with the spear.

Once converted, the Tongans made Progress in the classic eighteenth-century sense. Guided by the missionaries, they abandoned Idleness and Fornication, and began to wear clothes. (The latter custom is tersely enshrined in the Tongan constitution: 'All Tongans shall clothe.') They went to church on Sunday, which was observed as a day of rest, and wrote Polynesian–Wesleyan-style hymns and read the Bible in Tongan. Taufa'ahau took the name George, after the King of England.

King George I, surnamed Tupou, ruled from 1845 to 1893. His temporal authority was secured by the moral legitimacy of religious leadership, a union of cross and crown: *Dieu et mon droit* – God and [hence] my right [to rule].

The Kingdom of Tonga was never conquered or colonized. King George realized that the only way for Tonga to preserve its independence would be for it to develop the forms of statehood which an imperial power could easily recognize as 'civilized' – that is, that resembled its own: a homoeopathic repellent. In 1876, a year after it adopted a constitution, Tonga negotiated a treaty with imperial Germany, followed by similar ones with Great Britain, two years later, and in 1888 with the United States. It owes its survival as an independent state in large part to this history of treaty relationships.

On the advice of the Wesleyan missionaries, George introduced a constitution that established legal rights and the rule of law, a judicial system, a parliament and an established church (Methodist, of course). No imperial power could now be tempted to conquer Tonga by the desire to conduct a civilizing mission. This assimilation of Western trappings and institutions proceeded from the King's belief that 'if there be anything in foreign lands, which will be useful to us, it is right for us to desire to get it, but it is also right if there is any Tongan custom which is useful, for us to preserve it.' Among the things from foreign lands he felt it appropriate to have were a crown, a throne, a royal palace, a coat of arms, a flag and a national anthem. He gave the most important chiefs the title 'Baron'. Tonga convincingly *looked* like a nineteenth-century European monarchy.

Also among the measures which King George introduced was a law (still in force) forbidding the sale of Tongan land to foreigners. He closed an early speech to parliament with a statement of policy that rings with the force of a nationalist slogan: 'Tonga for Tonga.'

Guiding George Tupou I during this formative period was an English clergyman named Shirley Baker, who came to Tonga as a Methodist missionary and became the King's close political adviser and then Prime Minister. The two worked together to make Tonga into a credible state, until Baker – who had severed his connection with the Methodist conference by then, and was leading a campaign to establish an independent Tongan Church – was forced out of the kingdom by the British. This happened at a time when something like civil war had broken out in Tonga between members of the contending Churches.

King George's speeches (as rendered into English in the official record) show a graceful style of English much influenced by the language of the King James Bible. This is the beginning of his speech at the opening of the Legislative Assembly (parliament) in 1880. It is a lament on the death of his only son, David:

The first thing I shall refer to is the calamity which has fallen upon our land to the man – David. You know he went to New Zealand with Mr Baker, to seek health, but the Lord has been pleased that he should die in the land of the stranger. Truly, this is a heavy blow which has fallen upon my house; but, nevertheless, the Lord reigns, and it is with him what shall happen, and His will has been done. But it is for me to say, 'Lord, Thy will be done,' for Jehovah has taken away, but blessed be the name of Jehovah.

But I stand here today to thank Mr Baker for what he has accomplished, in bringing David to be buried in the land of his ancestors. Thanks to Mr Baker and his love, and I am also truly grateful to the Captain of the German man-of-war and the Emperor of Germany, because of David being brought in the German vessel of war, and also for the respect which was shewn to him – a proof of our being a nation.

David – Tevita in its Tonganized form – was buried on the island of 'Uiha in Ha'apai, the group of islands north of Tongatapu. The circumstances of his death and repatriation are recorded in Tongan on his gravestone.

On the occasion of Tonga's signing a treaty with Great Britain, in 1878, the King told the assembled nobles of the realm, 'Great Britain has acknowledged us as a kingdom. I have requested Sir Arthur Gordon [the British governor of Fiji] to take my words and thanks to Queen Victoria, in that she has been graciously pleased to ratify the said treaty, and also because of the love she has manifested to myself and my land which is the least among the kingdoms of the world.'

These constitutional institutions and trappings did not, however, ensure that the Tongans were competent to manage their own internal affairs after the death of George, especially as these affected British interests within the country. In 1901, during the reign of George Tupou II (the only weak link in the Tupou chain), Tonga was forced to become a British 'protected state', with a resident minister who controlled its foreign affairs and advised on financial matters. This situation lasted until Tonga rejoined 'the comity of nations' in 1970 as a genuinely independent state.

Still, it never became a colony. Full independence was restored during the reign of the present King, who acceded in 1965 on the death of his mother, the famous and popular Queen Salote Tupou III.

Negotiating Tonga's return to full independence was King Taufa'ahau Tupou IV's first significant political accomplishment. Since then, the king has built on this with a policy of cultivating diplomatic relations with the 'great powers', in the way established by his great-great-great-grandfather, George Tupou I.

For example, in 1975, while Crown Prince Tupouto'a, the King's eldest son and the heir to the throne, was the Tongan High Commissioner in London, he began to talk to Soviet representatives about establishing diplomatic relations between the Soviet Union and Tonga. In the spring of the following year, the King revealed that the Tongan government had been talking to Soviet diplomats in the Pacific about long-hankered-for development projects, particularly an international airport. The public alarm among God-fearing Tongans was such that by August the King felt the need to go on the radio and invoke the venerated name of George Tupou I to assure the people that a treaty with the Russians would conform to old-fashioned Tongan diplomatic practice: 'Tonga is not entering into negotiations with the Soviet Union in a change of policy, but in a continuation of the policy adopted in the days of King George Tupou I, i.e. to create friendly relations with all countries of the world, particularly the major powers.'

The negotiations never got very far, probably because of public opinion. Later that year, the King took advantage of the fortuitous expiration of the 1876 treaty with Germany to rekindle relations with the Germans instead. At the closing of the Legislative Assembly, the King announced a German undertaking to help build the international airport. The Soviet promises were allowed to fade into the background and were never mentioned again. In April 1987 the Federal Republic of Germany came through with a grant worth T$10 million. King Tupou is the last of the great nineteenth-century statesmen.

The royal palace was a modest white mansion with a pointed red roof, surrounded by a deep porch. Alisi said it would be more accurately described as a 'royal residence' than as a palace. A lawn led down to the rocky seafront. A rickety wooden chapel stood beside it, held together with scaffolding, a victim of Hurricane Isaac, which tore through the islands in 1982. In a circular flower-bed there was a stone statue of an angel in flight, straining toward the kind of heaven anticipated by nineteenth-century English missionaries. A soldier in a white uniform stood in a sentry-box by the main gate, looking miserably bored. The palace and grounds were surrounded by a low wall that kept in the royal chickens and geese.

Access to the palace was arranged at the palace office, which was next door. This was a whitewashed wooden bungalow with a porch and a large sign on the roof saying PALACE OFFICE in foot-high capitals.

One of the principal techniques for establishing distance between a king and his subjects is to make people wait. Except in Tonga. I found this when I approached the palace office to request an audience – or rather an interview – with the King. The deputy private secretary opened the engagement book, nodded, and pencilled me in for an appointment later the same week. 'You will receive a telephone call this afternoon to confirm,' he said. The call promptly came after lunch.

The King is the exemplar of Tongan civilization, Tonga's culture hero, the kingpin. Politically, his position is secure because he is not only King but has also held all the top government jobs, including Prime Minister and Foreign Minister, and has more innate political talent than anyone else in Tonga. As King, he makes all cabinet appointments. If he vetoes a bill passed by the Legislative Assembly, it stays vetoed. He writes his own speeches for the ceremonial opening and closing of the Assembly, setting and commenting on its legislative programme. Nothing would happen in Tonga unless the King made it happen.

He is the first Tongan to hold a university degree. He devised a standardized Tongan orthography, which is now universally used. He is also a scientist. He proposed a solution to the mystery of the Ha'amonga trilithon, Tonga's Stonehenge – an ancient structure of two upright coral slabs supporting a horizontal slab in eastern Tongatapu. He theorized that it was used for astronomical observations for navigation, because of a notch in it that lets a ray of light through on the longest and the shortest days of the year. And no one has disagreed with him. It was previously thought to be the gateway to a royal compound. *Tupou as athlete*: he also holds the national pole-vault record. *Tupou as inventor*: he devised a goalpost which can be used for both soccer and rugby. It too has been universally adopted in Tonga. *As agriculturalist*: he experiments with new strains of food crops, and has a small flock of sheep – the only sheep in Tonga – which he grazes on the grass of the royal burial-ground.

But the forces of discord are swirling around the base of the throne. Tonga's problem is that the King is the only political figure of any calibre, and the nobility are reactionary and corrupt. According to Tonga's original constitution of 1860, they hold the majority of seats in the Legislative Assembly. A minority is held by elected 'people's representatives', who are younger and much better educated than the nobles. These younger politicians are agitating for reform, and challenging the old order of Tongan society in which the majority obey their superiors without question. The new representatives are powerless to do anything except make noise. Change depends on the mind of the King, but the mind of a king is necessarily a universe in itself, a sphere of untrammelled, unpredictable, pure human will. Tupou's mind especially.

That mind works in isolation because it has no peer. It is free of constraints, and is subject to whims and enthusiasms, which he can indulge because he is King. For example, he recently considered buying 30 million cast-off tyres from Washington State to burn them as fuel for electricity production, at a cost of $25 million. He suggested draining the freshwater lake in the middle of the remote island of Niuafo'ou and turning it into a huge reservoir for crude oil for use by Japanese tankers. He insists there is oil in Tonga itself, and has drilled for oil in Tongan waters every year since the 1973 oil crisis, without success.

The royal mind is innocent. 'He doesn't think anyone is going to tell him lies,' a resident diplomat told me in a tone of exasperated disbelief. This means that he too often listens to carpetbagger entrepreneurs and religious fruitcakes.

On the morning of my interview, I appeared at the palace office half an hour early. Mercifully, the waiting-room or antechamber contained several edifying curios to study while I waited to be admitted to the Presence. There was a fragment of moonrock mounted on a plaque bearing the engraved signature of President Richard Nixon. Beside it was a photograph of the King and Queen in extra-large Japanese kimonos. There was a model of an old TWA airliner on a stand, and bookcases full of dusty volumes of Tongan law.

An aide-de-camp appeared, in a uniform so brilliantly white in the blazing Pacific sun it was hard to look at him. He led me across the lawn and into the room in which the interview would take place. It used to be the Privy Council chamber. There was an electric fan and a map of the world, and a large boardroom table with a huge chair at the head of it bearing the royal crest. A large bust of Bismarck stood on a sideboard, under portraits of three of the King's predecessors, King George Tupou I, King George Tupou II and Queen Salote Tupou III.

At eleven exactly the ADC gave me the signal to stand up. An inner door swung open and Tupou emerged.

He wore a white Mao-style tunic and a large *taovala*, and walked with the aid of an aluminium walking-stick. He sat himself in the big chair with the royal crest.

I recalled reading Saint-Simon's account of an audience with Louis XIV. The Duke was afraid for his position at court, having been excluded from certain royal excursions, and he sought the audience as a last chance (as he saw it) to restore himself to the King's favour. A silence or a frown on the King's part could be a fatal sign, so Saint-Simon carefully scrutinized the King's mask-like expression for glinting expressions of favour or displeasure and recorded Louis's every response. 'I thanked him as I approached for the favour he was so good as to grant me, and I prolonged my compliment a little, in order to better observe his air and his attention; the first seemed to me stern, the second complete.'

Tupou seemed loftily indifferent to my presence, like a giant Polynesian idol made of stone, before which one trembled in atavistic fear. I had brought him a present, and offered it to him, like a propitiation. It was a book by Tip O'Neill, the former Speaker of the US House of Representatives. I thought something on American politics would be suitable. (I had tried to get him a letter from Mayor Ed Koch of New York, but Koch's press office had said, 'He don't do dat. Nice try.' The New York Jets only gave signed footballs to terminally ill children.) The King took the book, saying nothing. His hand covered it, but he did not even look at it. Traditionally, the King does not acknowledge presents. He owns everything already.

It is something of a shock to find oneself face to face with a king for the first time. My overwhelming impression was one of embarrassment. Possibly this embarrassment arose from a feeling that there was something improper in interviewing a king. I wasn't interested in knowing what he was like beneath the surface, which is what interviews are intended to discover: I wanted to know what he was like on the surface. Moreover, I had not come before him in any of the constraints of rank in which Tongans would come before him. I was bound by no taboos. I could ask him whatever I wanted. Even the prospect of this seemed improper. But, unlike anyone else in the Tongan hierarchy, the King has a Western politician's grasp of the importance of publicity. Because he's King, he is confident that people are interested in anything he cares to say, however delphic. He freely *vouchsafed* his perceptions – something only a king can do – speaking from the realm of pure kingly will and intelligence, not acknowledging my presence at all.

I began by asking him about the white plaster bust of Bismarck that glowered down from the sideboard. The King's voice was deep, booming and adenoidal. He spoke with an aloof self-absorption, like a child playing alone in a room full of splendid toys. The interview veered wildly from one subject to the next under my terrified direction (I think this approach pleased him), beginning with a long, strangely rambling discussion of nineteenth-century European history. He is the only person in Tonga who has been able to cultivate such a range of interests.

'Well, first of all, that bust was presented to me by the German magazine *Bunte*,' the King began. 'And in 1876, when Bismarck was Chancellor, the German empire under Wilhelm I and Tonga signed a treaty of friendship, which became 100 years old in 1976, and we renewed it with the Federal Republic . . . We also had an old treaty of friendship with France – Napoleon III – and Queen Victoria too. And in 1888 Tonga signed a treaty of friendship with the United States which is becoming 100 years old next year.

'Bismarck,' he went on, 'united Germany under Prussian leadership. And my ancestor united Tonga also under one administration, under one constitution. Our constitution was [adopted] in 1875, but Germany has had many changes. Because, whereas we are an archipelago in the middle of the Pacific, Germany was surrounded by big powers, so sometimes she lived with them in peace, sometimes in war, and that made a difference to her history, of course. Bismarck fought three wars: one against the Danes, one against the Austrians, and one against France.'

I observed that A. J. P. Taylor, in his biography of Bismarck, had suggested that Bismarck was responsible for the idea of European nation-states within fixed boundaries.

'Yes, yes. Well, you see, his policy was to safeguard the empire he created. And in order to do that he created a triple alliance with Austria and Russia. ["The secret of politics? Make a good treaty with Russia." – Bismarck.] The mistake his successors made was to allow Russia to grow. They retained the Austrian connection but they allowed the Russian treaty to lapse. When that happened, of course, France started courting Russia, and after that Russia became the ally of France. France was looking forward to a time when she might recover Alsace and Lorraine, and she hoped that by making Germany fight on two fronts Germany would ultimately be defeated. In the meantime, of course, she made the Entente Cordiale with Great Britain, which caused the confrontation between the Central Powers and the Allies.'

'As soon as he died, the kind of peace that he managed to broker died with him, it seems,' I said.

'The policy was a good long-term policy for Germany,' the King replied. 'But his successors were not as able. They only spoke German. He spoke English, French and Russian as well, so he understood Europe and the position of Germany in Europe. But his successors wanted to use the military might of Germany to threaten others, but they didn't understand that this military might carried a sense of responsibility. He was a good European. The others were simply Prussians or Germans!'

The giant, mirthful King laughed at the mistakes of history: a hearty, booming laugh. I had never heard laughter so loud, or so triumphant.

While he was talking, a servant had brought in glasses of passion-fruit juice on a tray. I hadn't touched the drink up to that point, observing the taboo about not eating or drinking in front of the King. 'Have a cold drink, before it gets warm,' the King said, and then began to drink himself. 'Good health.'

I drank.

I said that I had been interested in an article in the *Tonga Chronicle* describing how he had demonstrated 'the King of Tonga's addition method' to a group of visiting Christian businessmen. It was another of his scientific hobbies. 'Can you tell me something about that, Your Majesty – how that works?' I said, obsequiously.

He bellowed to the ADC to bring him his king-sized abacus. It was set beside him, and he began to push the beads around the wooden frame while explaining what he was doing.

'I've been doing some research on the origin of numerals, and how they came from India to Arabia to Europe, and I made some interesting discoveries – namely, that the idea of the abacus based on the ten, or tens as a base, probably originated in Egypt.'

'Oh, really?'

'Yes. And this knowledge was carried to India. The Indians invented the shape of the numbers. This instrument is a teaching abacus from Russia, where they use the abacus as much as China or Japan. And I discovered that the rules for using Arabic numerals that had been brought to Europe by the Arabs departed from the way the abacus operates and made the rules more complicated than they need to be. Whereas if we study the abacus again as a teaching tool the rules would be simplified. Watch carefully, then I'll tell you something about it. One, two – see, these are visual, instead of being abstract – three, four. When it's ten, of course, you transfer it to the next column . . . So, if you give me a piece of paper and a pencil, I can show you how it works.'

He took my notebook and pen and jotted down a column of numbers. His breathing grew heavy as he concentrated on the task.

3
9·
6
5·
7·
8
2.
1
8
<u>49</u>

'Three and nine is twelve, you see. Now I go to the base ten. So I put a little dot. That's ten, just carry the one, the two. That's twelve. Ten, take two. Eight, thirteen; I've gone over the base again, so that's the three, make ten, and nine. So there are nine units and one, two, three, four tens. See how simple that is?'

'I can't say I followed it, Your Majesty.'

He went over it again for my benefit.

'Eight and two make ten, and then one is nine. So you put the nine as the units over the multiples of ten and count the dots up – one, two, three, four. There are four tens, makes forty-nine. See?'

'Oh, I see. Yes, I see.'

'See? Very simple.'

He said that 'the King of Tonga's addition method' was already in use in Tongan primary schools and that he had demonstrated it on New Zealand television. 'I'm going to write a book about it. And there's a Swedish manufacturer who's going to arrange to have small models made in Hong Kong and made up into a little package, just a little model, for the child. Each child will have a little model, and a book of explanations. And we hope to produce some larger models like that for teachers . . . The number of primary-school children in the world must be several billion. So there's a huge big market for something that's easier, and will help them.'

I then asked him about various European royals, to gauge his sense of his position in comparison to theirs, to see if, as an absolute monarch, he might feel any pity or condescension towards constitutional monarchs, whose power has been reined in by history. 'They are monarchs in abstraction,' he said smugly. But Prince Charles, he allowed, was 'a very open-hearted young man'. He was amused to recall the fact that for the Prince's wedding in 1981 an American had given him a condominium apartment building in Florida as a wedding-present.

'At least he's not as frustrated as King Edward VII, because he was a grandfather by the time he became King,' the King said. 'In fact, he said something quite humorous. He said, "All Christians have an eternal father. I'm the only one who has an eternal mother!"' He boomed with laughter again.

I asked him about King Juan Carlos of Spain, surely a different sort of European ruler – one with real power. In an oblique, courtierish way, I was hoping to prise out of the King an insight into the mysteries of power; but all he talked about was toys. 'King Juan Carlos gave me a Spanish guitar when I was in Madrid last time. I went there to buy an aeroplane for the local service, and I had lunch with him and Queen Sophia. He's also a very nice young man.' He smiled a huge smile.

I wasn't really sure where the conversation was going. I asked him about his visits to the United States, and the topic turned to shopping, then to cars. We were on firmer ground here.

'I buy exercise benches and barbells, generally from Sears Roebuck. I buy bicycles. It's interesting generally to go shopping in the United States. It's a big industrial country – there's nothing you can't buy.'

'That's for sure.'

'I have a lot of American cars.'

'Yes, I've seen one – a black Lincoln.'

'No, that's a stretched Pontiac. It was taken from Detroit up to Toronto, and was stretched in Canada. I also have a Mercedes 600. I'm trying to sell it back to the factory and get another stretch car. I don't know yet if it will be a Mercedes. If it's a Mercedes, it will be right-hand-drive and kept in London, for when I go there, or some other car. But I've got to sell this other Mercedes first. It's just a question of arranging it, because the factory buys them back for several times their original price, and they overhaul them and hire them to the federal government for carrying VIPs. I have friends who are arranging this with the factory in Stuttgart.'

He also has a friend at the US Department of Agriculture who sends him seeds for his various agricultural projects.

The King was in a very talkative mood: to my amazement, we had talked for nearly an hour and a half.

Finally, I asked if I could take some photographs. As I snapped away, he told me about a yacht that was in Tonga for a few days. It was called *Sea Cloud*.

'She was built by Mrs Merriweather Post. I read in an article that she was the daughter of a millionaire, the widow of a millionaire and the wife of a millionaire.' He laughed at this. Being King made him an honorary member of the fraternity of millionaires.

'When she died, it was sold by the estate to the King of Sweden. He sold it to the dictator Trujillo. Then it was taken over by the navy in World War Two, then sold to a German company and refitted out as a sailing-ship, and that's what it is now. It takes selected wealthy people around the world. I went on board for a short while. I sat and talked to a friend of mine who was a passenger, and my son went all over the ship. He's a naval officer; he's interested in sailing-ships. He was trained in the British navy, then in the New Zealand navy, and he did some courses with the US navy in San Diego.'

'Your Majesty, I'm going to shoot this picture. All right?'

'Right.'

'Thank you. I'd like to take one more of you standing there in the doorway.'

'I see, that's all right.'

It was very odd to be directing the monarch to move now here, now there. I took one picture of him standing on the porch, pointing out to sea with his aluminium walking-stick.

Saint-Simon judged his audience a success. He wrote in his journal, 'What I said was received with a readiness that surprised me, and showed plainly that I was restored in his mind . . . He waited a moment to see if I had anything more to say, and then he rose from the table.'

At the end of my audience with Taufa'ahau Tupou IV, the King said, 'Fine, wonderful. Goodbye,' and shuffled back into the palace. My position was secure.

★

It was the day of the opening of Tonga's first brewery, an event of great national significance. The beer was called 'Royal Beer', and bore a portrait of an obscure nineteenth-century Tongan prince on the label. A king's portrait on a beer bottle would have been taboo, but the royal aura sold beer. The beauty of having a brewery in Tonga was that the beer could be sold in bottles with a returnable deposit, and replace Foster's Lager and Victoria Bitter, imported foreign brews whose empty, discarded no-deposit cans were overwhelming the islands. The King was to attend the official opening.

A canopy of palm branches had been erected outside the plant, and an enormous armchair – very deep and comfortable-looking – was set in the centre of it. The guests were a mixture of resident *palangis* – Europeans – in suits and dresses and Tongans in *taovala* and *vala*. They sat on folding chairs under another, larger, canopy, facing the King's tent. The Tonga Police Band played Western pop tunes as the dignitaries arrived. These included the resident diplomats, the visiting Swedish Ambassador, whose country helped set up the brewery, and the brewery's directors, including Crown Prince Tupouto'a.

The King's motorcade approached; the royal standard was run up the flagpole and the band played the national anthem. The King's usual manner on ceremonial occasions is to plod through them like any job of work. He got out of his car, and walked slowly to his chair, supporting himself on an aluminium walking-stick. The short distance between the car and the chair he was to sit in was covered with a path of *tapa* cloth, as was the route he later took through the brewery itself. He wore a grey Mao-style tunic, and a grey *vala* with a large *taovala* over it. He wore dark glasses, and directed his glance grumpily downward as he walked, like an old man in England going to the corner shop for a packet of cigarette papers. He sat back in the deep chair and let the proceedings start, as if completely uninvolved with them, gazing straight ahead through his huge dark glasses, frowning. There was great beauty in this composure.

The Revd Bishop Fine T. Halapau, representing the Established Church, the Church of Tonga, led the opening prayers, which were followed by a reading in Tongan from the Gospel of St Mark (7: 14–16).

And when he had called all the people unto him, he said unto them, Hearken unto me every one of you, and understand: There is nothing from without a man, that entering into him can defile him [i.e. beer]: but the things which come out of him, those are they that defile the man. If any man have ears to hear, let him hear.

The Church having spoken, it was now the State's turn. The King stood up and breathed heavily and slowly into the microphone a few times, creating an effect of tension and anticipation (as well as the fear that he was having an asthma attack), preparing listeners for important words.

His speech was quite lively. The Tongans in the audience fell about laughing. None of the jokes were reported that week in the *Tonga Chronicle*, but he was at least reported to have said that he would continue to drink the low-alcohol beer he usually drank, despite the opening of the brewery, and would consider drinking the local brew if they made a low-alcohol variety.

It may seem odd that, at the opening of a plant that would reduce Tonga's foreign-exchange expenditure by meeting the country's unslakable demand for beer with a local product instead of beer imported from Australia, provide at least a few jobs, and wipe out the epidemic of beer-can litter by the use of returnable bottles, the King should say that he doesn't intend to drink the stuff himself, but such is the charm both of the Tongan sense of propriety and of the King's sense of humour.

Political theatre is a product of the Europeanized, Christianized era of kingship in Tonga. The argument (as put in one of the court masques presented to Charles I in his last stormy days on the throne) of the piece I was to witness was approximately as follows:

Discord, a malicious fury, appears in a storm, and by the invocation of malignant spirits, proper to her evil use, having already put most of the world into disorder, endeavours to disturb these parts, envying the blessings and tranquillity we have long enjoyed.

FURY

Blow winds! and from the troubled womb of earth,
Where you receive your undiscover'd birth,
Break out in wild disorders, till you make
Atlas [i.e. Tupou] beneath his shaking load to shake.
How am I griev'd, the world should everywhere
Be vext into a storm, save only here?
Thou over-lucky too much happy isle,
Grow more desirous of this flatt'ring style!

The setting of the drama was the Tongan parliament, the Legislative Assembly. Attending the proceedings of this body was far more difficult than interviewing the King. Its name in Tongan is *Fale Alea*, which means 'talking-house'.

The reason for my difficulty in gaining admittance was that a serious political conflict was in progress within it. The last elections had brought in a group of new members who were young and Western-educated and pressing for change against an unelected aristocratic old guard who formed the majority and liked things the way they were. The new wave represented a challenge to traditional authority in Tonga. They were a faction, pushing for reform, and what amounted to the nearest thing Tonga had yet seen to a political party. The 1987 elections had opened a new era in Tongan politics.

Pilimilose, incidentally, had played an early role as the herald and forerunner of this movement some years earlier. She was an intellectually precocious schoolgirl, and had graduated from high school at the age of fifteen. The same year, she won a public-speaking competition with an address entitled 'Is Tonga democratic?' Her verdict was that, no, Tonga was not democratic. No estate of the realm was spared her criticism: commoners, nobles, King – all were to blame for Tonga's lack of democracy. The speech was printed in the *Tonga Chronicle*, and it caused a scandal. Questions were asked in parliament. One minister stood up and said, 'I shall ask the Minister for Police to investigate these foreign influences in our country.' The only casualty of the incident was the editor of the paper, who was forced to resign. Pilimilose, for a while, was the best-known schoolgirl in the

Pacific; her picture appeared in newspapers all over the region.

Architecturally, the *Fale Alea* looks like a chaste white Methodist church transposed from Appalachia to the tropics, a modest wooden building surrounded by a neat floral border of flame-coloured blooms. The administrative office is in a kiosk beside it. It has a traditional Tongan shape, rounded at the ends, with a red roof shaped like an inverted boat. I applied here for permission to attend the Assembly as a spectator. The *Fale Alea* is not a parliament on the Westminster model; its proceedings are not open to the public. I encountered a grave official countenance, creased and furrowed with the familiar, timeless bureaucratic negative.

My efforts lasted several days. Sione wrote a letter on my behalf. Finally, the clerk handed me a letter in a small brown envelope. It was from the Speaker, and had been written on an old manual typewriter.

'What does it say?' I said.

'It says, "No,"' said the clerk, with a sly smile.

This is the text of the letter from the Speaker of the Legislative Assembly turning down my request to attend the proceedings of the Assembly, addressed to Sione:

Tangata'eiki,

'Oku ou faka'apa'apa mo fakaha atu, kuo ma'u 'a ho'o tohi 'o fekau 'aki mo ho8o kole ngofa ke hu mai 'a ho8o motu'a ko Edward Fox ki fale alea.

Kuou ma'u ha tu'utu'uni'ae Tama Palemia 'oku 'ikai totonu ke hu mai ha toko taha fai nusipepa kihe fale alea.

Kataki Sione, 'o Fakahoko lelei atu kihe motu'a, 'ae 'uhinga 'oku 'ikai tali ai ke hu.

Faka'apa'apa atu,

Here it was signed with a scribble, accompanied by a rubber stamp in purple bearing various state symbols encircled by the words LEGISLATIVE ASSEMBLY OF TONGA. I could make out the word '*nusipepa*' – 'newspaper' – in the letter which seemed to mean that the Speaker thought I represented a newspaper. I didn't.

Sione thought it was the silliest thing he'd ever seen. He said he'd see what he could do.

A few nights later I went with him to a reception given by the Ambassador of the Republic of China (Taiwan) in the garden of the main hotel in Nuku'alofa, the International Dateline Hotel.

The garden was illuminated with strings of coloured lights. None of the other resident diplomats was present, as none of them recognizes the Republic of China (Taiwan), even though its Ambassador was dean of the diplomatic corps in Nuku'alofa. The Ambassador wore a white dinner-jacket and greeted everyone effusively with outstretched arms as they arrived. He would grab each guest and hold him, or her, in place while his son took a photograph, as evidence of continuing Sino-Tongan relationships.

After the reception, Sione took me to a kava club patronized by the Hon. Baron Tuita, the Deputy and Acting Prime Minister. The actual Prime Minister, the King's younger brother Tuipelehake, was too ill to serve.

We left our shoes at the door and entered a small room with mats on the floor and framed sepia-toned photographs of ancient Tongan rugby clubs on the walls. In the middle of the floor was a wide wooden bowl full of kava. Around it, cross-legged, sat a group of men. We joined them, and Sione paid our fee, a few pa'anga notes which the treasurer put into an old metal box on the floor beside him. Cups (halved coconut shells) were filled and passed around to us. Kava is made from a pounded root mixed with water, and has a bitter, muddy taste. It numbs and soothes the nervous system but has no effect on the brain.

After we had drunk two cups, on Sione's cue we made our excuses and passed into the next room, where the Hon. Baron Tuita was sitting.

He wore a Hawaiian shirt, a *vala* and sheepskin slippers. His scalp was bald, and he had the familiar Tongan rugby-player physique and an air of compressed force. He radiated authority and lofty dignity. He held a huge fly-swatter shaped like the ace of spades. Every now and then he would violently slash the air with it to drive away a mosquito. Here in this private room, he had his own kava bowl, and a couple of elderly gentlemen to prepare the drink and serve it to him.

He and Sione spoke quietly. Sione was tense: he wrung his

hands. Finally the Deputy Prime Minister nodded, and turned to me. 'You have been in Fiji, I'm told?' he said suavely.

I said I had, on my way to Tonga. There had lately been a military coup in Fiji. Colonel Sitiveni Rabuka, in the name of indigenous Fijian nationalism, had overthrown the democratically elected government, which contained a narrow majority of Fijian Indians, and had promoted himself Brigadier in the process. Everyone in Tonga quietly sympathized with the Fijian action. Even the King had said as much.

'What was your impression of the situation in the country?' Baron Tuita asked.

I told him that I had seen soldiers at roadblocks in the vicinity of the international airport, but that was all.

Baron Tuita sniffed and grimaced. He seemed satisfied by the answer.

Sione then introduced the subject which was the purpose of our visit. He uttered a long monologue, very deferential and respectful in tone, apparently pertaining to my desire to witness the proceedings of the Assembly. The Baron nodded gravely. 'Be at the Legislative Assembly at ten o'clock Monday morning,' he said to me. Then he talked to Sione about farming. We paid our respects and left, our mission accomplished.

At ten o'clock on Monday morning an old blue Rover pulled up outside the Legislative Assembly, and from it stepped the Hon. Baron Tuita. I was waiting in the office outside the building. He carried a slim folder. As he ascended the three wooden steps to enter the chamber, I stepped forward.

'Oh yes. It's you,' he said in his sombre, sober baritone. He uttered a few terse commands in Tongan to a sergeant at arms – a giant in *vala* and black tailcoat – ordering him to admit me to the chamber and look after me while I was inside.

The sergeant at arms and I sat together at the back of the room. Now and then he would whisper a highly simplified translation of what was being discussed.

The chamber was dark and cool inside, lit by stained-glass windows and ventilated by open doors at each side. Framed photographs of past parliaments hung on the dark wooden walls.

The room had a clubby atmosphere, with a table in the shape of a horseshoe at which the members sat on armchairs covered in red velvet. The Speaker sat on a raised chair under a huge red and white Tongan cross.

The week's business began with fifteen minutes of prayers and hymns, sung *a cappella* in beautiful lilting Polynesian harmonies that filled the high-ceilinged chamber with angelic sound. When the roll was called, each member made a low bow from the waist toward the Speaker's chair.

The tone of the discussion appeared correspondingly well-mannered: Westminster-style heckling and the hurly-burly of the dispatch-box are not Tongan style. The first item of business was a discussion of how to prevent an invasion of Indian businessmen into Tonga in the aftermath of the Fiji coup. There was an element of xenophobia in Tongan nationalism.

They also discussed a bill that would allow the police to make arrests on Sundays. It was defeated.

The twenty-eight-member Legislative Assembly consists of ten cabinet members appointed by the King, nine nobles' representatives selected by the thirty-three nobles of the kingdom, and nine popular representatives elected by universal adult suffrage. These 'commoners' representatives' can speak but not vote on bills. In 1987, four new people's representatives were elected who had degrees from Western universities, bringing the total of university-educated popular representatives to six. Two of these new members sued incumbent members for extravagant misuse of government money. The representatives had used thousands of pa'anga to hold public meetings to explain a new sales tax. The meetings cost as much to hold as the tax would have brought in. At one point, these representatives were earning salaries larger than those earned by members of the US House of Representatives. The action was not entirely successful (one of the suits was thrown out by the Tongan High Court), but it was a turning-point because Tongan politics up to then had been distinguished by a tendency not to question authority. The young Turks also waged their campaign through revelations of corruption in a new independent weekly newspaper, *Kele'a*.

The King has always defended the right of Tongans to debate issues more openly than is natural for most of his subjects. But when one of these new firebrands unsportingly introduced a motion to impeach the Finance Minister while the Minister was out of the country, the King closed the session early, before the motion could come to the floor.

The closing of the Assembly, although precipitated in tense political circumstances, had a D'Oyly Carte atmosphere of stiff gaiety. All the estates of the realm turned out in their finery: the English judge in red robe and white wig; resident diplomats in white tie, tails and top hats; the Tongan nobles and notables in *vala*, *taovala* and black tailcoat. Everyone arrived in order of precedence. The pews filled up, and the ladies cooled themselves with palm-leaf fans as they waited for the King to arrive. A red carpet had been spread out from the kerb to the door of the Assembly building, and on each side of it children in white sat cross-legged on the ground. Behind them stood robust police-women, also in white. Military and police bands marched and played. The excitement was all in the waiting, the build-up.

At last there was a twenty-one-gun salute from the cannons pointing out to sea by the palace, and the King's long, black, open-topped Mercedes limousine pulled up to the door. He wore a white military tunic sagging with medals, with a sword at his hip, which got stuck in the car door. He yanked it free. With his usual grumpy look, he stomped up the red carpet and into the chamber. At the door, he held out his peaked cap. No one was there to take it, and he waved it with mock (or real) impatience from side to side until he was finally relieved of it. Then he stomped down the aisle to the throne, where he sat to read his speech. A very elaborate crown sat on a purple velvet cushion on a little wooden table on his right. He made his usual introductory huffs and puffs into the microphone, then the speech lasted about fifteen minutes, delivered rapidly in Tongan in a low, monotonous murmur. Then he marched back down the aisle and rode back to the palace, about a hundred yards away.

The geographical remoteness which has been the key to the

survival of the Tongan monarchy has also been one of Tonga's greatest liabilities. The idea of remote islands has an irresistible attraction for the Western imagination. Strangely, they are associated with freedom: they are places where the human imagination is paradoxically seen as completely liberated, as with Prospero and his desert-island books in *The Tempest*, or more specifically Gonzalo, with his prescription for a desert-island nation of dreamy idleness:

> All things in common nature should produce
> Without sweat or endeavour: treason, felony,
> Sword, pike, knife, gun, or need of any engine,
> Would I not have; but nature should bring forth,
> Of its own kind, all foison, all abundance,
> To feed my innocent people.

Swords, pikes, knives and guns were what Tongans wanted more than anything else in their first encounter with the European. Tonga has a problem with 'Anglonesian' adventurers of this disposition, who stay beyond the time allowed on their visas, who fall dramatically in love with the islands and the people, and who seek to show their love through highly delusive schemes of little benefit to the Tongan economy. A conspicuous example of this tendency was Mike Oliver.

The newspapers called him a 'right-wing millionaire'. Seeking an antidote to the social evils he saw in the United States – 'crippling taxes, riots, crime and drug addicts' – he sought to create a tax-free offshore utopia in the South Pacific. After a 'worldwide search', in January 1972 he settled on Minerva Reef, at the tentative edge of Tongan territorial waters. His idea was to claim it and declare it the sovereign territory of the Republic of Minerva. He and his associates sailed there and raised the flag of the republic, depicting a conch shell and a torch of liberty. He announced that he planned to build a condo paradise on the reef for himself and other millionaires with a similar political outlook.

Most of the time the reef is under water – it is not really a place at all. Building on it required a dredging operation of phenomenal cost. Oliver told the *Fiji Times* in February, 'The problem is that they [the dredging companies] do not want to start work until the end of March. It is now the hurricane season and they have difficulty getting insurance cover.'

Undaunted, Oliver wrote to 'every country in the world' asking for recognition of the republic.

On 3 February the *Tonga Chronicle* reported, 'Tonga will not recognize any claims to Minerva Reef, a government spokesman said this week, commenting on a claim for recognition by an international group and the setting up of a "Republic of Minerva" on the reefs. The government spokesman said that although the Kingdom had not made any formal declaration about the reefs, they were usually associated with Tonga.' As evidence of this association, it cited the episode, six years earlier, in which a Tongan yacht crew had spent 102 days on the reefs and had raised the Tongan flag there in memory of a lost crew member, though this was not 'a formal declaration of sovereignty'.

Eventually the Tongan navy, three ships strong, was dispatched to remove the troublemaker. Oliver reappeared in Vanuatu, where in 1983 he supported a rebellion against the government of Prime Minister Walter Lini. His plan was to create a 'free enterprise state on [the island of] Santo devoted to his ideal of totally unstructured *laissez-faire* capitalism'. He gave the rest of his fortune to opposition parties to support his project, and when his money ran out so did his influence. He vanished into obscurity.

Tonga abounds in stories that reflect the great universal theme of the desert-island idyll. A good one was told to me one night by Peter Warner, an Australian who runs a shipping business in Tonga. The story is really about how he came to start his business in Tonga in the first place.

One day in the summer of 1965, six boys from St Andrew's College in Tonga, a boarding-school, set out on a fishing trip, using a twelve-foot boat they had borrowed without the permission of its owner. The boys were from Ha'apai, where the people have a reputation as good fishermen. That night, while they were asleep in the boat, a storm blew up; the anchor broke, and the boat was carried far out to sea. When they woke up, they had no idea where they were. A gale was blowing, and the boat was taking on water. They were lost and about to capsize; they began to bail frantically to keep the vessel afloat, while the wind continued to carry them in an unknown direction. They drifted for eight days, bailing constantly, without any sight of land. Back in Tonga, they were given up for lost, and the search for them was called off.

After drifting for eight days, they sighted an island. As the boat fell apart around them, they used its boards as rafts and swam towards it. They swam for a day and a night, and at dawn they were washed up, exhausted, on to the island's rocky beach. Although they didn't know it, they had landed on 'Ata, the southernmost island of the Tonga group, a steep-sided mountain rising out of the sea, three miles from end to end. The island had been uninhabited since George Tupou I had evacuated its hundred or so residents in 1860, to protect them from Peruvian slave-traders.

For three months the boys stayed where they had landed, at the base of the island, on a shelf of jagged volcanic basalt. They slept in caves at night, and drank rainwater from rock pools. They caught sea birds and drank their blood, and ate shellfish. When they were strong enough, they climbed to the top of the island.

There they found traces of previous habitation. Taro and bananas that the earlier inhabitants had cultivated were growing wild and had spread in chaotic profusion among the tangled vegetation. Skinny wild chickens were running about, descendants of the domesticated chickens that had been kept a hundred years earlier. The boys didn't starve. They built huts to sleep in, with bedding made of woven banana leaves, set up pens for chickens, and brought the food crops under control in garden plots. On walks around the island they found two knives and some pieces of iron. By sharpening them on the rocks, they made the points of spears for fishing. After they had seen to the necessaries, they built a badminton court.

A routine developed. They would get up at dawn, say prayers together, and work in their gardens until noon. Then they would have their main meal of the day, invariably consisting of chicken or fish. In the afternoon they would either continue gardening or go down to the sea to fish or to gather shellfish from the rock pools. In the evening they would have a singsong. One of the boys made a guitar out of halved coconut shells with some pieces of wire he had found as strings. He composed five original songs in Tongan. After further prayers for their rescue, they would sleep.

Two mounds of firewood were maintained, ready to be lit as bonfires to signal to any passing boat or aeroplane.

The boys ranged in age from fifteen to eighteen. The two oldest became the leaders. One of the two assumed leadership in practical matters – he later became an engineer. The other one, who told Bible stories and led the prayers, was the spiritual leader – he later became an alcoholic. Whenever the two of them had an argument over something, one or the other would go off into the bush on his own for a day or so, and when he returned the group would carry on as before.

This is how they lived for a year and a quarter.

One day Peter Warner was passing through the area in his boat, looking for lobsters. Warner's boat was only the third the boys had seen since they had been on the island. The previous day the Australian cruise ship *Canberra* had passed, and the boys had lit one of the bonfires to signal to it, but it had continued on its way. Peter Warner thought the evidence of fire – a brown scar on the greenery, as seen through binoculars – on an island known to be uninhabited was rather mysterious, so he decided to go over and have a look.

As he approached the island, he saw a brown figure scrambling down the rocks. The boy was completely naked (as their clothes had all rotted), and his hair grew in a wild bush around his head. He dived into the sea and swam vigorously out to the boat. As he climbed over the side, and was pulled on board by members of the crew, he said, in perfect English, 'I am one of six castaways. I estimate we have been on this island for eighteen months.' Amazed, Warner asked the boy his name and the names of the other castaways. He radioed to Nuku'alofa and asked the authorities if they knew of these six boys. 'Oh yes,' came the crackly reply. 'They are all dead. Their funerals were held more than a year ago.'

Warner and a crewman went on to the island and climbed up to the boys' camp. They dined with them on 'rubber chicken' and taro, and spent the night there, as it soon became too dark to climb back down.

In the morning, Peter Warner brought the boys back to Nuku'alofa. No sooner had they arrived back in civilization than the boys were arrested and put in jail, charged with the theft of a boat.

Warner telephoned Australian television. He had the idea of having the castaways re-enact their adventure for the cameras. After they had been in jail for ten days, Warner bailed them out and paid the owner of the stolen boat the 120 pa'anga he was demanding.

Warner was not impressed by the television crew. There were two of them. They wore tight trousers and pointed shoes. They couldn't swim and were bad sailors. By the time they, the boys and Warner reached 'Ata, the journalists were incapacitated with seasickness – they had to be carried from the boat and passed, like sacks of potatoes, along a human chain in the water formed by the Tongans. They shot the material they needed for their programme, but left one roll of film on the island. If you go there now, you will find one can of film and a jar containing fish-hooks and matches left by Peter Warner for the convenience of future castaways.

After bringing the camera crew back to Nuku'alofa, Warner brought the boys back home to Ha'apai to be reunited with their families.

In Ha'apai, there were five uninterrupted days of feasting. Pigs, chicken and, indeed, lobsters lay piled up on top of each other on twenty-foot-long heaps of food. As Warner's original intention in coming to Tonga had been to find lobsters, he kept asking, 'Where did you get the lobsters?' No one would tell him. Or else they wouldn't tell him just then. 'Later,' they said.

When the time came, the Ha'apaians showed Warner how they caught lobsters. All they did was wade out on to the beach at quarter tide, pick them up by hand from the rock pools, and drop them into sacks. That's all there was to it.

Upon his return to Nuku'alofa, Warner was summoned before the King. The King thanked him for rescuing the boys and, as a sign of his gratitude, asked him if there was anything he could do for him in the Kingdom of Tonga. Warner tugged his forelock and said, 'Well, Your Majesty, I was thinking of starting a fishing business.'

'Done,' said the monarch, like Prospero waving his magic wand, and, lo, the red tape parted like the Red Sea before Moses. Peter Warner now owns what has become one of the most successful shipping businesses in the region, Warner Pacific. Mighty is King Tupou and glorious are his works. Long may he shine in the pupil of the All-Powerful.

CHAPTER 2

Absolute Kingdom – Oman

SULTAN QABOOS OF Oman stood proudly yet quietly apart from other Arabian rulers. He did not rule by consensus, as first among equals in an oligarchy of merchant princes, as in Saudi Arabia or Bahrain, or hold the traditional Arab *majlis* – the open court to which anyone has the right of access – or self-effacingly dress almost identically to his subjects, or profess nostalgia for the old ways of the desert. His rule was absolute and solitary, and his personality shone like the sun into every crevice of his dominions. He wore beautiful costumes and presided over spectacular ceremonials. He was more like a Persian king than an Arab sheikh; he had the spark of charisma that the sheikhs lacked. He was the miracle of Omani history: the bright pearl on an undistinguished string of predecessors, ruling a country that for most of its history had been a hot and impoverished backwater, but now was transformed through Qaboos's administration of the miraculous wealth produced within two decades by oil.

As distinct as Qaboos from other rulers, Oman was so different from the other countries of the Arabian Peninsula as to be hardly part of it at all. A relief map of Arabia conveys its singularity. The south-eastern quarter of the Arabian peninsula contains two dominant features: a mountain range and a desert. Beside this, the modern boundaries of Oman enclose 1,700 kilometres of coastline. These features, like Tonga's, have shaped Oman's history and culture. The mountains and desert isolated Oman from the rest of Arabia; the sea connected it with the cultures of India, Africa and Iran.

Muscat, capital of the modern sultanate, in the past was approached by sea, and the sight of it formed most travellers' first impression of the country. This is how the British Consul-General in Muscat described it in a report to the Political Resident, Bahrain, in 1960 (the history of Oman is preserved in the fine epistolary style of two hundred years of British imperial correspondence):

> In the foreground is a horse-shoe shaped bay, flanked by forts which the Portuguese built before the Armada, on crags which fall sheer into the sea; at the head of the bay a walled and gated city on a crescent shore; in the background, mountains everywhere, the nearest looking like huge lumps of clinker from a furnace . . . [The air of the town had] an atmosphere of a hot saline bath, pervaded by a smell in which old fish and spices struggled for mastery.

This was written in the days when the country was called Muscat and Oman. The capital was turned away from the rest of the country, and looked seaward, surviving on a trickle of trade with the outside world. The mountains in the background were the peaks of Oman, another country, landlocked, whose truculent inhabitants were trapped in an ancient cycle of intertribal warfare. In those two black forts, Murani and Jalali, the old Sultan, Qaboos's father, kept his enemies incarcerated, in the dark, in shackles. He ordered the gates of the town locked every night three hours after sunset, and after that anyone walking the streets had to carry a lantern. Sunglasses were illegal because the Sultan liked to see a man's eyes when he talked to him. He preferred to let the country rot than to modernize it, arguing with suave confidence in the best Indian English that his people were not ready for development. Everyone who heard him was charmed. He was cursed by everyone else.

This prospect of Muscat has gone. Qaboos overthrew his father and transformed the town. He built a flamboyant palace with blue and yellow columns shaped like trumpets on a landfill extending into the harbour. He cleaned the place up, moved the trade out to nearby Muttrah and the new town of Ruwi, whitewashed the buildings, introduced a one-way system, and built government offices. Few people live there now, apart from Qaboos. Now Muscat bay serves not as a harbour and entrance to a commercial town but as the architectural setting for Qaboos's palace.

Now one's first impression of Oman is the highway that links the airport with what has become the greater Muscat conurbation. I'm no connoisseur of highways, but this one really is spectacular. Mighty, broad and straight on the way in from the airport, it swoops over and through the jagged stony hills when it approaches the formerly separated areas of Qurm, Muscat, Muttrah and the villages beyond. Belts of grass in the median and verge are tended carefully by Indian labourers in orange overalls. If you throw a cigarette end out the window of your car, someone will pick it up within fifteen minutes. The road is decorated with arches showing Qaboos's face and scenes of Omani progress. Its intersections are adorned with roundabouts displaying concrete sculptures of objects linked with Omani history and culture: a fountain made of a cluster of gigantic coffee-pots endlessly pouring welcome, an antique boat eternally cresting a blue cement wave.

Roads and roundabouts are the distinctive post-oil Arabian art form. This is what you quickly learn when studying the imagery of power in modern Arabia. Qaboos's greatest monument to himself, his Arc de Triomphe, the Renaissance Tower, is built on a roundabout where the highways link coastal Oman with the interior. Why roads should have become the showpieces of development, not just in Oman but all over Arabia, is a mystery. Perhaps they represent the ultimate triumph over the former hardships of desert travel. Certainly, it was the love of blacktop (rather than high-flown imagery) that inspired this poem in praise of Qaboos, published in an Omani newspaper at the time of his twentieth anniversary of power in 1990:

> A bold leader develops our land;
>   in twenty years Qaboos has developed it.
> He started when nothing flourished in the land;
>   and in a short time he developed it:
> With roads smooth with tar,
>   joining its villages to its towns . . .

I beheld this highway in a taxi from the airport to my hotel on my first visit to Oman. It was the end of Ramadan, and I was fleeing Saudi Arabia, where I worked for an oil company as a member of the international Gulf petroletariat, for a fistful of petrodollars. I was only a few hours out of the oppressive Saudi kingdom, and already feeling as if my head had been released from a vice. In a few hours, or whenever the Muslim divines of Oman decreed that astronomical conditions determined it, Ramadan would be over. Hailing the cab outside the airport, I was hit by the same hot damp air that HBM's Consul-General had noted thirty years before, damper and hotter than Dhahran. My driver, plump and contented, with a neatly clipped grey beard, wore a green gown and a purple embroidered cap. Once we had got under way, he pressed a button which turned on an incense burner, filling the inside of the cab with fragrant smoke. He drove the air-conditioned cab in the cool, unhurried manner of one browsing in a jewellery store, occasionally dipping his fingertips into the ornate gold and green plastic box of multicoloured tissues lodged between the burgundy-velvet seats. This was a modern Omani.

The other thing you notice immediately in Oman is that the Omanis themselves *look* different from other Arabs, in their ample, pastel-coloured gowns and distinctive Baluchi-style square caps and colourful turbans. This is the national costume that Qaboos has commanded Omanis must wear. There is none of the drab uniformity of attire that prevails so depressingly elsewhere in the Gulf, the ill-cut white *thobe* and the white or red-and-white headcloth.

The following day, lying on my bed in the Muscat Intercontinental Hotel, I saw the following brief item in the English-language *Oman Daily Observer*. It was the last paragraph in a story listing the heads of state from whom the Sultan had received holiday greetings:

> His Majesty Sultan Qaboos ibn Sa'id will greet wellwishers after morning prayers at al-'Alam Palace on the first day of the 'Eid al-Fitr.

That was tomorrow. I resolved to go and gaze upon him.

By eight o'clock the following morning I was standing in the courtyard of al-'Alam Palace, sweating in my blue-and-white Brooks Brothers seersucker suit under a hot, milky sky, having timidly approached the gate and, unchallenged by the guard, passed through it. In the road outside, a line of purring black limousines flying national flags on their bonnets waited to collect the diplomats who were in the palace paying their respects to His Majesty. I was surrounded by a crowd of Omanis, mostly very old men and small boys, who had come to greet the Sultan in their turn. The men carried glittering swords and proudly wore their best curved jewelled daggers around their waists. Apart from a quartet of Indians in Western-style suits, nervously fingering their loosely knotted polyester ties, I was the only foreigner.

As I was a foot taller than anyone around me, my view was unimpeded. All the estates of the realm, in order of precedence, had turned out and were filing into the palace to murmur their respects to the Sultan: Muslim divines in heavy brown robes and white turbans and beards; some American navy officers in gleaming white dress uniforms, with sweaty, beaming red faces; suave government officials in billowing, gauzy robes of gold-edged black. We, the popular masses, were corralled in place by a black-gowned palace official with white gloves and a growling walkie-talkie.

Once the last of the dignitaries had passed out of the palace, an inner gate was thrown open to admit us. There was a certain amount of pushing, and the officials had to maintain order. A manageable number were allowed through, and then the gate was closed again and those of us who remained outside continued to wait. A guard in a gauzy black cloak first told me to hold my Jermyn Street pseudo-Panamanian hat by my side, then, on second thoughts, took it away from me completely, just to be on the safe side, in case it had a neat little pistol inside which I could whip out the moment I came face to face with the Sultan and – *Wallahi!* – shoot him dead. Why I should want to do that, though, was above my level of security clearance.

At last we were allowed into the palace, through a vestibule decorated in an opulent Ottoman style, and sent in a queue up a flight of broad stairs. The throne room was like the interior of a gigantic Fabergé egg. It was of Palladian proportions, with very high walls bisected by a gallery that ran around the four sides. At the far end of the room, on a raised red throne ornamented with gold, with a backdrop of curtains behind him, sat the Sultan, the focal point of the room's grand perspective. The floor was made of black and white marble squares suggesting parallel lines meeting at a vanishing-point of royal infinitude, and facing the throne there were rows of chairs upholstered in green velvet.

He wore characteristic attire: a light-brown cloak over a simple white gown, and his stylish turban, as worn by all members of the royal family, of blue, purple, crimson and orange cloth tied with a jaunty blue tassel hanging down the left-hand side. His grey beard was neatly trimmed, and he wore an ornate Omani dagger around his waist.

The palace officials attending him stood at a distance from where he sat. In public, Qaboos is never physically close to anyone else, to dramatize the solitude of his power. Up on the gallery, facing the throne, high above the line of well-wishers and invisible to them unless, as I did, they turned back and looked upwards, were about thirty youths. They stood in a disciplined row, shoulder to shoulder, with their hands behind their backs, dressed in baggy-trousered costumes that made them look like extras from *The King and I*: court pages or favourites.

The Sultan, sitting before us in splendour, could see them and us, and they could see the Sultan and us, but we could only see the Sultan and not them. Their presence on the gallery was a court secret shared by the Sultan and the pages, I reasoned. We, for our part, were there solely to feast our eyes on the Sultan on his throne. I stepped forward.

The scene was an emblem of vision and power in an absolute monarchy; it was, in Roy Strong's phrase, 'power conceived as art'. Two dramatic rituals were being performed simultaneously that spoke of the nature of this power. In one, the Sultan was the sole spectator: from where he sat, he could see us, and the pages, and the whole of the room, arrayed in the hierarchy of which he was the apex. There was only one position from which this order could be viewed, and he was occupying it. This ritual recalled the court masques of Charles I, who sat in a similarly exalted position to view fanciful theatrical evocations of the splendours of Britain under his own absolute rule.

The other dramatic ritual was Qaboos's exhibition to us of his person, in order that we might feast our eyes upon it. The king displays the royal body not to convey information about himself, of course, but to dazzle us. Rule through splendid display is one of the basic techniques of kingship, for to be impressed is to obey. It arouses an aesthetic appetite in us that can be satisfied only by the continued reign of the king. It turns the king into a cultural force we come to identify with the culture of the nation itself, making him indispensable to it.

Still, feast or no, I couldn't spend too much time looking around, as the line was moving forward. There were only a few boys between me and the Sultan, so I had to compose myself. For these kids it was like seeing Santa Claus in a department store. I, for my part, exploded with sweat inside my suit.

At last I was before him. I bowed, and reached out to take his hand. He flinched when he saw me, fearing, perhaps, the assassin's blade. His hand was soft and plump, and it rested on his knee to spare him the exertion of lifting it for each of his however many thousand well-wishers.

I said, in Arabic, 'Happy and Blessed '*Eid*, O Sultan.'

He replied, with a flicker of a smile, 'Thank you.'

Having feasted, I walked back to collect my hat from the usher, reflecting smugly on the Sultan's flinch. He feared me more than I feared him – at that instant anyway. His flinch momentarily revealed the fearful, mortal self that hitherto lay concealed within the ritual and theatre that established the illusion of Qaboos's kingly distance from us. I wondered who Qaboos's enemies could be: certainly not me. Surely he had none! He had been wise enough to buy them all off after the civil war of 1970 to 1975, pouring the sultanate's money and resources into the rebellious southern province of Dhofar, so that the Dhofaris had no reason to complain about anything. He had been fortunate enough to possess the means to do so.

Still, everyone around me was wearing a dagger, and it would be natural to assume that these daggers were sometimes used. They had an ironic appearance, these gem-hilted blades – urbane, elegant, lethal. They were curved, which suggested an aim on the part of the bearer to inflict especial internal damage to the recipient of the glinting stab, the swift, clean movement that brings justice, settles scores. To be a man in Oman was to carry a weapon. Even the old fellows who did the xeroxing in the Wali of Sohar's office wore belts of antique bullets around their waists, in case a misunderstanding over office etiquette should escalate into a firefight.

Historically, daggers did emerge from their scabbards from time to time. The dagger's vindicating power is used to best advantage where there is an audience, where its unexpected flash becomes a gesture of maximum explosive historical power, as in 1803 in the Saudi capital Darʿiyyah, when the Saudi king ʿAbd al-ʿAziz was murdered by an Iraqi Shiʿite as he kneeled at prayer in the main congregational mosque one Friday noon. In the zeal of conquest and expansion, the Saudis in 1801 had sacked the sacred Shiʿite shrines at Karbala, and massacred most of the town's inhabitants. After two years waiting for the right moment, a Shiʿite avenger pretended to be a member of the Saudis' Wahhabi sect in order to gain entry to their prayers, then plunged a dagger between the prostrate king's shoulder blades. Every ruler is afraid of something like that happening. It's why the Tongan King struck with a stick the knees of anyone who came too close to him.

Qaboos has built a golden age on ruins. He is the fourteenth ruler of the Al Bu Saʿid dynasty, which has ruled at least some of what is now Oman since 1741, when Ahmad bin Saʿid Al Bu Saʿid led a campaign to expel Persian invaders from the port of Sohar and was elected Imam, or Leader. Old Oman reached its peak in the first half of the nineteenth century under Seyyid Saʿid, who ruled a little empire of the Indian Ocean stretching from Pakistan to Zanzibar, which became its capital. After Saʿid, it went into a decline which hit bottom during the reigns of Qaboos's grandfather and father. The word 'renaissance', officially used to describe Qaboos's rule, mainly denotes a contrast with those harsh decades.

The ruler of Oman was not always called 'Sultan': the title was introduced by the British in 1861, when the government of British

India divided Oman and Zanzibar into two separate states (the Canning Settlement). As a gesture of their equal stature in the eyes of the British, they gave each ruler the same title. (The dying ember of the Zanzibari sultanate was eventually extinguished in the 1964 Tanzanian revolution.) Qaboos is the first Al Bu Saʿid ruler to use the title 'Sultan' exclusively: even his father used the traditional Omani style, 'Seyyid', in tandem with the British title. The title itself is the Arabic word for 'power' and was first used to denote a secular ruler who was effectively independent of the Caliph after the breakup of the Islamic empire at the end of the Abbasid era, although nominally subject to his authority.

The title 'Imam' has deeper roots. When Ahmad bin Saʿid assumed it, he was taking over the leadership of a theocracy modelled, in theory at least, on the original Muslim community led by Muhammad at Medina. In its isolated corner of the Arabian Peninsula, Oman was the haven for an Islamic sect, the ʿIbaḍiyyah, that had kept its flinty doctrine unaltered for centuries. It emerged in southern Iraq in the leadership disputes that followed the Prophet's death; the ʿIbaḍiyyah were a faction of a faction that fled Iraq to escape persecution under Hajjaj ibn Yusuf, the psychopathic grammarian-governor of Basra and Kufa. They came to Oman in the eighth century CE, cutting themselves off from the rest of the Islamic empire, bringing with them the belief that they were the only true Muslims on earth; everyone else was in error. The ʿIbaḍi state's sole purpose was the salvation of souls, and its leader was called simply '*imam al-muslimin*', leader of the Muslims. The ʿIbaḍis professed a strict egalitarianism: any man could be Imam who set the right example of piety and leadership. If he deviated, or became too autocratic, the community was obliged to remove him. State institutions were kept to a minimum. 'We do not allow *kings*,' they said.

But Ahmad bin Saʿid was elected Imam not for his piety but for his military ability, and his successors were chosen not by election but from his family. The imamate, consequently, died out, and the Al Bu Saʿid ruler called himself 'Seyyid' instead, which means, roughly, 'Master'. By this time the capital had moved from the interior of Oman (Oman proper) to Muscat. This left the ʿIbaḍi community leaderless, while the Seyyids built up a maritime empire. A split between the ʿIbaḍi interior and the Al Bu Saʿidi coast was established which lasted until the reign of Qaboos, causing centuries of war and instability.

Culturally, the people of the interior grew reactionary, xenophobic and trigger-happy, while the coast supported a mixture of nationalities and cultures. This cultural split noticeably persists in modern Oman. The fortresses and castles the feuding warlords of the interior built are still there, beautiful sand-coloured structures rising up among the palm trees of the once isolated oases. They have been renovated by Qaboos and now serve as symbols of a country unified under his rule. And it is mostly in the interior where the rusty Martini rifle and bandolier are still the favoured fashion accessories for male attire.

The British established relations with the coastal sultanate in the late eighteenth century, leaving the interior to its own devices, and after the loss of Zanzibar Muscat became just another of the Persian Gulf principalities forming the glacis of British India. By the beginning of the twentieth century, the country was poor, the Sultan was weak, and a new imamate had been established to oppose him. In 1920, when they brokered a treaty between the coast and the interior (the Seeb Agreement), the British were supporting, according to a soul-searching report by the Political Agent, Muscat, 'a ruler against whom most of his subjects were in open rebellion, who was theoretically independent and yet who would be driven into the sea in a day if it were not for us'.

This ruler was Qaboos's grandfather, Sultan Taimur. Taimur hated his hopeless position as Sultan and the oppressive climate of Muscat so much that he spent ten years trying to abdicate, as his father, Sultan Faïsal, had done before him.

The official correspondence, now in the India Office Library, London, shows the British and the Sultan trapped in a political farce in which the country couldn't be governed without the Sultan, because of its nominal independence, but the Sultan didn't want to govern and did his best to avoid all official work. 'He hankers after the joys of civilization as represented by India, loathes his own country and is determined to be as idle as possible,' the Political Agent wrote. As a result of Taimur's aversion to responsibility, a 'regency council' was appointed to run the country, led by the British explorer Bertram Thomas, who had a talent for politics but none for financial affairs.

The Political Agent, Muscat, described Taimur as 'not unintelligent' but 'incredibly weak and incurably vain'. Taimur, for his part, loathed being a British puppet. In 1932, after nineteen years as Sultan, he was finally allowed to resign, in favour of his son, Sa'id.

Opening the records at 1920, we find Taimur begging the administration to allow him to go to India, to be cured of unspecified ailments. Reluctant consent was given only after several months' tedious correspondence. Hypochondria was Taimur's favoured weapon of self-defence against his British patron-captors. They noticed that his fevers would leave him immediately on his setting sail from Muscat.

Once in India, Taimur on this occasion pleaded not to have to return.

> The cause of this is, that when we reached Karachi I put myself under a Doctor for treatment to cure me from the diseases which I have for a long time and I fear from their bad consequences. Secondly it is not a secret that doctor's treatment must take time, and I have got a medical certificate to that effect. Undoubtedly the Government would not allow badness of my health and it would be great assistance to me if I would be cured of my these [*sic*] dangerous diseases.

The Political Agent gruffly concluded, 'He will do his best never to return to Muscat.'

To make good his escape, Taimur fled to the coolness of Kashmir. The British tracked him down and in September 1920 forced him to attend a meeting at Parry's Hotel, Ambala. By this time the Sultan was travelling in disguise. He appeared at the hotel wearing a European suit and a sheepskin fez.

> The interview lasted six hours and was extremely difficult and trying. His Highness showed a mule-like obstinacy in sticking to his original request to abdicate at all costs . . . His attitude was a combination of

terror at having to return to Muscat even for a day, and of a pathetic desire to get as much money out of his state as possible for his own personal use.

Just when the British thought they had secured Taimur's grudging agreement to return to Muscat for a few weeks to participate in the fiction of his authority, the uncooperative sultan announced instead that he was buying a house in Dehra Dun. '[We] found a suitable one having a garden in it. It has electric lights also.' Clenched fury seethes through the code-words in the ensuing British telegram:

FLUSTRIS SOTTOPONI FOVIAMUS AGAIN EMGALLA SECAMEN LIRARENT VENDITUM AUGNINO REDOLISCO ADVANCE MONEY PERFLUIMUS HOUSE UDAREMUS SAYS PERFLUXIUS REDUCO IN DEHRA DUN TOXIGLOSSA EXPRESSLY GIVEN TO TAMARIGIA LAEDEREMUS ABSEGMINA TRAFELANTE SEE MY NOTE . . .

The Sultan had written asking for money to make a deposit, the telegram said. 'He was expressly given to understand by me that no action will be taken in this way . . . I would be glad if you would telegraph instructions. Stop.'

Taimur felt that the British little understood the tribal situation that was the cause of conflict in Oman, yet would not allow him to deal with it his own way. So he gave up. Meanwhile, the state's meagre treasury dwindled as a result of his constant demands on it:

Political Agent, Muscat, to Political Resident, Bushire, 22 September 1921: 'It is by no means certain that the state in the future will be able to stand the strain of paying out three and a half lakhs a year, nearly a third of the revenue of the state, to the Sultan and his useless family, none of whom do a hand's turn of work.'

Skipping ahead nine years, we find the same music being played without variation: the Sultan still pleading from India to be allowed to abdicate, on the familiar grounds of ill health, and the British responding with the same weary scepticism:

Agent, Karachi to Political Resident, Bushire, 4 September 1930: 'As he is fit enough to go tiger shooting this excuse hardly holds water.'

Political Resident, Bushire, to Agent, Muscat, 20 October 1930: 'It would be humorous if it were not so annoying.'

After abdicating, Taimur seems genuinely to have led a much happier life. Spies kept an eye on his movements, reporting in 1935 that, under the anonymous-sounding name 'T. F. T. Said', he had sailed to Japan and China on unknown business. At first they feared he might be running guns to Dhofar, Oman's southern region, which was in perennial revolt; then they concluded that he was only harmlessly involved in 'some small commercial venture'. In 1936, Special Branch, Singapore, reported that 'Alsaid is shortly leaving again for Japan, chiefly at the request of a Japanese geisha girl who fell in love with him when he was last in Japan and has been urging him to return to her.' He married her, and they had a Japanese–Arab daughter named Buthainah.

In 1943, we read, the unnamed geisha died, leaving Taimur in Bombay with six-year-old Buthainah. Taimur died in Ceylon in 1965, thirty-three years after his abdication, having lived the better part of his life outside of Oman and free from the affliction of the kingship of a buffer state.

Taimur had shrugged off the sultanate on to his son Sa'id when Sa'id was only twenty-one. By this time Sa'id had been Chairman of the Regency Council, established to run the country in the light of Taimur's indifference, for three years.

The British hoped Sa'id would drag Oman out of the stagnation into which it had drifted, that he would assert his authority, subdue the tribes and unify the country. He had been carefully groomed for this role since childhood ('He is an intelligent and excellent mannered little boy of eight to ten years old, who can read and write Arabic and who is as yet uncorrupted by his horrible surroundings,' the Agent and Consul, Muscat, wrote to the Political Resident, Bushire), and had been sent to Mayo College in Ajmer, the 'Indian Eton', where Indian princes were prepared for their roles as traditional rulers.

On his accession, Sa'id signed a statement promising to abide by British guidance. In the first years of his reign he did nothing to disappoint his patrons. Things seemed quiet, if only because of the isolation of the palace and the consulate from the harsh landscape beyond them.

In 1948 the Sultan was thirty-eight years old and wrote his official letters by hand. 'The weather here is nice and cool, especially at night,' he wrote to the British Consul. Money was in rupees. Petroleum Concessions Ltd was prospecting for oil. The Sultan's letters show how the government of this scorching backwater was a personal matter between him and the British Consul:

The sardine season is good and the dhows from Aden side began to arrive here. I am expecting my 'Jeep' station wagon to arrive here from Aden at any moment.

I have received my account sheets up to 20th August 1947 from the Lloyds Bank London but no credit is shown from His Britannic Majesty's Government for rent, etc.

I am sending you through my secretary some bananas, papayas and a bottle of brown sugar the produce of Dhofar. I hope they will reach you safely and enjoy eating them. I am glad to let you know that we have discovered an Iron Ore near Murbat and I have sent to India for analysis and the result shows that the ore has 94% iron. I am advised that we should have a million tons for commercial purposes. I wonder if some one will be interested in this iron!

But Saʿid had the same problem his father had, and it ultimately overwhelmed him too. After trying and failing to subdue the perennially rebellious interior, in 1946 Saʿid had asked the British for military support in a new campaign. He wanted RAF planes to bomb the mountain strongholds, but the British refused. So he too gave up the governing of the country as a hopeless cause, and left it to the British. He had never liked the Seeb Agreement anyway, which had conceded too much to the uncouth interior tribes.

Saʿid's subsequent decline into apathy and eccentricity can be traced partly to his disappointment at the unwinnability of the war against the interior. Like his two predecessors, Saʿid was the ruler only of the coast, while the British maintained the fiction that he also governed Oman proper. But the bad climate of Muscat, his own Anglophile cultural predisposition, timidity, laziness, and a solipsistic sense of princely grandeur also played their part. He made one final campaign against the interior in 1954. Four years later, he retreated permanently to his palace in Dhofar and stayed there until he was overthrown by Qaboos twelve years later.

The legends of the cruelty of Saʿid's rule originate from this period. It is as if he had tried to kill Oman by a combination of deliberate neglect and active repression. In the solitude of his power, Saʿid practised a corrupted form of classical Islamic absolutism. If he had practised it correctly, he might not have been overthrown.

The model of classical Islamic absolutism is to be found in the 'mirrors for princes' that were written by philosophers and officials for the independent sultans who came to power in the Middle East and Asia after the breakup of the Abbasid dynasty. Works in this genre would have been as familiar to Saʿid as Bagehot to a Westminster MP.

They say, in essence, that the ruler must set an example of piety, consulting frequently with religious scholars; he must be generous and magnanimous (according to one writer, the king should not even mention sums of less than 1,000 dirhams); he must be just; he must be accessible, yet dignified; he must know everything that goes on in his kingdom; he must possess physical beauty; and he must know how to prosecute war.

One of the points made frequently in the Islamic 'mirrors' is that the ruler must observe everything that happens in his realm. In the *Siyasatnameh* ('The Book of Government'), the Seljuk Vizier Nizam al-Mulk lays down a firm line: 'if anybody wrongly took so much as a chicken or a bag of straw from another – and that 500 parasangs away – the King would know about it and have the offender punished, so that others knew that the King was vigilant.'

Sultan Saʿid followed this policy exactly. In order to know what was happening however many parasangs away, he used telescopes set up inside his palace in Salalah to watch what his subjects were doing. Writing with the inflamed imagination of a youthful Marxist, Fred Halliday described the eccentricities of Saʿid's personal system of intelligence gathering:

One man in Salala built an outside lavatory on to his home and government officials arrived the next day to knock it down, saying the Sultan had seen him contravening regulations . . . In the 1950s [before he retreated to the southern capital] he often telephoned the British Consulate in Muscat, across the harbour, to complain if he saw anyone smoking on the veranda.

In this way the ruler imposes his personality over every square inch of his kingdom, spreading like a gas, evenly and pervasively over the land, even into the chambers of the hearts of his subjects.

An early Arabic 'mirror', translated into Latin and then into English as *The Book of the Secret of Secrets*, has ten pages advising the king on how to read men's thoughts and intentions in their eyes. The book purports to be an epistle from Aristotle to Alexander the Great, advising him on the art of kingship during his conquest of Persia, written because the Sage was too old to accompany him in person. It was in the spirit of this kind of all-seeing autocracy that Saʿid is held by legend to have banned the wearing of sunglasses in his presence.

But Saʿid failed to observe two other important principles of classical Islamic absolutism. The first is put vividly in the 'mirror' of the north African scholar al-Maghili (died 1504), the *Taj ad-din fi ma yajib ʿala al-muluk* ('The Crown of Religion Concerning the Obligations of Princes'): 'The height of affliction is the isolation of the ruler from his subjects!' For to stay alone in the palace breeds conspiracies. Saʿid did just that. For four years most of his subjects thought he was dead: that he had been murdered in 1966 in what was in fact an unsuccessful assassination attempt.

Second, he was a miser with his swelling treasury. By 1970, oil revenue was coming in at a rate of about £35 million a year, yet Saʿid allowed little of it to be spent.

As for physical beauty, he was about average. He was a small man of just over five feet, with a white beard that encircled his face, which was jovial. He dressed simply, usually in a white robe and turban, and comported himself modestly.

Before long, a conspiracy overwhelmed him.

Ignorance and disease were his people's bread and roses. The British called his state 'a machine for the repression of fractious sheikhs'. Sa'id told Hugh Boustead, the British Development Officer, 'That is why you lost India: because you educated the people.'

By 1970, there was complete opposition to Sa'id's fossilized regime. While Sa'id waited for the 'Ibadi sheikhs to starve to death, rebels were mining the roads and inciting the population with an adapted version of Maoism. Throughout the 1960s British supervision of Muscat and Oman was preoccupied with analyses of the problem of the 'personality' of Sa'id, as part of a diffident strategy of nudging him into agreeing to allow the most minimal development in the country. 'His hobby is astrology and numerology. He solemnly told me that he always consults his books of numbers before taking a decision on any important matter and that he has found this practice of great help in coming to the right decision.'

His palace in Salalah was a labyrinth. He had five hundred slaves and a hundred and fifty concubines, and secret stores of weapons.

He was *lonely*. In 1960 the British consul wrote, on the eve of Sa'id's annual secret visit to London (where he stayed at the Dorchester, his only luxury), 'He admitted that he had felt somewhat isolated in London last time and if it hadn't been for the television he would have been bored. This time he wanted to get out and about a bit and go up to Scotland if possible. When asked what else would interest him he said that he wanted to ride on a bus and in the Underground and *mix more with the people* [!]'

The leader of the conspiracy that overthrew him was his son, Qaboos, who had been kept a prisoner for six years in the palace, compelled by his father to study Islamic theology and law, concocting his fury in his breast, and carefully laying his plans. Sa'id had hardly seen Qaboos since his son had returned from his years of education and military service in Europe.

Qaboos was born amidst a question over the succession, and he will certainly die in one. In 1940 there had been discussion in the official correspondence over who should succeed Sa'id in the event of his untimely death. Although he was not yet thirty, the British were concerned that he had no son, a natural successor. At first it was reported that Sa'id did not even have a wife; this false impression was corrected in a later memo. (Qaboos's mother died in 1992. She had been living in poor health in the palace in Salalah with her own entourage, frequently consulted by her son.) Dated 4 December, the following letter appears in the file, neatly handwritten by Sa'id to HBM's Consul, Hickinbotham.

My dear and valued friend:

Very many thanks for your kind letter of this evening and for your cordial congratulations on the good news which I have received from Dhofar this afternoon. I join with you in the prayer that God may watch over and protect him and enable me to bring up the boy to the proper standered [*sic*] of life.

It is very kind of you indeed to feel the pleasure of this happy event. I wish you every happiness and success.

I am
Your very sincere Friend
Said bin Taimur

The problem was solved: Qaboos was born. His name appears again five years later in a letter from Sa'id to the British Consul in which, in closing, Sa'id mentions deliberations concerning Qaboos's education: he has been in touch with King Farouq about having the boy educated in Egypt.

Instead, Qaboos was tutored privately in the palace in Salalah. When he was eighteen he was sent to a small private school in England, near Bury St Edmunds. The headmaster, an old India hand, introduced him to European classical music. One of the few personal details on record about Qaboos is that he has an enormous collection of classical LPs.

The loneliness of the Al Bu Sa'id rulers emerges again from these sparse details of Qaboos's early life. 'Qaboos writes to his father [1959] that he is enjoying himself in Suffolk. He had not had any contact with young men of his own age (now 17) in Salalah – only the Wali and his tutor.' (Actually he was nineteen in 1959.) This *Wali* was described as 'a charming old man' but 'distinctly past his prime'.

The *Bury Free Press* reported that the young prince was taking evening classes in art at a local school. Meanwhile, the British discussed the succession. The cloistered prince did not figure in their reckonings. 'I think his son Qabus is one of the few people the Sultan really cares about,' the Consul wrote to the British Resident, Bahrain; but 'I do not think Qabus would stand a chance [to succeed Sa'id] unless we decided to support him, and in fact impose him on the Family Council and I don't imagine we would do that . . . Qabus has never been to Muscat or Oman in his life, as far as I know, and many of the Family do not know him.'

In 1960 Sa'id came to England for a two-month holiday, staying in his 'usual suite' in the Dorchester. He was invited to the royal box at the Royal Tournament, but declined suggestions that his son might accompany him.

The British arranged for Qaboos to go to Sandhurst, then to join the Scottish Rifles (Cameronians), an unglamorous, soldierly British regiment. He rose to the rank of adjutant. Later he spent two years working in local government in Bedfordshire.

On his return to Oman in 1964, after his years in Europe, the gentle youth with a taste for classical music, now twenty-four, was back in his father's hands. The Western part of his education was over; his father now saw to it that Qaboos received an Islamic education to complement it, the proper training of an Islamic ruler. A cook and a tutor, a *qadi* (an Islamic judge), were appointed. He was denied servants, lest he succumb to delusions of grandeur. Qaboos remained detained in this way for six years.

Sa'id's half-brothers were placed under similar restrictions: after education in Europe, they found themselves back in Oman living in enforced leisure. Some of them are now ministers in Qaboos's government.

'Qaboos' is an unusual name in Arabic. There is no one with that name in Omani or Arab history (although the classical dictionary *Lisan al-'Arab* names a certain Abu Qaboos al-Nu'man bin al-Mundhir 'king of the Arabs'), and I have never met anyone else called Qaboos. In classical Arabic dictionaries it is an epithet for a man meaning 'good-looking and with a handsome colour'. In modern Arabic it means 'nightmare'.

Curious about this, I wrote a letter to the Sultan to ask him why he was given this apparently unique name. My lengthy question was rewritten as a single sentence by the Ministry of Information and conveyed to the Royal Diwan. In due course the answer came back:

Question: Is there any significance in the fact that His Majesty was named Qaboos?
Answer: There was no particular historical significance in the choice of the name Qaboos for His Majesty. The choice was made by his mother, and accepted by his father. It means, as you probably know, 'the light of dawn'.

No, I didn't know that, although I was flattered that His Majesty (or his British press officer) should assume that I did. Nevertheless, it was not an entirely satisfactory answer. The name was a bit more interesting than the officials of the Diwan and the Ministry of Information were willing to allow, in the slanting light it cast on the Persian dimension of Qaboos's style of rule. It doesn't mean 'light of dawn'.

According to the *Encyclopedia of Islam*, at least, the only other Qaboos in history was the Persian ruler Qaboos ibn Washmagir ibn Ziyar, who ruled in Caspian Sea provinces of Tabaristan in the late tenth and early eleventh centuries CE. His two reigns were distinguished by the splendour of his court, where astronomers, philosophers and poets found patronage, and by bloody campaigns to stamp out all forms of Shi'ism in his dominions. 'Eventually there remained not a single Baṭini [transcendentalist, i.e. Shi'ite] in all Khurasan and Transoxiana; the religion collapsed completely and its adherents were all forgotten' (Nizam al-Mulk, *Siyasatnameh*).

Qaboos ibn Washmagir was famous for the elegance of his Arabic epistolary style, and for his poetry in Arabic and Persian. Yet he was vindictive, paranoid and cruel, and would order execution for the slightest offence. Eventually he was overthrown by his officers and left in an exposed castle to freeze to death.

He is immortalized by his tomb at Gorgan, about two hundred kilometres north-east of Tehran, a bizarre cylindrical tower made of brick, like a Jules Verne rocket, noted by Robert Byron in *The Road to Oxiana*, and by the *Qabusnamah*, a 'mirror for princes' written by Qaboos's grandson, the prince Kai Ka'us ibn Iskandar ibn Qabus, for his son Gilanshah, in 1082. Kai Ka'us held Qaboos to be the exemplar of pragmatic kingship, and sought to impart its principles, as he saw them, to his son.

In conception, the *Qabusnamah* is like a crowded chest of drawers. It contains everything that one individual learned in his life that he feels is worth preserving, important or trivial, neatly packed, but without any organizing theory or hazard as to what it all means: such is the wisdom that man hands on to man. Posterity is what we dread to throw away because some day it might come in useful.

He advises his son to worship God, to tell the truth whenever he can, to honour his parents and not to succumb to pride; also to drink wine moderately, to avoid playing chess with awkward customers, not to have sexual intercourse when the weather is too hot, or when it is too cold, and to dry his hair immediately when getting out of the bath. Ministers must have large beards, to make them look impressive. Do not let your bodyguard consist of a single race, he advises, to prevent conspiracies. In war, you must 'breakfast on your enemies, before they dine on you.'

A king anywhere is subject to two conflicting imperatives: on the one hand, in order to rule effectively he must be accessible to his subjects. On the other, he must inspire obedience through awe and fear, and do this by remaining aloof and inaccessible. Accessibility belongs to Arab and Islamic tradition; aloofness is characteristic of an older, Persian, style of kingship. The *Qabusnamah* reflects the latter:

> Expose yourself to the general gaze only rarely, and so prevent yourself from becoming a spectacle commonplace in the eyes of your troops and people, taking heed not to esteem yourself too poorly.

In this Persian style of kingship, the king seems superhuman, a force of nature. All time and history revolve around him. He is depicted in Persian art with his head surrounded by a kind of flaming halo called *farr*, the divine effulgence of the rightful ruler.

It is in the Persian royal tradition that we find early versions of the perennial metaphor of the sun-king, a kind of divine being. Early in the Persian epic the *Shahnameh* ('Book of Kings'), for example, we find Shah Jamshid attaining solar apotheosis:

> . . . by his royal Grace
> Made him a throne, with what a wealth of gems
> Inlaid! which when he willed, the divs [Mazdean demons] took up
> And bare from earth to heaven. There the Shah
> Whose word was law, sat sunlike in mid-air.

Vainglorious Jamshid eventually came to believe himself a god and lost his kingdom. (The Persians always had a tendency to go over the top in their approach to kingship. The ceremonial crown of Khusrau II was so heavy – it weighed ninety-one kilograms – it had to be hung by a chain above his head.)

The king can bring paradise to earth, fructifying the land and subduing it at the same time. This is from the *Wisdom of Royal Glory*, an allegorical Turkish 'mirror' written in the Persian tradition:

> When the Khaqun assumed the throne, the World breathed easy and began to shower him with kingly gifts. Birds descended out of the lofty ether, some from the Raja of India and others sent by Caesar, vying with pride and joy in praising him and calling out his name. Flowers covered mountain and valley, hollow and ridge, with green and blue, so many ornaments scattered over the ground . . . Fortune herself came and stood at the gate ready to serve.

This is closer to the Pharaonic idea of the divine king. It is very different from the ideal of Islamic rule, which subordinated the ruler to God. The Muslim philosopher and theologian al-Ghazali (died 1111) harangued the ruler to whom his *Nasihat al-Muluk* (or 'Book of Counsel for Kings') was addressed:

> God on High owns a house called Hell, and He has made you the janitor of that house. He has given you three things: the Public Treasury, the

sword, and the whip. He has told you to keep people out of Hell with these three things.

Al-Ghazali admonished the ruler to see the world as a Sufi ascetic would see it, as something corrupt and corrupting, to be transcended through piety. He warned him that 'the harshest torment on the Resurrection Day will be for the unjust Sultan.'

Qaboos's education in the mysteries of kingship is always mentioned in his official biographies. In the same letter in which I enquired about the significance of the name Qaboos, I sought to know what the young prince read during his years of confinement. The response conveyed the charming image of a prince in a tower piously studying scripture.

Answer: During his time in Salalah on his return from Europe, His Majesty principally studied the Koran, and he also read widely, in Arabic books, on the history of his own, and the Arab people in general. This was the only literature permitted to him, and he has described it as his only consolation during his years of confinement. The guidance provided by the Koran has undoubtedly provided a complete structure within which His Majesty has led his life, both as Sultan and as a man. His Majesty would certainly advise a ruler of any Islamic country to make the guidance provided by this literature the foundation of his own rule.

On 23 July 1970, Qaboos confronted the unjust Sultan in his labyrinthine Salalah palace. In his years of imprisonment, in addition to his reading of improving books, Qaboos had been quietly planning this moment, sounding out political support. His original idea had been to accumulate power gradually, but the British, whose support Qaboos needed, advised a quick take-over. A gradual approach posed too much uncertainty, especially as the country stood on the threshold of undreamed-of wealth due to oil. Qaboos's education was over.

The spark that set plans in motion was a night attack by rebels on the army garrison at Izki on 12 June. It was the first rebel attack in Oman proper. Until then, the rebellion had been limited to the remote southern province; now it was spreading.

The coup was led and organized by Qaboos, and the participants were all Omanis, many of them tribesmen from Salalah. They surrounded the palace and cut the electricity. With the palace in darkness, Sa'id's slave bodyguards were easily overpowered. A small SAS detachment, in the country already to fight the rebellion, entered with Qaboos's party, officially to see that the shooting was kept to a minimum. The Omani army – the Sultan's Armed Forces, led then by British officers – arrived later to maintain law and order around the palace.

The Sultan pulled out a revolver, but was so unpractised and frightened that he shot himself in the foot. Qaboos ordered his men to arrest him. Sa'id protested that he would surrender only to British officers, allegedly afraid of what his own people might do to him. The injured despot was sent in an RAF plane to Muscat, thence to Bahrain, and finally to his usual suite at the Dorchester.

Two years later, while travelling to New York on an ocean liner with his friend Brigadier Pat Waterfield, his former Defence Secretary, Sa'id had a heart attack on a staircase. He returned to London, and died there at the age of sixty-two. He was not bitter towards his son and had hoped to make peace with him before long.

News of the coup was announced three days after it had taken place. Qaboos issued a proclamation stating that he had overthrown his father because of 'disquiet and growing anger' over Sa'id's 'inability to make use of the country's new riches to meet the people's needs.' He had the support of the royal family and the armed forces.

Qaboos arrived in Muscat, for the first time in his life, in triumph. His Defence Secretary, Colonel Hugh Oldman, told *The Times*, 'There was overt joy and sheer jubilation. In fact, the Sultan had a great deal of difficulty in getting everyone to go back to work.'

Qaboos's first speech, on 9 August, reflected great excitement, urgency and hope. He appealed to Omanis who had left the country during Sa'id's reign to come back. Among these was Seyyid Tariq, Sa'id's half-brother, who had long been spoken of as a possible successor to Sa'id but had left the country out of unhappiness with Sa'id's policies. Seyyid Tariq, the young Sultan said, would return to Oman to serve as Prime Minister as soon as he had settled his private affairs.

Qaboos quickly set about building schools, hospitals and roads. Since then, he has built public housing on Islamic architectural principles. He has built roundabouts and fountains. He built a stately pleasure-dome of a luxury hotel on top of a fishing village, and made all the villagers rich. He put fibreglass replicas of the Arabian oryx – made extinct by hunting early in the century, but now reintroduced – on crags overlooking the Muscat highway. He built a promenade on the waterfront at Muttrah, with a fake waterfall in the rock beside it.

Qaboos synthesized an original Arab–Islamic–Persian-style absolute monarchy on the ruins of an exhausted Indian-style princedom. He gave himself the title 'His Majesty', as a step up from the style 'His Highness' borne by his father and by the other Persian Gulf rulers, and dropped the old title 'Seyyid' that his father had used.

He established the myth of 1970, according to which all was darkness before 1970, and all was light afterwards. In fact, many of the country's big development projects – notably the harbour at Muttrah, Mina Qaboos – were started by Sa'id and only finished by Qaboos.

It took Qaboos five years to consolidate his authority over the country, eventually prevailing in 1975 in a war with rebels armed and inspired by communist South Yemen. This war was Qaboos's testing. His reign has been conspicuously without a serious crisis ever since, except a minor one in the mid-1980s when the price of oil plunged to eight dollars a barrel.

In 1975, Qaboos married. The *Times of Oman* announced the event in its usual fulsome Indian-English prose style.

It shall add to the joy and jubilation of the people of Oman and outside the Sultanate to hear about the happy news of marriage of His Majesty Sultan Qaboos with the respected daughter of Sayyid Tariq bin Taimour of the Royal Family. [And what was her name?] His Majesty the Sultan was married at a private colourful ceremony here last week, which was attended by members of the Royal Family and ministers of His Majesty's cabinet.

The marriage was like a gift to the nation after five years of war. It also served to restore relations with Seyyid Tariq: the experiment of having a Prime Minister had not been a success. But the marriage was later dissolved, and there were no children. The Sultan's ex-wife is said to live quietly in London.

Qaboos governs in the same way as his father did: the Sultan's rule is a projection of his personality over the whole country. The difference is in the personalities. The Sultan likes Western classical music, so there are five minutes of classical music on television every evening before the news. He likes Western art, so on 14 November 1990 the evening news on Omani television carried an item about how a Van Gogh painting had failed to reach its reserve price at auction in London – a revelation that was probably received without comprehension in Jebel Akhdar.

Qaboos's interest in music is worth a digression. Before 1970, music was virtually illegal in Oman. A retired government official told me that during the oppressive reign of the previous Sultan, a man who was found in possession of an *'oud* was brought before a judge who ordered his precious instrument – acquired abroad at great expense – publicly burnt. The judge called it 'the Devil's craftsmanship' and sent the owner to jail.

Since 1970, music has become an important instrument of Qaboos's policy of creating a new, single Omani national identity transcending regional allegiances, one in which (in the words of his impassioned first speech as Sultan) 'there is no longer any difference between the coast and the interior and the Eastern Province'. He has directed the invention of 'Omani music', in which the disparate musical styles of Oman's regions are officially encouraged and considered together, in a way that links folk culture with patriotism. Official ensembles have been formed, like the Royal Band for Music and Folklore, based in Salalah, which play an original hybrid style combining Arab classical music with Omani folkloric elements, for presentation at official occasions.

The high point of this propagandistic use of traditional music was the performance of 'The Symphonic Music of Oman' in 1985. This was a group of works commissioned by Qaboos for a Western orchestra and Omani traditional musicians, and written by the Director of the Oman Centre for Traditional Music, an Egyptian musicologist. The pieces were performed in the auditorium of the Boustan Palace Hotel for Qaboos and an audience of VIPs, and were reverently filmed by a British TV company. The Omani musicians blew oryx-horn trumpets and beat drums, and at one point banged out a rhythm on a crushed five-litre oil can, while the orchestra laboured to whip up a suitably gorgeous string sound around them from an opaque score. It was designed to be seen as 'a step which has pioneered the development of Omani music from the folkloric level to that of the symphony', in order to show 'the great progress achieved by Oman' since 1970.

That the music was, by any standards, pretty awful was of not the slightest consequence. Everyone clapped anyway, once the Sultan started clapping. The point had been made.

Driving through Salalah, the Sultan notices that the place needs brightening up. He tells someone to see to the planting of trees along the main roads. The newspapers later report that following a 'directive' by His Majesty Sultan Qaboos bin Sa'id, a new programme for tree-planting in Salalah has begun. Policy is either inaugurated by the Sultan or agreed by him, but nothing can move forward without him. He delegates little, and rarely smiles.

There are no glaring human-rights violations in Oman – Omanis don't live in fear, with soldiers patrolling the streets and the ruler's portrait is not plastered over every wall, as in Syria or Iraq – but there is no public discussion of politics. It is illegal for an Omani to marry a foreigner, and air-conditioners must have wooden boxes around them to hide their ugliness. This is Qaboos's will. His is the only conspicuous personality in Oman. There are no dissidents, intellectuals or stars. (There is a frustrated popular singer called Salim 'Ali Sa'id who covets Western-style stardom, but he will never achieve it in Oman.)

A resident diplomat told me in hushed, awed tones that Qaboos is rumoured to go out disguised as a taxi-driver, casually soliciting his subjects' views about their ruler and how the country is being governed. At first I dismissed this as a yarn from the *Thousand and One Nights*; then I read the following in one of Qaboos's rare interviews:

Q: You keep a watchful eye over many things. It is said that you even drive yourself in the evenings, incognito, and if you see rubbish in the streets, ministers hear about it the next day. Is this true?
A: Absolutely true. I make a point of going around incognito. I can't succeed all the time; sometimes I'm discovered! (Laughs) . . . One enjoys doing these things, and I keep people on their toes. They know that I am keeping an eye on things. I move from one area to another. I don't stand still in the capital. I move. Some days you will see me driving into the interior, others I go to the south. When I have a few days free from the pressure of work, I move elsewhere. I do not like sitting in one place.

Politics are muted, hidden. Influence in Oman means having the Sultan's ear. There are no discernible factions, although Qaboos has been careful to balance the influence of Dhofar with that of Oman. Unlike other Gulf monarchies, the royal family is small and not very powerful. There is no one in it of stature comparable to Qaboos.

Under Qaboos, Oman is enjoying a golden age, the like of which has never been seen in its history, and will probably never be seen again. In 1990 it was estimated that the sultanate could produce oil from existing fields for another twenty years. If oil ran out then, Qaboos would be seventy. It is possible that Qaboos and the oil that has underwritten his golden age will expire at about the same time. With his death will come uncertainty, not least because of the lack of an obvious successor. The official line on this is that 'the family will decide when the time comes'.

So completely is Qaboos identified with modern Oman that his birthday and Oman's national holiday are celebrated on the same day. *L'état? C'est lui!*

Officially, the link between National Day and Qaboos's birthday is understated. At Qaboos's own directive, Omani propaganda subordinates imagery of the person of Qaboos to a more abstract symbolism of Oman itself, to create a sense of nationhood that goes beyond the traditional obedience to the ruler. (Unlike other Arab states, which idolize the image of the ruler, whether king or president, there is a specific directive in Oman banning the image of the Sultan on wristwatches.) But to ordinary Omanis the link is clear enough. They call the occasion '*'Eid* Qaboos' ('Qaboos Day'), not by its official name, '*'Eid Waṭani*' ('National Day').

In November 1990, for the twentieth anniversary of Qaboos's rule, and of modern Oman, and his fiftieth year, a gold coin was minted, as a token of the golden age, in a denomination of twenty rials. It showed Qaboos surrounded by the fruits of his reign, emblems of industry, agriculture and learning: a classic gesture of absolutist grandeur and triumphalism.

The anniversary festivities were spread over a week, and journalists from all over the world were invited. I managed to wangle a place in the press entourage, which was billeted in the Muscat Intercontinental Hotel. Politically, the events were to culminate in Qaboos's National Day speech, in which the Sultan makes his main policy statement of the year, in a stadium, accompanied by great pomp.

But the *real* centre, the aesthetic nucleus of the celebrations, was something more esoteric: the ceremonial presentation to the Sultan of a rose named after himself. The rose was a new breed that, like Qaboos himself, could thrive in both a temperate European and a hot desert climate. It had been bred by the Dutch landscaping firm contracted to work on the grounds of Seeb Palace. The rose was to be presented to Qaboos by Mrs Susan Begg of Argentina, President of the World Federation of Rose Societies. The Ceremony of the Rose was to take place on the lawn at the back of the palace, before an invited audience of about a thousand of the Sultan's closest friends.

The press was denied access. Every one of the foreign journalists, without exception, asked to attend the ceremony and received the same peremptory negative reply from the Ministry of Information. The rose was not for the general gaze: it was a symbol of the mystical dimension of royal power, kept apart in a walled garden, like some secret of occult science reserved for the adepts of the royal court. In his work on alchemical symbolism, *Mysterium Coniunctionis*, Carl Jung quotes Figulus's *Rosarium novum Olympicum*: 'I will not forbear to admonish thee not to reveal to anyone, however dear, the treasures of our secrets, lest the stinking goats browse upon the red and white roses of our rose-garden.' This could be Qaboos addressing the Minister of Information.

Secrecy is a necessary attribute of the royal rose: it is the thorn that protects it from violation. But because of the ardour of our desire for the Invisible Rose, the Ministry of Information organized a viewing of it for us in the palace grounds before the ceremony took place. We would be allowed to bask in its rays for thirty minutes, but must then leave, a separate and unworthy caste of devotees. Then we had to go by bus to a perfume factory.

Stern officials from the Diwan shepherded us on to the lawn, an oval of perfect green overlooking the bay of Muscat. On one flank Jalali fort, where Sultan Saʿid left his prisoners to rot in shackles, stood on the rocky promontory; on the other, the graffiti of British sailors could still be seen: HMS *Falmouth* had been there. The green of the lawn contrasted starkly with the red-velvet chairs and white-covered tables that had been set out on it. The green, the white and the red of the rose together were the colours of Oman's national flag.

The rose itself was an ordinary-looking red rose, with rather tough dark-red petals. A multitude of the roses had been arranged in an eight-foot cone. Behind it the royal-blue and gold trumpet-shaped columns of the palace rose up into the overhanging roof. We photographed the specially commissioned Limoges teacups adorning the tables (bearing the sultanate's emblem of a curved dagger on crossed swords under an Indian-looking crown), and we photographed each other, and we photographed the rose. We had been especially warned not to try to remain behind after it was time to leave and thus violate the sanctity of the ritual by, for example, hiding under a cloth-covered buffet table.

Had I been hiding under a table, I would have seen with my own eyes what was shown on the TV news that night. Qaboos wore a modest and unflamboyant military uniform, with the shy smile of a boy taking his first Holy Communion. Under the gaze of his guests, Qaboos faced the President of the World Federation of Rose Societies, an English-looking lady wearing a blue dress and a broad-brimmed white hat, who made a speech and handed him a single stem of the flower; it was wrapped in ribbons of red, white and green. The guests clapped politely. The camera then cut to a long close-up of the rose resting on a green velvet cushion, reposing in solitary splendour. The rite of the ruler and the rose was consummated and complete.

In contemplating the Sultan Qaboos rose, Sultan Qaboos metaphorically contemplates himself: essence contemplating essence, Pure Beauty mingling with Pure Power. The rose symbolizes his perfect attributes: it was presented, according to the Ministry of Information, 'in recognition of his work for the welfare of his people, his contribution to world peace through his efforts to bring about a cease-fire in the war between Iraq and Iran, his achievements in protecting the ecology of his country, and his support for human rights'. These acts were the flowers of his rule; in the Ceremony of the Rose they were translated into a real flower, one that in Islamic tradition represents divine wisdom, beauty and love. In the Ceremony of the Rose, Qaboos both commands and accepts that these attributes be seen as part of himself; they come to him, in the Presentation of the Rose, but they also come out of him: wisdom, beauty and love approach what they resemble. The ceremony confirmed this metaphysical union, through the office of a priestess in a broad-brimmed white hat.

So when the Sultan's yacht *Fulk as-Salama* steamed into Muttrah harbour on 17 November, an enormous metal rose on a raft floated out to greet it, accompanied by a smiling portrait of the Sultan, festooned with balloons, on a second raft, and the United Nations emblem on a third. The rafts were powered by outboard motors and steered by concealed operators. The yacht was being used as part of a UNESCO project to retrace the ancient silk routes, which centuries ago passed through Oman.

I had hoped to see more of the Sultan than I actually did during the 1990 National Day celebrations. I attended every event at which he was scheduled to appear, hoping to catch a glimpse of him, but he was always too far away.

It was for this purpose that I went to a football game at the Royal Oman Police stadium near Qurm, at which he was to award the cup, and watched a very slow match between two local teams. I saw much histrionic heading of the ball, and a lot of players lying on the pitch as if mortally wounded, writhing in pain. Stretchers were in motion constantly, always unnecessarily, as the injured player would bounce back miraculously as soon as a stretcher appeared. The crowd were very well-behaved – except at the end, when they pelted the winning team with full litre bottles of mineral water during their lap of honour around the stadium. But I never saw the Sultan, nor even worked out where he was sitting, and he left by helicopter.

Even on National Day itself I was disappointed. Journalists mustered outside the Muscat Intercontinental at 6.00 a.m. on the day, to be bused to the National Stadium for a programme that began at 7.00 a.m. After a long military tattoo, involving an equestrian display, battalions of bare-chested Dhofari tribesmen brandishing swords and obsolete rifles, and helicopters spewing coloured smoke, the Sultan made his speech. He spoke in classical Arabic, preceding each point with the phrase 'O countrymen,' and announced the formation of an elected assembly, a cautious step toward popular representation in government. He wore a splendid uniform, decked in gold braid and medals, crossed by a sash and set off by a sword at his hip. But he stood inside an enclosure of smoked bulletproof glass, and even my camera's zoom lens made him seem no bigger than a toy soldier from the place to which I'd jostled to photograph him. I complained bitterly to the man from the Ministry about not being admitted among the official photographers, who stood like gulls at an effluent pipe in front of the enclosure, down on the floor of the stadium, hoovering in images of the royal person standing exhibited before them.

To see how golden-age Oman has produced its own unique forms of modern royal ceremonial, we now look at the grand finale of the National Day events: the celebration of the Sultan's birthday by the massed schoolchildren of Oman, in the Sultan Qaboos Sports Centre at Baushar, outside Muscat – yet another of the stadiums that have been built in the capital area in the past two decades.

The event involved thousands of schoolchildren performing for Qaboos (and a multitude of spectators) spectacularly choreographed idealized representations of life in Oman under his rule. Those in the terraces facing him created the kind of mosaic-like pictures, through the synchronized display of thousands of rectangles of painted board, that are best known as the product of Mao's China, where they dramatized the unitary creativity of a disciplined proletariat. Here the technique had been turned to the glorification of absolute monarchy, with portraits of Qaboos (for whom the experience must have been like looking into a gigantic mirror), quotations from the Qur'an and scenes of an idealized, industrialized modern Oman.

Down on the stadium floor, dancing and marching routines glorified aspects of Qaboos's reign. The creation of an Omani workforce, one of Qaboos's priorities, was reflected in a parade of children carrying the tools of trades whose development is state policy: agriculture was represented by children carrying toy sheep, fisheries by nets, mining by picks. Girls carrying incense-burners symbolized national heritage. Rule through splendour: it was as if by performing these things, they could be brought into existence.

The sports centre was equipped with a TV system which allowed the projection of video images on to an enormous screen at one end of the stadium. On this from time to time the Sultan's approving expressions were shown on this Milky Way of white lights as he sat in the royal box observing the proceedings. When a group of children parading past the box waved in his direction, the screen showed him waving back, the leading actor as well as the key spectator.

But now a pink-and-white birthday cake on wheels, with a crown on top, twinkling with fairy lights, was approaching, and his face, thrown up on to the screen in a million light-bulbs, reflected stonily the pressure of kingly dignity afflicted by acute embarrassment. The cake-carriage was pulled by a pink-and-white tractor, and on it sat two little girls in shocking-pink dresses. Each little girl carried a box on her lap, wrapped in white paper tied with pink ribbon. These were their presents to the Sultan. What were they giving him? Socks? He hates socks. A tie? He has loads of ties, and he never wears them. Meanwhile, from a ring in the centre of the stadium, where children had built a prefabricated model of the Renaissance Tower, the country's most famous roundabout sculpture, a procession of girls in white, like bridesmaids, was filing towards the royal box with bunches of flowers. The Sultan was being brought bouquets, after all – the flowers of the Renaissance! He departed with these by helicopter, and then we were allowed to stream out to the parking-lots.

Such shows are 'the outward expression of the magnanimity and liberality of princes'. Bravo!

The Amir of Bahrain, Shaykh 'Isa, is the last ruler in Arabia to hold the traditional open *majlis* at which anyone who wants to can come and see him, either to present a petition or to pay respects to him. This is the Arab tradition of access to the ruler. Al-Ghazali wrote, 'The Arabs have a saying that nothing is more damaging to the subjects and more prejudicial and sinister for the king than royal inaccessibility and seclusion; and that nothing impresses the hearts of the subjects and officials more than ease of access to the king.' So, every Friday morning at seven o'clock, Bahrainis of all stations and foreigners of all nationalities come to the Riffa' palace outside Manama to greet the Amir. Visitors sit around the large room on sofas, and queue up before the Amir's low, comfortable chair, either to shake his hand or kiss his cheeks and shoulders, or to give him a petition in an envelope, which he passes to an aide. Servants distribute cardamom coffee in tiny cups, and tea, and splashes of orange water, and waft a censer of incense before each person, so that one can fan the fragrant smoke into one's robes and beard. Some people come merely to sit and be with the Amir, to show loyalty to him. It is enough to sit and stare blankly into space. After an hour or so he swishes out to prayers in a rustle of robes, followed by a train of attendants.

There is no such institution in Oman, but a suitable alternative has been invented for Qaboos. In the early part of the year the Sultan makes a tour of the country to meet his subjects. It is called the Meet the People Tour. He wears a simple robe and drives his own four-wheel-drive Mercedes. He is accompanied by his ministers, all dressed likewise, their opulent garb left behind in Muscat. Everyone carries a gun, for appearance's sake. The official explanation of the tour is that it allows Qaboos to find out directly from his subjects what their needs are. A mat is spread on the ground and Qaboos meets them face to face, in a manner suggesting the simple, honourable egalitarianism of Bedouin life.

Its name suggests that it was devised with British help as a device to generate goodwill through exhibiting the royal body and satisfying the appetite for access to the ruler. But no advance warning of where Qaboos is going to appear is given; no one has time to prepare a question, and there is no guarantee that he is going to come at all.

While it is officially intended to establish the consent of the governed by facilitating contact with the ruler, it achieves the same result through the very different technique of the spectacle of the royal progress. The tour is like a military campaign. The Sultan travels with an enormous retinue of tents, trucks and military vehicles, which establish bases along the route of the royal itinerary, as if he were conquering his own territories anew.

I was in Oman at the time, travelling around the country officially engaged in the recording of Omani traditional music. I wanted to see Qaboos 'meet the people', and to feast my eyes on him once more.

People said the tour would begin 'after the rains'. I waited; I kept my eye on the churning clouds for a clue to the Sultan's intentions. The waiting was an ordeal of aborted time, energy, expense, spirit. Oman was hoovering money out of me as I waited, and the Ministry of Information was saying nothing about when the tour might start. It was 'for Omanis'; journalists were kept away. Every day I would buy the tedious English-language newspaper for clues. The Sultan addressed a convention of businessmen, stressing the 'Omanization' of the economy. The wind raised menacing sandstorms. The first sign that the tour was about to begin was the beginning of a national military exercise called 'Daring Adventure 2', in which the Sultan's Armed Forces used the whole country as an adventure playground. The highways were full of formidable sand-coloured vehicles, laddishly driven at the highest possible speed by elated soldiers.

Then, one day in early February, driving on the Batinah coast road, I stopped on the outskirts of a place called Saham to have a despondent lunch at a Baluchi restaurant among the tyre-repair shops. Chicken curry with rice: one arthritic dwarf knee-joint in a sea of sauce. Outside, the sand blew and the sky grew very dark. It was like being in some desperate Mexican border town of the imagination. In the filthy lavatory, I reflected that by now I knew the word for cockroach in about a dozen languages. It began to rain very heavily, then to hail. The rain fell solidly for three weeks.

Water poured down the mountains of bare rock and flooded the highways. Dirt roads became pools of mud. Wadis in the interior that were cracked and dry for most of the year were now overflowing; their currents were strong enough to sweep away camels and palm trees. On the urbanized coast, the lightning knocked out power lines. Still I waited, twisting in the wind.

And then the skies cleared. The sun began to shine again in all its fury, on to a landscape renewed by a veil of green. The tour began.

I reasoned that, since his previous year's itinerary had begun in the west, this year he would begin in the east, and when the first report was transmitted on the TV news that night I learned that I was right. I set off east in my rented car, towards Sur, to find him.

I eventually found his camp, on a flat, white, gravelly plain beside the highway. The scene was like a combination between a military campaign, with forces arrayed on the battlefield, and a fairground, with parked cars and Omanis in colourful costumes drinking soda and eating. The air was filled with the sound of drumming. Around Omani flags planted in the ground, large groups of men were performing the *razha* war dance. A metal barrier, patrolled by policemen, bisected the plain; beyond it lay the Sultan's camp.

After I had been there for about two hours, as the sun grew fierce, I asked two teenage boys where the Sultan was.

'Over there.'

'When will he come out?'

'Five o'clock.' People were ready to wait all day to see him.

By two o'clock the crowd had thinned out. By five o'clock I was on the verge of sunstroke. It was obvious that he wasn't going to appear, so I returned to Muscat without having seen him.

My hotel overlooked Muttrah harbour and the corniche. The room was dark and had mildewy walls. I disconsolately ordered beer, and a light-bulb for the empty socket of my bedside lamp. In the evening I watched the news. Omani TV showed the same film-clip every night: the Sultan's Mercedes driving down the centre of the road, with people on either side waving and throwing flower petals. We were never told where the Sultan was going to be the next day.

That night I dreamed that I entered the Sultan's tent and had a long talk with him. He sat very close to me, with his bare foot pressed against my shod foot, and showed me plans for a new village that was about to be built.

For a week I set out every morning to hunt for the campaigning Sultan. At the end of the day, I would return unsuccessfully to Muttrah and my dismal hotel.

In the evenings, the Muttrah corniche belonged to Indian men. At night the Omanis would withdraw from the town centre, leaving it to the foreigners. Together, we foreigners hovered on the periphery of Omani prosperity, far from home, attracted like moths to the glow of the petrodollar. Usually alone, sometimes not, the Indian men would soothe the loneliness of their expatriate servitude with an evening walk. The Omanis were all at home indoors, with their music and food. The Indians ran the hotels and restaurants, and most of the businesses, and did most of the manual work – pumping petrol, building roads, humping cement, mopping the floors. All were between twenty and fifty; there were no old men. They were not allowed to bring their families. They would work for years, and many of them – particularly those at the bottom of the heap – would go back little better off than when they started, with a cassette-player or a video machine in a torn cardboard box.

In the Gulf, a foreign employee of whatever nationality is a kind of bondsman, the property of his employer. Sometimes one of them escapes, and the employer puts an advertisement in a newspaper, of the type which in the antebellum American South would have been headed RUNAWAY SLAVE:

NOTICE

Mr X, holder of Indian passport no. 008752729 and whose photograph is appended alongside [looking glum and blurry in a long-ago photo booth] has been absconding since 30th August 1990. As he is urgently required to discuss his position, anyone knowing about his whereabouts is requested to inform the General Manager, Services.

Oman Daily Observer

In hotels, consequently, the service tends to be rather surly, due to homesickness and what the French call *cafard*.

Every night I would watch the clip of the Sultan's tour that indicated that it was still in progress. I consoled myself that it was worth watching TV in Arabia. The Arabs had all the best equipment, and were slowly developing television as a distinctive cultural form. Naturally, in an Arabian monarchy, TV fits squarely into an evolving tradition of royal panegyric and protocol. In the future, travel books will be written without leaving the hotel room and will simply describe what is seen on local TV.

The news is intended to sedate rather than to stimulate; when there is an official visit, news serves as a branch of diplomacy. When the Emir of Kuwait came to Oman, the whole of the evening news was devoted to his visit. The first image was of an empty sky, in which a dot appeared: the Emir of Kuwait's plane entering ceremonial airspace. Up there, in the royal-blue yonder, the Emir's jumbo began its gracious descent towards the welcoming tarmac terra firma of the sultanate. A military brass band serenaded the friendly skies. The Sultan stood alone under a ceremonial awning. Then the plane landed, the Emir emerged, and he and the Sultan exchanged fraternal Arab greetings on the red carpet. Then the Emir shook hands with the long line of government officials who had turned out to greet him. It was like watching the grass grow, but it was dignified: the thirty-second news bite isn't part of the political theatre of Arabia.

Arabian television is the modern equivalent of the panegyric of the court poet of classical Arabic literature, like al-Mutanabbi, who praised the ruler in fulsome and elaborate terms for his wisdom, his valour and particularly his generosity. These were the only permitted themes of public discourse in Arabia, and they still are.

> Whither do you intend, great prince? We are the herbs of the hills, and you are the clouds;
> So may you be blessed for the rain shower that you are, whereby it seems to me our skins sprout brocade and embroidered silks and fine woven garments, and for the liberal giver you are . . .

Some weeks earlier, at a party at the home of a senior government official, I had sat in a room full of rapt Omanis before a huge projection TV while another government official recited a poem in praise of Qaboos on the occasion of the opening of the Sultan Qaboos University Medical Centre. The thirty-two-couplet poem was printed in the newspaper *Oman* the following day.

> You raise the glory of Oman, O Lion of the Colocynth; you make a sacred place out of what would otherwise be a heap of stones.
> You stand out among the kings of the world; honours and glories incline toward you.
> You vow, Qaboos, to advance toward the stars, and you are true to all your promises.
> Five floors of beds where people are cured! The pens are all broken trying to record your achievements . . .

After a week's fruitless searching, I had had enough. I slumped over my steering-wheel at the side of the road near the Sultan's camp and gave up. If only I didn't have to tell the truth! Then I would describe how I had disguised myself as a member of Qaboos's court, and watched him reclining on cushions in his tent, listening to Mozart with a company of young companions, discussing military affairs, firepower and horses, while soldiers guarded the entrance. Perhaps I would even have joined in the conversation myself, throwing in an appreciative pleasantry for the Sultan's amusement. I would have been quite good at it.

Obviously, there was an experience of Oman which I was

striving for but which I would never capture. I was skating over the surface, and the quixotic nature of the enterprise haunted me like a direct question I was evading. The real Oman was a closed country, which belonged to Omanis and to long-serving, loyal expatriates – mostly British – who worked for the oil industry or the military and who liked to keep the secrets of the place to themselves. Oman allowed no freelancers; everyone was there at the pleasure of the Sultan, and no matter how hard I tried to insinuate myself into that king-centred world I could never do it.

And why I was slumped over a steering-wheel in an expensive rented car running around impertinently after a head of state was a matter for a psychiatrist. Lost father-figure, perhaps. I was adrift, like a lost satellite. One comes to the desert to chase mirages and to find oblivion, and I had found it. It began to get dark. It was time to drive back to Muscat. If I stayed there any longer, I'd be arrested.

In manic-depressive psychosis, the patient alternates phases of sometimes unbearable exaltation with periods of even worse depression. A patient in a manic state experiences highly elevated self-esteem, a sense of limitless opportunities and heightened powers. The patient's thoughts race; he stays up for days until overcome with exhaustion. Often this state is accompanied by delusions, conventionally classified as delusions of special abilities, delusions of wealth, delusions of a special mission and delusions of grandiose identity. In delusions of grandiose identity, patients believe they are a king or queen or of royal blood, or are divine in some way: the second coming of Christ, Moses, an archangel. The religious and the royal, as guises of the triumph of the self, are, here as elsewhere, close neighbours. I saw in a textbook a self-portrait of a patient in a manic state: her head was surrounded by a halo – the symbolism used to denote not only holy people in the Christian tradition, but also, in the iconography of ancient Iran, the king. The treatment for disorders of this type is 800–1600 grains of lithium daily.

In *Clinical Lectures on Mental Diseases*, an out-of-date medical textbook published in 1883, Dr T. S. Clouston described an asylum patient who wore a multicoloured crown he had made himself, 'each part of which had a symbolic meaning. He was so picturesque a character about the place, and was so striking a clinical illustration of monomania of grandeur, and withal so harmless and useful in the garden, that I never ordered him to be discrowned.' Clouston made an assertion of a kind that the psychiatrists of a century later are cautious to avoid: 'This imaginary grandeur and power has a physiological foundation in the brain workings of every man.' What physiological foundation is that?

In 1972 a book was published in Britain entitled *Dreams about HM the Queen and Other Members of the Royal Family*. It was a sampling of dream-accounts of ordinary Britishers; usually they involved having a nice cup of tea and a pleasant chat with her. 'You dream about royalty', the author theorized, 'because exalted, regal figures compensate for the dullness of a routine existence.' Only in Britain would such an explanation be thinkable.

In manic-depressive psychosis, the feeling of exaltation the patient feels in the manic state, with its accompanying delusions, is thought by psychiatrists to flow from a sense of triumph over the restraining force of the super-ego, the authority figure in the psyche. In this sense one can see kingship as being an outward show of an inner state of exalted freedom of the self rather than of despotic power over others. Note that Qaboos overthrew his own tyrannic father before assuming the trappings of splendour.

It is amazing to me that there can be people in whom such symptoms are not pathological but the reflection of a real state of affairs. It shows how strange a being a king is. Qaboos is not treated with lithium for sitting on a throne. Anyone else would be. One wonders how he manages to keep a cool head, and not fall from the sky like Shah Jamshid. Indeed, the *Qabusnamah* warns, 'Strive against becoming intoxicated with the wine of kingship . . . no king who becomes intoxicated with kingship regains sobriety except with its disappearance.'

While Qaboos, the world-adorner, adorned himself with signs of exaltation, I at my steering-wheel, at the edge of the desert, with the sun nearly set, represented the nadir of the manic-depressive cycle, Pluto in the underworld of depression, as the result of circumstances as real as Qaboos's aura of triumph.

I thought it was time to make my excuses and leave.

CHAPTER 3

Innumerable Kingdoms – Nigeria

IN SOUTHERN NIGERIA – the land of the Yoruba – the god Eshu was my patron and tormentor. In the Yoruba pantheon, Eshu is the god of crossroads, highways and markets. He oversees a realm of uncertainty and confusion, the web of random comings and goings that fill a public thoroughfare, and the numberless crises of losing and finding one's way that each individual passing through it experiences. Eshu is inscrutable, unpredictable and undependable. He has no form and no morality. 'If you look for him around the roof-beam, he squats under the ground-nut leaf. If you look for him under the mat, he towers so high above you that his head goes through the roof.' You can only pray to him in the negative: '*Eshu ma se mi*' – 'Do not injure me, Eshu'.

He favours sacrifices of baby goats and black chickens. His symbol is a mound of earth.

Eshu travels with the stranger. He was with me at bus stations, taxi stands, palace gates and markets – everywhere I went as I made my endless journey in search of the Yoruba kings.

In Nigeria, gods and kings are innumerable. Some say there are 201 Yoruba gods, others say there are 401. There might be 700 Yoruba kings, though some are more important than others. This is to say nothing of the traditional rulers of the Igbos and Hausas.

A Yoruba king – *oba* – is the immortal and immaterial soul of a Yoruba town. Most of the temporal powers the *obas* once had have been taken over by the government of Nigeria. What an *oba* retains is influence on local and sometimes national government, money, a palace, prestige and elaborate supernatural powers. A Yoruba can explain to a stranger the *oba*'s role as guardian of the traditional Yoruba religion. He will tell you that, although the *oba* must represent all of his subjects, Christians and Muslims, he leads the worship of the Yoruba gods. What he cannot explain is the divine spark the *oba* embodies, which seems to place the *obas* among the gods themselves.

A reigning *oba* is the living embodiment of a single spirit, passed from king to king. After an *oba* dies, his successor eats his heart (dried, in soup) and drinks from his skull, and performs a miracle, and becomes the *oba* – if he is following the tradition. He then can speak of his predecessors in the first person. Of a battle that took place three hundred years ago, he can say, 'I slew them left and right as they came,' even if, like the king of the town of Iragbiji, the Aragbiji of Iragbiji, in whose domain I began my investigation, he might be a retired employee of the trading firm John Holt, and a Christian.

The Aragbiji of Iragbiji's name is His Highness Oba Timothy Oyelade Adepoju II. Iragbiji is a large village in the north-eastern part of Ọ̀yọ́ State. It wasn't on any of my maps.

Iragbiji is hidden deep in the heart of Yoruba country, an unvaried, mostly flat geography of red earth, tangled forest and stone hills. It is not virgin forest but 'secondary growth': what has grown back after centuries of bush farming. The forest ensured the isolation of the Yoruba over the centuries, and covered up the tracks of those who came to the Yoruba lands from elsewhere: this is where the secrets of the Yoruba are hidden.

I met the Aragbiji in the compound of Muraina Oyelami, a well-known Yoruba artist and musician whom I had met in London. Muraina's daughter Bimpe was getting married the day I arrived from Lagos.

Bride and groom were dressed in matching pink-and-silver costumes. They stood under a canvas tent at a table strewn with plastic flowers and bottles of Coke and Fanta, and cut an enormous blue cake. There were drummers and acrobats. All day, Muraina pulled money out of his robes to 'dash' the performers.

That evening the Aragbiji of Iragbiji favoured the proceedings with his presence. He arrived in the compound in his second-best car, a yellow Toyota with a licence plate that read:

OY 2 E

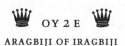

ARAGBIJI OF IRAGBIJI

His black Mercedes (licence plate OY 1 E) was back at the palace.

The Aragbiji and an *oba* from a neighbouring town sat together in an upstairs room which was bare except for two bulky armchairs, borrowed for the occasion from a carpenter, and put there for their use. Food had been set before the *obas* on a low table: glutinous *eba*, like unbaked bread dough, and a soup of the slimiest okra.

Their cream-coloured robes were stiff with beadwork, and they carried beaded walking-sticks, the emblems of *oba*-ship. Deep in their armchairs they sat, very still, receiving visitors and nodding to them distantly. When you enter a room to greet an *oba*, you are supposed to fling yourself on to the floor in a prone position on the threshold, as if performing press-ups; usually to get down on one knee while deeply lowering the head is enough.

The Aragbiji, whose title means 'owner of Iragbiji', was the older of the two kings. His features were fine and wizened, making him look almost Chinese. He wore a gold watch, and gold rings on his fingers. He had been *oba* since 1974.

I stood in the outer room among the drummers who were serenading the *obas* as they sat in splendour. The Aragbiji spotted me and summoned me in with an elegant wave of his hand.

I bowed and said, 'Kabiyesi!', which is how you address a Yoruba king. It can be translated as either 'May you have long life' or 'You cannot be contradicted.' It's one of these Yoruba expressions whose etymology depends on the imagination of the person who is explaining it to you. This is one of the principles of the interpretation of Yoruba culture: it's impossible to get to the bottom of anything. The further you burrow, the more numerous and tangled the roots become. Likewise, a white person is called '*oyinbo*', which means either 'one who comes from over the sea' or 'someone without skin', depending on whom you ask.

It is the same when dealing with the problem of the origins of the Yoruba. There are three possible answers, all mutually contradictory. (a) They came from somewhere else – i.e. the savannah. But where did the people of the savannah come from? From Egypt. But where did the people of Egypt come from?

From somewhere else. And so on. Inquiry leads into an infinite regression: the inward-curving boundary of the universe of the knowable. (b) They came from heaven. (c) No one knows.

Any one of these is the right answer, but it's the wrong question. Why look for a chicken behind the egg? The chicken (or whatever bird it was) disappeared into the forest long ago, leaving behind a marvellous egg of mysterious provenance. It is better to consider the mysterious egg alone. Ifẹ̀, for instance, the cradle of the Yoruba, where the world was created, gave the world the Ifẹ̀ bronzes, perhaps the greatest treasures of African art. These sculptures, most of which are now in the National Museum, Lagos, are human figures of breathtaking sensitivity. The jewellery and crowns which the figures wear suggest the art of a royal court. The sculptor seems to be recalling the image of a person dearly loved; each bronze is the evocation of fond memory, idealized but true. They have warmth and nearly the breath of life.

The Ifẹ̀ bronzes have no equal in the art that followed, and no antecedents. They cannot be placed in history more exactly than in a four-century band of time from 1000 to 1400 A.D. A refined court tradition seems to appear fully formed out of the darkness of unrecorded time.

I told the Aragbiji about my mission in Nigeria. He listened and nodded, and invited me to call on him at the palace. Then his features went icy and still, and it became clear to me that I had been dismissed. Although only a minor *oba*, he was a master of the art of royal distance and hauteur.

The day after the wedding I went to the palace ('*afin*' in Yoruba) with Muraina's eldest son, Tajudeen. We walked along the red dirt road until we saw an arch of painted cement over the road that led to the palace. On the arch was written 'AFIN OF THE ARAGBIJI OF IRAGBIJI'. A mural had been painted on the wall beside the arch, showing the Aragbiji sitting in splendour, with his subjects prostrating themselves before him.

A palace servant showed us into the Aragbiji's private reception room upstairs. It was dimly lit by green fluorescent tubes. Deep, low armchairs surrounded the room; the walls were decorated with a clock, a calendar ('Sons of Iragbiji Benevolent Association') and portraits and photographs of the Aragbiji. A child brought us bottles of Star beer. Downstairs we could hear shouting: the Aragbiji was settling a domestic dispute. The electricity went off for fifteen minutes, then came back on. We waited for an hour and a half for the Aragbiji to appear, which he eventually did in a rustle of maroon robes.

He apologized for being busy. He gave us kola nut, then bitter kola. He broke the pink kola nut into segments and shared them with us. Kola contains nicotine: it gives you a lift. 'It dries the mouth, no?' the Aragbiji said, chewing. 'Now drink some beer. It will sweeten the mouth.' The biggest kola nuts, with four lobes, are called '*oba*'s kola'. He sat in one of the deep, threadbare armchairs.

'We usually live very long,' the Aragbiji said, 'before we go where our fathers go.' He was speaking of his predecessors, of whom there had been fourteen. *Obas* do not die: when an *oba* 'passes away', he goes 'where his fathers went'.

Iragbiji, like every Yoruba town, has a foundation myth. The first Aragbiji, Ogba, came from Ifẹ̀ on a hunting expedition. When the hunters saw a leopard, they chased it into a hole in a stone outcrop. They ran in after it, and chased it through a narrow, winding passage. The leopard ran out the other side, and the hunters caught up with it and killed it. Where they emerged from the rock, they founded Iragbiji. They sealed up the hole, and every year the Aragbiji leads the people of the town back to this place to worship at the shrine of the deity who guards the spot.

The Oyelamis' compound was built on the slope of a hill, and from the balcony of the upper room where the Aragbiji sat on the day of the wedding the forest stretched away as far as one could see. Granite outcrops jutted out between the houses and the trees. It was the rainy season, and the sky was heavy and grey.

The compound was enclosed by a high concrete wall with a wrought-iron gate that was locked at night by a night-watchman. Inside there were buildings for the members of Muraina's extended family. Water was drawn from a well with a bucket made out of inner tube. I found it very difficult to discern who was related to whom there and how. Among its inhabitants was a small child who screamed with terror every time he – she? – saw me.

Muraina had a friend called Shango, who ran a beer parlour. Shango introduced me to the mysteries of the Yoruba religion. His real name was Adeleke, but he had taken the name of the god of thunder and lightning.

The Yoruba religion has no orthodoxy. As a theological system, it is whatever a Yoruba's imagination says it is. It is a shared dream-world in which all act out the supernatural drama of their lives. Nothing is fixed. The gods control our lives, but their way of doing so is as confused as human affairs on earth. Their favour can be bought with sacrifices – if they are in a good mood; but you can never tell what kind of mood they are in. The supreme god, Olorun, is an absentee landlord who takes no interest in human affairs. The gods below him have no hierarchy. A god's personality and characteristics are what each devotee perceives them to be. The identities of the gods blur and merge. Their reputations rise and fall depending on how well they are seen to deliver benefits to human beings.

Shango, if you don't bless me, the shame is your own.
Shango, if I don't serve you, the shame is mine.
Shango, if you don't bless me, I will go and make an Ogun image.
Shango, if you don't bless me, I'll go and turn Christian.

Shango – Adeleke – was an artist, a musician, a dancer and a farmer. He was small in stature and sinewy in build, and had a wispy moustache and beard, which he often twisted in thought when spinning his version of Yoruba religion. Much of it came to him in dreams. The octagonal diagram of the Yoruba cosmos that he built into the floor of his beer parlour had come to him in one of these dreams. It was a mosaic of pebbles and cowrie shells pressed into the cement, for future archaeologists to discover and puzzle over.

Hanging from the walls were batiks he had made illustrating scenes in the imaginary struggles of Yoruba gods with supernatural forces. I couldn't see anything except dark, swirling abstract designs. For him they were windows into that other world.

'What's that, Shango?' I said once, over a large bottle of Guinness Foreign Export Stout (a malty version of Guinness, brewed in Lagos). His wife was asleep on a bench beside him.

'That is Ogun [god of iron weapons and machinery] fighting a snake.'

To me it looked like a diagram of molecules in Brownian motion, or the universe when it was two kilograms of matter.

His answers were glimmers from a complex and dangerous supernatural realm. I asked him to tell me the name of the god worshipped at the Irioke festival, at the cave where Iragbiji was founded.

'I can't tell you,' he said.

'Why not?'

'I don't want to die.'

Of the giant black snails the country people sell at the side of the road, whose blood is white and is a traditional symbol of the amniotic fluid, the fluid of life, Shango said, 'If you have one of those in your house, you will never get sick.'

Of the dried black fish, bent into a circle, that we ate with our hands, with our okra soup and doughy *amala*, he said, 'Eat it – it is from a good river.'

I told him about the American blues guitarist Robert Johnson, and his famous song 'Crossroads'. According to the legend, this is a song about a pact with the devil. To become a blues player, you must take your guitar to a crossroads just before midnight. 'A big black man will walk up there and take your guitar and he'll tune it. And then he'll play a piece and hand it back to you.' After that you can play anything. The Robert Johnson myth suggests that he broke the pact he made with this figure, and died in mysterious and tragic circumstances as a result. The big black man was an embodiment of Eshu, god of the crossroads.

Shango said it made perfect sense. 'When you want something from a god, you have to pay for it, and the more you want it, the more you have to pay. It's the same for drummers here.'

Yoruba religion is like gambling: it only works if you are in it so deep that the only way to break even is to put still more into it.

Later I told Shango I wanted to consult Ifa, the Yoruba oracle.

He gave me a serious stare. 'When you are ready,' he said, after a moment, and returned to his beer.

Money is more than a medium of exchange for the Yoruba: it is a sacrament. The design of the twenty-naira note, bearing the face of Murtala Muhammad, the assassinated military ruler of Nigeria (who ruled briefly from 1975 to 1976), is printed on to fabrics for clothes and on to the enamel crockery you buy in the market and is painted on to the sides of trucks and buses. People ask you for money as freely as they might ask you the time.

One night I went to Shango's and drank a calabash of palm wine. It gave me bad dreams and upset my bowels. In bed later, I dreamed I was watching people being hacked to death while some very loud drumming was going on. At about 2.30 a.m. I woke up, in my pitch-dark, windowless, airless room. The dream evaporated, but the drumming was still audible. In a room like that, though, you can't be sure if you're awake or asleep, so I fumbled for my torch and switched it on. The sound continued.

I hoped the compound gate was locked. I tried to tell if the sound was getting closer, but I couldn't. The talking drums were saying something, but of course I didn't know what.

The chanting stopped at around dawn, and I slept for an hour. At eight o'clock I rose and set about my ablutions.

I asked Nike, Muraina's other daughter, about the singing and drumming I'd heard.

'It was from the Cherubim and Seraphim church,' she said.

'A church? What were they doing at church in the middle of the night, singing and drumming until dawn?'

'They were praying to God.'

'?'

'To help them.'

'?'

'To give them money.'

She was a 'freethinker' herself.

The Aragbiji of Iragbiji demonstrated the real powers of an *oba* when he rescued me from the clutches of the Nigerian security police, the State Security Service, the SSS. He cannot be contradicted! May he have long life!

The incident took place in the nearby town of Ikirun. Shango and I had gone there to see the newly installed *oba*, the Akirun of Ikirun, exhibiting himself to the multitude. It was a very crowded and noisy celebration. Great beery multitudes of people, drummers, acrobats and sellers of cheap commemorative souvenirs had gathered outside the palace. The palace grandees, who sit permanently on the palace porch, welcomed us and we were pushed upstairs to greet the *oba*. We were shown to armchairs along the walls of a big reception room. A drunken trumpeter put his bottle aside and his bugle to his lips and blew a wobbly fanfare to announce the *oba*'s entry. Prostrations. The *oba* sat, waved his flywhisk, and summoned us forward. We exchanged courtesies. The *oba* invited me to come back the next day to interview him. He was an accountant and the managing director of a bank in Lagos.

As we were leaving the palace, a plain-clothes SSS agent in a white costume stopped us and began to ask a lot of impertinent questions. He demanded to see my passport. I said I wasn't carrying it, and wouldn't have shown it to him even if I had been. I had no idea who he was and wanted to walk away, but Shango was trembling at the knees. The man was tall, heavily built, vicious and young enough to be a real nuisance. 'Come with me,' he said.

Shango was dismissed, and I was taken to the police station, where the agent and the Ikirun police took it in turns to question me. I sat at a wooden desk and faced my accusers.

'Are you a spy? Are you the one who is stirring up the students at the university?'

'Are you carrying a pistol?'

'Where is your residence permit?'

'Who gave you permission to enter this area?'

'Why aren't you carrying your passport?'

'Do you know we have a law against wandering in this country?'

'Why are Nigerians treated so badly in the United States?'

So that was it! I was a scapegoat for US immigration policy.

Everyone in Nigeria wants a visa to the United States, but only a fraction of those who apply get them. I read later, in a Lagos newspaper, that 25,000 visas to the United States were issued annually in Nigeria, but 80 per cent of the applications were accompanied by false documents.

One of the SSS men said he had seen me the week before in Iragbiji. This made me appear doubly suspicious. The agent left, and I waited. A young Igbo policeman named Lucky sat beside me to prevent me from escaping. We had a nice chat. He had been in Ikirun for two weeks and couldn't stand it. He spoke no Yoruba. 'The people here are heartless,' he said.

Night fell and it began to rain. The revellers were still thronging the street outside. A tout came in and said, trying to keep a straight face, that when my questioning was over I was to go to a particular guest-house that he represented. Then the lights went out.

Lucky lit an oil lamp, and made apologies for NEPA, the chaotic Nigerian Electric Power Authority. The tout shuffled back and asked for two naira instead. Lucky said he only had two naira left and he needed it to buy some maize.

The man in white returned and ordered me to get into a car with a smashed windscreen covered in tape. Two other agents were inside. Personally, I've never liked driving with strange, hostile men in battered cars down dark country roads, especially in politically unstable foreign countries where Americans are unpopular.

'Where are we going?'

'Get in the car.'

I saw Shango standing in the rain, shivering.

The interrogation continued. 'What is your mission in Nigeria?'

They drove me to a remote police station, where the SSS man unsuccessfully, despite some threatening talk, tried to persuade the duty officer to incarcerate me. 'It is above my power,' the officer replied, in the often charmingly formal Nigerian dialect of the English language. I hadn't been charged with anything.

'I am asking you again, do you refuse to take this man?'

The officer stood his ground.

'What is in the bag?'

My belongings were arrayed on the counter. My notebook attracted the first agent's attention. He opened it at random and stared at the illegible script, pretending to read. I was allowed to put the other things back into my backpack, but he kept the notebook.

'Get in the car.' We drove down roads with no houses or people in sight, just tall grass and junked machinery on either side. I was going to be deported tomorrow, he said, just so I would waste the money I had spent on the ticket. I was sure they were going to beat me.

We seemed to re-enter the town, and pulled into a driveway. There were houses on both sides of the road, which was reassuring, but if the agents beat me up in full view of those modest people, cooking on outdoor fires, no one would try to stop them. The car stopped. An older man in his underwear came to the window. It was a superior officer. I had no idea what they were saying.

We drove back to Ikirun and found Shango, who suggested that the Aragbiji would vouch for me. We drove to his palace.

Shango pounded on the palace door. It was 10.00 p.m. and raining.

'What do you want?' said the silhouette in the window.

'We would like to see Kabiyesi.'

'He's asleep!' (The king is always asleep when you call unexpectedly. It's the Yoruba equivalent of the secretarial evasion 'He's in a meeting.')

'Er, there are some policemen here,' I called back.

A shirtless young man came out and led us in. The *oba* sat regally on the corner of his desk in the dark, clad in a single piece of purple cloth thrown over one shoulder, with the other one bare.

After the case had been put before him, the Aragbiji nodded curtly and turned to me in his best peremptory manner. 'Come here,' he said.

I stepped obediently forward three paces. 'Kabiyesi.'

'I saw you at Oyelami's house, did I not? And you came and greeted me. Later you came to me here, did you not?'

'Yes, Kabiyesi.'

'What else?' he said, with both palms upward.

He ordered us all to go upstairs, where he told me to take pen and paper and write.

'I will dictate. "I – write your name – promise to bring my passport – write the number – to Ikirun tomorrow. If I don't, – write your friend's name – agrees to bear the full consequences and punishments." Give him back his notebook. What else?'

The matter was settled. Praise to the Aragbiji of Iragbiji!

His neck is long – because of beads!
His arms are long – because of weapons!
He wears his crown bravely in the midst of war!
He makes a boundary with Eshu!
He is so rich in brass – he uses it to pound yam with!
No one will dance in the town without the Aragbiji taking part in it!
He will dance even in the presence of death!

That night, sleeping on Shango's floor, I was bitten by a female anopheles mosquito. Two weeks later I came down with malaria.

I moved on to Ifẹ̀, and stayed at the guest-house at Obafemi Awolowo University, southern Nigeria's main university.

The futuristic campus of Obafemi Awolowo University rose out of the forest like an Aztec ruin. It is said to be the most beautiful in Africa. It was built in the glory days of the early 1960s, soon after Nigerian independence, when the continent was aflame with the idealism and hope of the New Africa. Its architecture reflected that optimism: the buildings were set out in a proud and coherent geometry at the foot of a noble green mountain, with swooping planes of concrete that presented an enthusiastic synthesis of European modernism, Eastern Bloc severity and African motifs, symbolic of a time when all of those forces seemed to be coming together to carry the continent forward into independence and prosperity. Thirty years on, the future had become history. The concrete of the OAU campus was crumbling in the humidity, tall plants grew out of the cracks, and lizards scuttled over everything. Construction projects launched when the country was awash with money, in the late 1970s and early 1980s, stood half-completed, with rusting scaffolding and girders, half-hidden in the churning vegetation.

There were 13,000 students at OAU and they demonstrated at least once a year. The government would close the campus and arrest some students and professors. The police would be sent in, and they would fire tear-gas and some bullets and arrest people and occasionally kill one or two. Two professors and a handful of students were still in jail when I arrived. The students lived in crowded halls of residence and never got enough to eat.

The academic calendar was thrown into confusion by the frequent closures of the university. Few of the professors had been able to take a summer break in years and they were very badly paid.

The OAU Conference Centre Guest House, where I stayed, was far from the life of the campus, on the edge of the forest. I had to cross a stream on a log to get to it. It consisted of a cluster of octagonal buildings built around a central courtyard with a fountain that didn't work. The forest was doing its best to recapture the territory. There were few guests, and lizards a foot long trafficked the lobby. They had lead-coloured bodies and flame-orange heads. During the day they would scuttle across the sun-blasted concrete, pausing abruptly to raise and bob their heads like someone straining to see over a wall. At night, red bats flew in vast helices over the treetops. Huge moths clung to the concrete walls, basking in the chilly electric light. During the day the dead ones, half devoured by ants, lay scattered about in the sun like broken phonograph records.

It was a good place to stay. It had a very good bar, and it was there that I often sat with the professors in the evenings, drinking Harp Lager and Guinness. The professors had all earned their PhDs at universities in the United States and Britain. They were nostalgic for those days, especially now that the country was suffering economic catastrophe after a few years of squandered boom.

One night, as we sat in near darkness on the terrace of the bar, one of them said, 'I earn 1,000 naira a month [about $100]. I will never own a car, and I can never hope to own a house. On Friday I went to the bank and arranged an overdraft of 250 naira. I went to the market and bought food for my family, and today I have ten naira in my pocket. That food will not last until next week – and then what am I to do? Take out another loan for 250 naira? How can I buy a house when I have to borrow money to buy food? To build a house you need at least 50,000 naira. How long would it take me to save 50,000 naira?'

'Build a wooden house,' a wag said.

'Ah!'

'Build a house of bamboo with a thatched roof. It is much cooler.'

'Look, if you tell a man to cut you 100 bamboo sticks he wants 100 naira.'

Meanwhile, the rich of Nigeria lived high on the hog on hard-currency income from their investments in London and the United States. Their Mercedes Benzes were symbols of Nigeria's poverty.

Another time, as I was sitting in an OAU car waiting for someone, the driver translated the words of a Yoruba song that was coming out of the radio:

> I don't want any more poverty in this life,
> I don't want any more loss in this life.
> There is no money in trading.
> Enough is enough.
>
> I don't want to marry another man's wife,
> I want my own wife.
> I want my own wife through the power of God,
> I don't want another man's wife through the Devil.
>
> I suffer from tiredness of praying.
> I've had enough of this tiredness of praying.
> If God would only give me the power,
> I'd pray all the time.
>
> God can do anything, he can put an end to poverty.
> I would pray to God to put an end to poverty.
> God is turning the world as he likes.

He could turn all Nigerians into good people.

Then we would all pray to God.
In our eating and drinking, we would pray to God.
Then we would all live good lives.
Then everything in life would be peaceful and comfortable.

One night, on my balcony at the OAU Conference Centre Guest House, I watched thunder and lightning tear up the sky. The god Shango was hurling his spears at us in anger. The rain stampeded down. And then the lights went out. The guest-house staff distributed candles and matches.

There was no electricity for four days, and the whole campus was blacked out long after the rest of the town had had its power restored. The rumour spread that someone had driven a car into the cables that supplied the campus and had broken them. It was impossible to read – it was too dark – but the beer stayed blessedly cold because it was kept in large, powerful freezers, although by the fourth day the bottles were beginning to lose their bloom of condensation.

Down in the hell of Lagos, the rain had been falling so hard that the 300,000 residents of Maroko, one of the world's largest slums, were evacuated by the military government of Lagos State and their wretched dwellings were bulldozed to prevent the occupants returning to them. Truck-drivers charged the refugees triple the usual price to move them and their belongings. The cleared land was expected to be sold off to the rich.

Lagos has no system of drainage apart from ditches along the road, which are soupy green with algae. When the rains come, the city floods and the water flows to the lowest ground, which is at Maroko, where the land was cheap. Then the mosquitoes breed, particularly the malaria-carrying female anopheles mosquito. Half the population of the country suffers from at least one bout of malaria every year. Malaria is an unavoidable fact of life in Nigeria.

The insects that carry this parasite are the hand of God in West African history. Because of them, the British, when they named the land Nigeria and absorbed it into their empire in the late nineteenth century, chose to establish an administration that used the bare minimum of officials. Instead of imposing a complete government and bureaucracy on the country, as in India, they ruled through traditional rulers, supporting and manipulating them to make the country safe for British trade. There was no colonization of Nigeria, because of the susceptibility of the white man to 'ague, phrenzy and fever'. The only thing that permitted British penetration at all was the dodgy prophylactic quinine, a bitter medicine derived from a Peruvian tree-bark. It made European survival in West Africa barely possible, as opposed to completely impossible, but even with quinine the region was still 'the white man's grave'.

In his *Records of Captain Clapperton's Last Expedition to Africa* (1830) Richard Lander ('his faithful attendant, and the only surviving member of the expedition') describes a doomed expedition from Lagos to Sokoto in which the members were sick for the duration of the journey, almost from the moment they landed in Africa. His book is the record of the movement of a convoy of invalids, borne on hammocks across a dismal tropical landscape ('Captain Clapperton . . . being still severely indisposed'), who die off one by one until Lander is the only one left and must carry the leader's remaining personal effects and diary to the coast and from there sail back to England. It is written in a compellingly melancholic tone. Lander describes his life as one 'devoted . . . to perpetual wandering, and chequered by a thousand misfortunes'.

Once the British protectorate was established, the consuls spent as much time as they could away from their posts, on leave in England. Richard Burton described the residence of the Consul, or Governor, as 'a corrugated iron coffin or plank-lined morgue, containing a dead consul once a year'. ('Consul Campbell died in 1859; his successor, Mr Brand, died in 1860; and Mr Foote died in 1861.' – quoted in Sir Alan Burns, *History of Nigeria*.)

Through the Institute for Cultural Studies, I engaged a research assistant named Bayo. Although his official title at the university was Cultural Officer, Bayo's vocation was commerce between the sublunar and the supernatural realms. He was a traditional chief and a sorcerer. In the course of many years teaching primary school in rural areas, he had acquired a large body of knowledge of magic and traditional medicine from hunters and traditional doctors. He walked about the campus as if it were a village, bowing and genuflecting in greeting to whoever he passed, the model of fine, almost dandyish, Yoruba manners. From me he demanded five dollars a day as 'remuneration of the informant'. I offered ten.

One day he took me to his house in the town of Ifẹ̀ to see his ju-ju pharmacopœia. On the porch outside, his wife was grinding meal in an electric grinder, surrounded by children. She genuflected to him as he went in. We entered his private room, which was dominated by a high iron bed. Every shelf and cabinet was covered with dirty jars and grubby stoppered bottles with smudged labels. One contained an oil which was consumed to command attention and respect when appearing before a group; another, one to attract benign spirits. He took down the jar of oil to attract benign spirits and invited me to taste it. After I had diffidently put my fingertip into the oil and licked it, Bayo thrust his hand into the jar and voraciously scooped the oil into his mouth. There was a gourd filled with powders to protect the bearer from accidents; incense to promote good luck; potions for good memory; and a charm to protect against physical attack. This last was a curious little sculpture made of three short, straight twigs wrapped in string, with a cowrie shell tied at each end.

I saw a bag filled with razor-blades wrapped in Cellophane and asked what they were for. He showed me thin scars, an inch long, on the inside of his forearms. 'There are some people called witches. Did you know that? They can see wider than other people. They can see these marks, and if they do they will not harm you.' He pulled up his shirt and showed me a similar mark on his solar plexus. There was another one on his back.

He could make me a belt which, when worn, would render me invisible to armed robbers, or a charm to protect my home against burglars.

I asked him to make me a charm against burglars. He took powders from one jar after another, and blended them in his palm. Then he took a boll of raw cotton, and meticulously picked out the seeds. 'I will use these later,' he said, putting them aside. He wrapped the powders in the raw cotton, and tied it up with black and white threads, winding them around the boll of cotton until it looked like a ball of string. I asked him what the powders were.

'It is jaujoko leaf, dried bush rat – the smallest you can find – horse dung, and attar of alligator pepper,' he said, handing me the charm. I paid him twenty-eight naira ($3.50) for it.

(I think I finally fell afoul of Bayo by paying him less than he expected when I left southern Nigeria, and that he cast an effective spell on me. Two days after I returned to London, I was beaten up by a gang of kids who took my wallet and broke my nose as I walked down a dark street in the East End.)

Commerce with the supernatural greases the wheels of everyday life in Yorubaland. The newspapers would report the more excessive instances without making a distinction between the real and the imaginary. After a while the distinction became meaningless: in Nigeria, the way things seem is how they really are. Scientific rationalism gets you nowhere in trying to understand Yoruba culture. I read the following item in the *Sunday Tribune* of 12 August 1990:

WOMAN BEWITCHES OWN SON

Two years ago, a young-man who had just bought a brand new *Peugeot 504* saloon car drove to his home town, Okitipupa, to break the good news to his parents.

But unknown to him, his own mother was unhappy with that achievement and she bewitched the car leading to its destruction in a fatal accident in which her son barely came out alive.

This wicked act was revealed last week by the mother, one Madam Ako (nee Akindele) 60, while confessing to various acts of evil using the power of witchcraft.

Madam Ako who was exorcised by her elder brother, High Chief Igbayemi Akindele, the Uwanwe of Idepe Quarters, Okitipupa at the family shrine (Imole) also confessed to causing instability in her household by the power of witchcraft . . .

The *Sunday Tribune* learnt that the Imole god prescribed that Madam

Ako should go round the town confessing her atrocities as punishment.

She was seen with a gong walking the streets and relating her various wicked acts to anyone who cared to listen while the exorcist, Chief Akindele followed closely behind beating her with two horsewhips.

The world is a dangerous and haphazard place, a dark, tangled forest with no permanent paths and full of hidden pitfalls. There is no order in it, no consistency and no boundary between the real and the supernatural. To find a path through this world, one consults the Ifa oracle. So I went to see the *Babalawo* of Ifẹ̀, accompanied by the sorcerer Bayo.

Ifa is the god of truth, the light that shines through the forest of existence. His gift to humanity is a corpus of 256 poems through which this truth is revealed. These poems, the *Odu*, consist of hundreds of lines, and they are memorized by the priests of Ifa, called *Araba* or *Babalawo*, in the course of a long period of apprenticeship. To discern the future, or the will of the gods, the questioner asks the *Babalawo* to find a poem that applies to his predicament. The *Babalawo* throws sixteen flat stones, and the pattern of their random fall corresponds to one of the 256 poems of the Ifa corpus. Alternatively, he can cast the divining-chain, a kind of necklace with eight discs, which fall in a pattern of heads and tails, pointing to an *odu*.

There is an obvious comparison with the I Ching, but, like so much in Yoruba culture, the question of origin leads darkly back to the Middle East. The word *araba* echoes the Arabic root *'araba*, which means 'to state clearly' and 'to make plain or clear'. *Babalawo* means 'Father of Secrets'.

The *Babalawo* of Ifẹ̀ lives in a house beside the Ifa temple in the old quarter of the town, not far from the palace of the *oba* of Ifẹ̀, the Ọ̀ọ̀ni. The Ifa temple is built in the ornate Brazilian style introduced in the last century by returned slaves. It stands on a mica-strewn hill which it must now share with a tall telecommunications pylon. The pylon seems like part of the temple, a newfangled steeple to draw down the messages of the gods.

Ifẹ̀ is the birthplace of the world; it is where the land and mankind were made. The site of Creation is opposite a Total petrol station, and is marked by an enigmatic monument: a modest finger-shaped granite object about eight feet tall, marked with a mysterious lengthwise pattern of iron studs. Ifẹ̀ is 'the cradle of the Yoruba race' and the centre of Yoruba culture. The Ọ̀ọ̀ni of Ifẹ̀ is the 'grandfather' of all the other Yoruba kings and one of the richest men in Nigeria.

The palace and the Ifa temple are in the oldest quarter of Ifẹ̀, which used to be the centre of the town until buildings multiplied along the Ifẹ̀–Ibadan road and erased the traditional layout. From the hill on which the Ifa temple stands, the town looks like an infinity of rusting corrugated-metal roofs, with treetops billowing between them. Walking from the main road to the temple, one passes ramshackle shops selling the usual fare of Nigerian markets: tomatoes, chilli peppers and onions in neat piles; kola nuts and wooden matches; cheap manufactured goods from China ('Double Rabbit Brand' mosquito coils and enamel crockery); detergent and soap; liquor sold in counterfeit brands; and traditional medicines – dried leaves of different kinds, dried caterpillars, chameleons and mice on wooden sticks. One-room businesses have eye-catching hand-painted signs:

Action Boy, Doctor of Shoe.
A2 Socialist Tailor: Diploma of Tailoring: Try it and See.
Sir Confidence: Fashion Tailor.
Sir Million Naira: Principal agent for Bristol Pools – Fixed Odds.

The Ifa temple is at the end of this street, and has a sign at street level that reads WORLD TEMPLE OF IFA. A path leads up to it and branches off to the *Babalawo*'s house.

Bayo and I entered the house and took off our shoes. The room was lit only by a shaft of sunlight that came in through an open window. The father of secrets sat on a mat with his back to the wall, beside where the parallelogram of golden light fell. He was eating maize pudding and beancake from a banana leaf.

The *Babalawo*'s mystical objects, relics of the god Ifa, were enclosed in urns in an alcove. Bayo prostrated before them as we entered. Some slogans were written in chalk above the threshold:

MOLE KI IJOKO
IFA MO ERO OKAN RE
THINK B/4 YOU DO

which means 'Enter and sit down. Ifa knows what is in your heart.'

We bowed to the *Babalawo* in greeting. Bayo explained my purpose in coming: from Ifa I sought direction in my search for the Yoruba kings, and a glimpse of what fate held in store for me.

The *Babalawo* reached for the canvas bag that contained his divination instruments. Bayo told me to take a one-naira note, whisper to it what I wanted to ask Ifa, touch the note to my forehead, and place it on the mat in front of the priest.

The *Babalawo* threw the divining-chain. The discs fell in a pattern which indicated the *odu* IKA-OWUNRIN. He said, 'This is very good.'

Bayo translated. He said, 'Great riches lie in store for you. In the course of your journey in Nigeria you will find yourself at a crossroads and not know which way to take, but Ifa will guide you. There is a woman in England waiting for you, and your souls are like two stars of equal brightness. When you perform the sacrifice, she will feel a jolt in her body, like electricity, and she will shiver, and she will think of you. You will come into possession of a large sum of money, but in order to enjoy that money you must make a sacrifice to your spirit double for longevity.'

All I feared at that point was being shaken down heavily for a sacrifice. When this demand came, I was told that the god wanted five cocks, some kola nuts, some maize pudding, some red palm oil and 'twenty-naira notes in five places' – i.e. 100 naira. Bayo bargained this down to 80 naira. I like a deity you can do business with. Total cost: 240 naira. It was the most I'd spent at once since I'd been in Nigeria. I peeled off the notes from the wad that I carried in a pouch around my neck (which made me look pigeon-chested, especially when I'd just been to the bank) and gave them to Bayo, who would make the necessary purchases in the market.

We came back in the afternoon to perform the sacrifice. The chickens were in covered baskets. The fortune-teller's assistant took out the biggest one and decapitated it by placing his foot on its head and pulling the body sharply up. Like a movie gangster pouring a sloppily opened bottle of champagne, he poured the gushing blood from the chicken's neck on to little piles of maize pudding, red palm oil, chicken feathers and kola, set out neatly like sushi on taro leaves in a row on the fortune-teller's mat.

The *Babalawo* recited the verses Ifa had chosen for me. He spoke in a high-pitched, broken voice. It was an allegory, in which I was a pangolin, a toothless, scaled mammal which looks like a baby crocodile.

Akika, the pangolin, consulted Ifa, and the oracle told him that he would soon inherit a chieftaincy title, but only if he made the proper sacrifice.

The sacrifice the *Babalawo* prescribed included a measure of wood ash. The pangolin had no idea what this meant, or why the *Babalawo* asked for it.

In order to achieve the chieftaincy title, the pangolin had to cross a stream and, once on the other side, swallow a magic bullet.

This stream had no bridge. The only way across was by a very narrow branch.

The pangolin's enemies wanted him to fall into the stream, so the chieftaincy title would go to their candidate. They spread slippery okra on the branch to make the pangolin lose his footing and fall into the stream.

But the pangolin had made the sacrifice of wood ash! On Ifa's instruction, Eshu, who carries the sacrifices to the gods, took the ash and spread it on the branch, so the pangolin could get a sure footing on it and cross the stream in safety.

He crossed the stream and swallowed the bullet! All his supporters on the opposite bank cheered him, calling, 'Walk back to us now, majestically, in style! That's it, that's it!'

Moral: Ifa will guide you. Payment due: 240 naira.

That night Ifa appeared to me in my dream, a formless body in a fan of amber-coloured light, and directed me to the coronation of the Akarigbo of Ijebu-Remo.

The morning Bayo and I set off for the coronation, which was in Shagamu, a town about two hundred kilometres away, the newspapers reported that a disappointed aspirant to the throne had won a High Court injunction preventing the coronation from taking place, after all the arrangements had been made, programmes and other commemorative paraphernalia had been printed, and tents had been set up in the grounds of the Methodist High School. In quick response, the Military Governor of Ogun State had put his foot down and overruled the court, issuing a decree which determined that the coronation should proceed as planned. The Nigerian Bar Association grumbled about this outrageous disregard for legal process for weeks afterwards, but it was probably a relief to the people of Shagamu. Military government in a place like Nigeria is sometimes not such a bad thing.

The challenge fitted into the pattern of Yoruba coronations. There is almost always an aggrieved claimant who challenges the succession in court. For this reason, interregnums can last for years while disputes simmer.

Normally, the *oba*-ship of a town is rotated among its 'royal houses', to ensure that every eligible family gets a chance to supply an *oba*. The candidate is chosen from the family whose turn it is by a body of 'kingmakers' who nowadays tend to choose an *oba* on the basis of his wealth and professional background, rather than knowledge of his own royal tradition.

The selection of an *oba* has a supernatural dimension that is shrouded in occultism and secrecy. The public coronation that we were on our way to see was the public event that followed an earlier ceremony that was closed to all but a small hieratic circle.

We travelled to Shagamu by bus, via the monstrous conurbation of Ibadan, a sprawling slum city of over a million people.

The Ifẹ̀–Ibadan road was a narrow, straight corridor through the bush. We were jammed into a minibus with sixteen other passengers. The bus looked as if a kerosene stove had once exploded inside it.

A brutal philosophy was expounded in the slogans painted on the buses and trucks that we passed: 'ENDLESS STRUGGLE', 'NO MONEY NO FRIEND', 'THE BRAVE MAN IS ALWAYS IN DANGER', 'LIFE IS WAR'. There is 'NO FRIEND IN TIME OF DISABILITY', 'HATE AND JEALOUSY ARE NATURAL', but 'NO CONDITION IS

PERMANENT'. And 'I AM AFRAID OF MY FRIENDS – EVEN YOU!' (The shops were the same. You could dine at the HUNGER CLINIC near Iragbiji, or buy furniture at the DOWNFALL OF MAN IS NOT THE END OF HIS LIFE FURNITURE CENTRE near Ibadan.)

Country folk would stand at the side of the road selling game: pygmy antelope, bush rat, snakes, striped squirrels. Women held out bunches of still writhing giant snails, joined together with a string through holes bored in their shells. One day a woman boarded the bus in which I was travelling with a basket of live catfish, wrapped in leaves. Their soft grey skins were slimy and leathery, and their gills throbbed. They looked robustly alive, and I was frighteningly aware of some ancient reptile intelligence in their watery eyes: in America, I remembered, they are said to creep across highways, and to have phosphorescent bumps on their heads, and to be able to give electric shocks with their whiskers.

The queerest creature of all was the pangolin. Small children would dangle these shy, wriggling, coiling animals by the tail.

At times, passing through this landscape of swamps, vine-choked vegetation and rusting auto parts, I felt I had returned to some primeval prototype of Mississippi. Here, it seemed, was the origin of every aspect of the culture of the Deep South: even Yoruba food was like some ancestral version of Cajun cooking, favouring catfish, okra, yam and plenty of pepper.

And Yoruba music was like some spooky, prehistoric version of the blues. It was music reduced to bones and blood: a drum rhythm, persistent, enervating and darkly elaborate, below a tense, wailing, gargling vocal line, drowning in fear and pain. These microtonal vocal contortions, to my ear, had no beginning and no end, especially as I tended to catch them on the breeze as I trudged through the streets of Ọ̀yọ́ State. The drumming produced a single plateau of sound with no development, while the singer struggled with cosmic forces.

One day, as a cassette blared from a car's tape-player, I asked the driver what the singer was saying. He listened for a moment and answered, 'He is abusing those who make sacrifices to Shango and Ogun and telling them that they should worship God.'

My view of south-western Nigeria was formed during uncomfortable hours squeezed into a crowded minibus. The drivers of these vehicles and their conductors were devotees of Ogun, the god of iron and machinery. The buses were held together by a precarious web of welding, the windows either didn't shut or didn't open, and the windshield was usually cracked in several places. Passengers were likely to have to abandon one out of every ten journeys, because of insuperable mechanical failure. The boy conductor bawls the destination to anyone he sees, in the hope of squeezing in one more fare. The fares are cheap; the bus crews work with a quiet and desultory economy. The dream of every driver or conductor is to stop this kind of work and own his own bus and employ someone else to do it. Until this happens – which is usually never – the bus crews provide one of the few comparatively efficient and dependable services in Nigeria.

To travel long distances this way usually involves transferring to other vehicles at stations varying in size from the forecourt of a filling-station to a large motor park. At any of these junctions a marketplace springs up, with women and children hawking goods they carry on their heads. Items for sale are thrust at the prospective customer through the window. If a girl wants to sell you a boiled egg, she reaches through the window and holds it in front of your face until her arm gets tired. Boys carry trays of brutally butchered meat: a horse's jaw, hacked in two, grey teeth and all, grimacing skyward like a figure from Picasso's *Guernica*; lumps of goat meat still covered in mud and fur; quivering, weirdly coloured offal. Beggars wave their stumps at the windows for alms, or recite prayers in a tone so monotonous that one pays them to go away. (Then they stop in mid-syllable.) Men sell underwear or newspapers or booklets on dreams or magic prayers to solve all life's problems. I followed the advice of a Lagos taxi-driver, whose nerves were as frayed as mine, on dealing with the hawkers: 'Do not talk to them. Do not even look at them.'

The streets of Shagamu were closed to traffic, and thronged with people. Inside the grounds of the Methodist High School, the Akarigbo, christened with the grandiose nickname 'The Emperor', sat on his throne under a canopy. His face was concealed by a veil of beads. About a thousand people in their best finery sat under tents to watch as the Governor of Ogun State presented the new *oba* with his staff of office. There was a long speech giving an account of his life:

'The new Akarigbo of Remo was born in Lagos in the royal house. Oba Michael was born with a silver spoon in his mouth. He grew up among his kith and kin, and socialized with rich and poor and all classes of people . . .

'He is a man of substance who has made an indelible mark on his profession. His intellectual calibre was shown by the specialist courses taken by him, such as a course he took in England in 1971 with an emphasis on petroleum administration. He attended a senior management course in Mount Cisco in the United States, and was nominated Nigeria's representative to the UN conference on tax treaties between developed and developing countries . . .

'He sponsored two persons to perform the Muslim holy pilgrimage, and on his own pilgrimage to Jerusalem took two persons at his own expense . . .

'He endears himself to all, affluent and downtrodden. He is a traditionalist and a man of peace.'

While King Birendra of Nepal was said at his coronation, by an English reporter who was for this act of *lèse-majesté* banned for life from that Himalayan kingdom, to have looked like an accountant, the Akarigbo of Ijebu-Remo actually was an accountant. His speech was like a report to a shareholders' meeting.

After it was over, the *obas* and other traditional rulers and dignitaries left in a long traffic jam of Mercedes Benzes. The hawkers and drummers took advantage of the immobilization of the vehicles to solicit for 'dash' through their open windows. Beside the car of an *oba*, a troupe of talking drummers performed their percussive panegyrics. I asked Bayo what the drummers were saying. He listened for a moment.

'They are saying, "The *oba*'s crown is made of money."'

'?'

'People here worship money,' he said.

On the way back I fell asleep in the bus and dreamed that I had been condemned to spend the rest of my life compiling an

1. King Taufa'ahau Tupou IV and his Russian abacus.

2. The King in his best-known role: riding his customized Sears Roebuck bicycle. This thrice-weekly ritual symbolized royal vitality and made him famous.

3. The Fale Alea, or Legislative Assembly.

4. The Palace Office, Nuku'alofa, where audiences with the King are arranged.

5. An official portrait of Sultan Qaboos, issued during celebrations for the twentieth anniversary of his reign in 1990.

6. Qaboos addressing the nation on Oman National Day, 18 November 1990, which is also his birthday. *L'état? C'est lui!*

7. Al-'Alam Palace, Muscat.

8. A flotilla of symbolism in Muttrah harbour greets the return of His Majesty's yacht: note the giant Sultan Qaboos Rose on a motorized raft.

9. The Sultan's birthday celebration, November 1990, at the Sultan Qaboos sports complex outside Muscat.

10. The Ataoja of Oshogbo at his palace. He was careful to make himself 'look big'. (Photo by Lindley Wilson)

11. The Aláàfin of Ọ̀yọ́, Master of Life and Death, emerges from his palace for the festival of Oru, surrounded by his *ilari*.

12. Abimbola Oyelawe, priestess of Oshun, the Yoruba Venus, at the goddess's shrine. Her father is the Ataoja of Oshogbo.

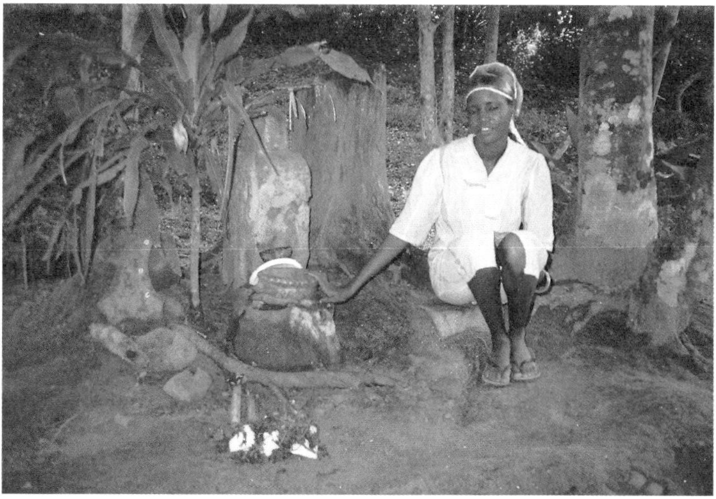

13. Swaziland's little-known other king: Maja II, king of the Mamba clan.
Unlike Mswati III, Maja II agreed to see me.

14. Maja II's *Indvuna*, or Governor, and his teenage son.

15. (*Above left*) Gateway to Kota Gede, home of mythical Javanese king Senopati's immortal blind albino catfish that can grant wishes.

16. (*Above right*) Bapak Sugiri, Keeper of the Yellow Pavilion at Kraton Yogyakarta, who told me he once saw a past sultan's spirit in the form of a snake.

17. The monument commemorating Sultan Hamengkubuwono VIII's attainment of mystical union with God. It once had a ball on top, symbolizing decisiveness, but it fell off in an earthquake.

18. Gateway to the inner city of Yogyakarta, at the centre of which is the Sultan's palace, the Kraton. The walls contain the Sultan's spiritual power.

19. Palace ladies carrying offerings to the shrines of past sultans through a courtyard inside the Kraton Yogyakarta.

encyclopaedia of all the Yoruba kings, a hopeless task which would never be completed because they are countless, and their numbers are increasing with the population, which is growing at a rate of 4 per cent per year, one of the highest in the world.

I felt I had unfinished business in Ikirun, where I had been arrested at the palace on the day of the new *oba*'s installation. The Akirun had courteously invited me to visit him there, so I decided to take up his invitation.

I found him in the same big reception room on the upper floor of the palace, holding court, in white robes, holding his horsetail flywhisk with a handle of green glass beads. We talked about the Council of Obas, the *obas*' trade organization, and other prosaic matters. When I asked him about traditions of kingship in Ikirun, he suggested I talk to a senior palace chief, the Ẹṣe, the highest-ranking chief after the *oba*. The Akirun knew nothing about such matters himself: he was only a Lagos businessman.

I found the Ẹṣe downstairs in family quarters hidden behind an old wooden door – dark rooms looking on to a covered courtyard with goats and chickens running in and out. An elderly, slow-moving, Yoruba grandee, he sat with me on the porch to conduct our dialogue. Several other chiefs and a score of women and children surrounded us and helped with translation.

The Ẹṣe described the *oba*-ship in ideal terms, as it ought to be, rather than as it was in the modern state of Nigeria. The Ẹṣe said that a new *oba* must spend three months in the home of the Ẹṣe, learning a traditional body of knowledge necessary to be *oba*. It was a Yoruba 'mirror for princes', completely unwritten. My question about whether the new *oba* had done this went unanswered.

Shango had disapproved of *obas* of this sort, who have no link with tradition and are chosen only because they are wealthy.

Unlike the Akirun of Ikirun, the Ataoja of Oshogbo, His Royal Highness Oba Iyiola Oyewale Matanmi III, did know about the traditions of his throne, and this presented him with a dilemma. *Obas* are supposed to be the guardians of traditional religion, but the extent to which an *oba* fulfils this duty depends on the disposition of the *oba*. The Ataoja of Oshogbo is the ruler of a town which happens to contain one of the most important Yoruba shrines, the shrine of Oshun. His problem is that he is a Muslim and doesn't believe in the Yoruba gods, but the Oshun shrine and especially the annual Oshun festival are an important part of the town's economy because of the visitors they attract.

By the time I came to the palace of the Ataoja of Oshogbo I was quite weary with the demands for money that a stranger was subjected to in days of hard times. I might as well have been dressed as George Washington on the one-dollar bill: when I walked down the street, people saw money on two feet.

In the palace office, I told the secretary I had written to the *oba* and would like to see him.

'What do you have for me?'

In bargaining, never be the first to mention a specific sum. It gives you the advantage.

'What do you want?'

'One hundred naira.'

I put ten on the desk.

Then I had to fill out a questionnaire, and write down my questions for the king on a separate piece of paper. This was taken to the Ataoja for his inspection, and after it had been approved I was brought to him.

I found the Ataoja of Oshogbo sitting on his patio. Two women sat behind him. He sat in grumpy splendour with a cordless telephone in his hand.

He hadn't slept in two days because of the Oshun festival, which was then in progress, and didn't want to talk at first. Then he reluctantly agreed, and we went into his office.

The Ataoja of Oshogbo's spiritual dilemma was made worse by the fact that the Ataoja's daughter, by tradition, is the high priestess of Oshun. She spends much of her time in the peaceful grove where the goddess's shrine is built. The Ataoja, for his part, had taken care to point out to the newspapers that 'the Oshun festival has nothing to do with religion. It is a celebration of the town.'

Someone who would not agree with this, and one of the town's great devotees of Oshun, is the Austrian sculptor Susanne Wenger, a forty-year resident of Oshogbo who has done much to establish Oshogbo as the modern cultural capital of the Yoruba. She is a devout worshipper of the Yoruba gods, and with the help of assistants she has turned the Oshun grove into an extraordinary sculpture park in the forest. The low point of her relationship with the Ataoja was when, without the Ataoja's permission, she had set up in the palace grounds a sculpture of a human figure with an erect phallus. Her style has been described as 'tortured Austrian expressionism in concrete'. The Ataoja is an articulate and educated man who is more concerned with the economic development of Oshogbo than with pagan mumbo-jumbo. But pagan mumbo-jumbo is what he stands for. As always, 'the *oba* must be above religion.' He must sit majestically above it.

Oshun is the Yoruba Venus – in human form, a woman of arresting beauty and sensuality. She is the goddess of the erotic, and of fertility. On earth she had many lovers. Among them was Shango, her second husband, the god of thunder and lightning and the ancestor of the Aláàfin of Ọ̀yọ́; and a python, which is one of her symbols. There are images of snakes all over the Oshun grove, and devotees of her cult wear a brass ring in the form of a double-headed snake in honour of her.

Sometimes Oshun appears in the forest gloom as an antelope wearing a brass necklace and earrings. In Brazil she takes the form of Our Lady of Candlemas. In Cuba, where her cult is especially popular, she is the Virgin of Charity of El Cobre. Ernest Hemingway gave her his Nobel Prize medal as an offering.

One day I went with Shango to visit Oshun's grove. We went to the shrine, where an elderly priestess gave us beakers of sacred river water to drink.

A graceful teenage girl, barefoot and slender, in a yellow cotton dress (yellow is the colour of Oshun), came and sat with us. She was the virgin priestess of Oshun, the reification on earth of the Yoruba Venus. Her name was Abimbola Oyelawe, the Ataoja's daughter. She carries the calabash of offerings to the river-goddess during the Oshun festival, something that can be done only by a virgin. She was obviously going out that night: her hair was covered in a plastic cap and she wouldn't shake hands because her nails, freshly painted with red nail varnish, were still wet. She had just graduated from high school.

Abimbola favoured us with a tour of the grove, and took us to places described in Susanne Wenger's book about the grove as being *verboten* to strangers. 'We are very lucky,' Shango whispered.

When we parted – we didn't shake hands, because of her nails – Shango whispered to me, 'Now you give her something.' I gave the virgin priestess twenty naira. She invited us to a party at the palace after the end of the Oshun festival.

'She liked you,' Shango said to me as we made our way up the dirt road back to the town. It was an intriguing prospect: being favoured by the Yoruba Venus.

> Owner of brass, owner of parrots' feathers, owner of money.
> My mother, you are beautiful, very beautiful.
> Your eyes sparkle like brass.
> Your skin is soft and smooth.
> You are like black velvet.
> Everybody greets you when you descend on the world.
> Everybody sings your praises.

Later I read in the newspaper about Abimbola's performance with the sacrificial calabash. The festival was a mob scene. As she led the procession to the shrine, no one could tell if she was in an ecstatic state or in a prima donna's fury, screaming 'Get those photographers out of here!' all the way to the water's edge.

The members and committee of the Ijesha Students' Union of the University of Ibadan – about fifty of them – came to Ilesha to pay homage to their 'father', the Owa of Ilesha, during the annual Ijesha Students' Week. (The Owa is the king of the Ijesha people. Their capital is called Ilesha.)

The Owa, Oba Adekunle Aromolaran II, Owa Obokun Adimula of Ijesha, received them in splendour in his throne room. He sat on an ebony throne upholstered in burgundy velvet, and an elderly shaven-headed servant fanned him with a peacock-feather fan. Half a dozen more elderly shaven-headed servants with heavy-lidded eyes lounged about like leopards on the floor at the foot of his chair. His face was completely expressionless and still, and his eyes focused in the middle distance, as if in disdain for a world of matter he had long ago subdued.

On his right was a chair for President Babangida; on his left a chair for the Military Governor of Ọ̀yọ́ State. But the Owa's chair was the most magnificent, the most gorgeously carved and upholstered.

The students' spokesman flung himself on to the floor and said, 'Kabiyesi, you who cannot be contradicted, may God bless you and give you long life and the same glory which he gave your brave forefathers. May you prosper and witness prosperity during your reign.'

The Owa nodded, and waved his ram's-beard flywhisk, with its handle of coloured beads. The students chorused, 'Amen!'

'Kabiyesi, we are members of the Ijesha Students' Union, and this is our annual week of celebrations and activities. We are all your sons and daughters, but some of us were born outside Ijeshaland and do not know about the kingdom to which we belong. We would like to ask you, Why is the King of Ilesha called the Owa?'

The Owa's chamberlain addressed the students first, a genial, smiling old man in beautiful robes. He blessed them and praised them and thanked them for coming, and wished them good jobs upon graduation. Then the king told the following tale about his ancestor, the first Owa, who lived a thousand years ago.

'The founder of mankind, Odudua, had sixteen sons, who were all made kings of the different Yoruba towns. When he became old, he gradually lost his eyesight, until eventually he was completely blind. He sent each of his sons on a mission to fetch sea water to cure his blindness. Of all his sons, only one accomplished the mission, which required travelling a long way from the forest to the sea and returning with a vessel filled with sea water. When the old king received his son, bearing the sea water, he said, "So, you are back," which is "*owa*" in the Yoruba language. He gave his son the Sceptre of Ilesha and the Sword of Victory which the Owa carries still.'

The Owa is the head of his own little empire of sixteen smaller kingdoms, with a quarter of a million people. He has a master's degree in development economics.

The Owa ordered servants to bring in crates of Seven-Up, Coke and Fanta to refresh his guests.

Later I talked to the Owa, in a private room behind the throne. He said, 'Do you want to change some currency? I have accounts in sterling and US dollars.'

Like Yoruba religion, Yoruba history has no orthodox version. If you ask someone from Ifẹ̀ for an account of the history of the Yoruba and the place of the Ọ̀òni of Ifẹ̀ and the Aláàfin of Ọ̀yọ́ in it, he will tell you that the god Odudua, son of the supreme god Olorun, came down from heaven when the earth was covered in the primeval waters and created land. The point on the globe where this took place was Ifẹ̀. It was here that he also created the first human beings. He had sixteen mortal sons, all of whom were kings. Odudua commanded them to spread out through West Africa and establish their own kingdoms. His favourite son stayed behind. On Odudua's deathbed, he gave this son the title 'Ọọ̀ni', which is a contracted form of the statement, 'You are the owner of it' – that is, of Ifẹ̀. Because he was the favourite son of Odudua, and his reincarnation, the king of the birthplace of the world and of the cradle of mankind, the Ọọ̀ni is the grandfather of all the other *obas*.

If you ask someone from Ọ̀yọ́ for an account of the history of the Yoruba and the place of the Ọọ̀ni of Ifẹ̀ in it, he will tell you that Odudua fled from Mecca to Ifẹ̀ with his sons. Olorun, the supreme god, created the world and its first inhabitants. At Ifẹ̀, Odudua dispersed his sons, who numbered only seven. They founded the kingdoms of Benin, Owa, Ila, Ketu, Popo, Sabe and Ọ̀yọ́. Ọ̀yọ́ was founded by Odudua's son Oranyan, and became one of the great West African empires. Adimu, the first Ọọ̀ni of Ifẹ̀, was merely assigned the task of guarding the treasures of Odudua. He was not a king. The title Ọọ̀ni means 'son of a condemned slave'. The king of Ọ̀yọ́, the Aláàfin, is the grandfather of the Ọọ̀ni and of all the other *obas*. The Aláàfin of Ọ̀yọ́ is the Lord of the World and of Life, the Owner of the Land, the Companion of the Gods. The thunder-god Shango was the fourth Aláàfin of Ọ̀yọ́, and every Aláàfin after him is his reincarnation.

The Ọ̀yọ́ empire reached its peak in the sixteenth century, and collapsed early in the nineteenth. This was followed by a century of civil war, fuelled by the slave trade: captive soldiers were sold to European and American traders.

'We want three things,' said a West African king at this time; 'powder, ball and brandy. We have three things to sell: men, women and children.'

The British came at the end of the nineteenth century and imposed peace treaties on the warring kingdoms. Legitimate trade replaced the slave trade. They established a protectorate and became the rulers of Nigeria.

The manuals for British rule were the *Political Memoranda* (1906 and 1916) of Lord Lugard. He devised indirect rule in Nigeria: the policy of governing through traditional rulers, using a minimum of resident British officials.

One of the problems with indirect rule in southern Nigeria was that the British chose to govern through kings who had lost much of their power to the military chiefs who had risen during the civil wars. But they preferred to rule through an institution that was familiar to them.

Another problem with indirect rule was that the Yoruba kings were not traditionally as autocratic as the Hausa emirs of the north, where the model of indirect rule was formed. A Yoruba king had to observe the consensus of his chiefs, and so was intractable as an instrument of British rule. Nor was there, after the decline of the Ọ̀yọ́ empire, a single supreme Yoruba king.

The Aláàfin of Ọ̀yọ́, as the heir of a great empire with its own administrative tradition, most closely resembled the kind of ruler the British could do business with. Lord Lugard wrote, 'The Oyo Province has accepted British Suzerainty, and its loyal and enlightened ruler, the Alafin, is anxious to accept the same status as the paramount Emirs of the North.' For this sporting attitude, the

British gave him the rank of number-one traditional ruler in southern Nigeria. They created a hierarchy of Yoruba *obas* and put the Aláàfin at the top of it. *Obas* were graded as first-, second- and third-class *obas*, which led to much competition among them, and this competition persists.

The British ranking of traditional rulers created an unstable, contentious and constantly shifting and expanding heap, at the top of which the Aláàfin of Ọ̀yọ́ was perched uneasily by the time British rule came to an end.

Since independence, in 1960, the Aláàfin has slipped from this position, and the Ọ̀ọ̀ni has come to be regarded as number one, mainly because of the historical and cultural importance of Ifẹ̀.

For almost as long as he has been on the throne, the present Aláàfin has been trying to re-establish the primacy he feels is his historical right. His field of war is now the Nigerian legal system. The object of his campaign, the throne now at the top of the heap, is the chairmanship of the Ọ̀yọ́ State Council of *Obas*.

It was two weeks before I saw the Aláàfin of Ọ̀yọ́ that the following story appeared in the Lagos *Guardian* of 19 July 1990:

> The Aláàfin of Oyo, Oba Lamidi Adeyemi and two other Oyo State obas, entangled in a legal battle with the Ọ̀ọ̀ni of Ife, Oba Okunade Sijuwade, over the chairmanship of the Council of Obas, since 1988, will tomorrow, know if they can amend their statement of claims after trial had begun at an Ibadan High Court.

There followed a leaden account of the Aláàfin's elaborately convoluted legal manœuvrings. His latest tactic was to request the court to withdraw historical evidence originally submitted to prove the supremacy of Ọ̀yọ́ and instead 'to test the legality of the appointment of the Ọ̀ọ̀ni as a permanent chairman of the council'. For it doesn't matter if a cat is black or white, as long as it catches the mouse.

Speaking on behalf of the Ọ̀ọ̀ni, the *oba* of Ilawe, the Alawe of Ilawe, said, 'in a philosophical [i.e. smug] tone': '"I am very surprised at Aláàfin's claim to pre-eminence because Ile-Ife is the cradle of the Yorubas . . . but when a child matures, there is nothing he cannot claim or say before his wife. Aláàfin is a grandson to the Ọ̀ọ̀ni."'

The Aláàfin might have better luck in challenging the Ọ̀ọ̀ni's permanent chairmanship of the Ọ̀yọ́ State Council of *Obas* on grounds that do not take him and his armies into the tangled forest of history and myth, for these considerations had nothing to do with the appointment of the Ọ̀ọ̀ni to the position the Aláàfin covets. This appointment was made in the turmoil of Nigerian politics during the days of civilian rule.

Traditional rulers were subjected to unprecedented indignities during the last civilian government, which was overthrown by the army in 1983. Military government, which has been the rule rather than the exception in Nigeria since independence, tends to suit them better. The Aláàfin was the victim of one such indignity. In 1980, he held the post he is now trying to regain. The civilian governor of Ọ̀yọ́ State felt that the Aláàfin was supporting an opposition party, the NPN, and took the chairmanship away from him. He gave it to the Ọ̀ọ̀ni, who supported the governing party, the UPN. In those days, politics was a violent and opportunistic business, in which those at the top mobilized mobs to riot and to burn the property of anyone who disagreed with them or who threatened their licence to plunder the state for all they could get their hands on. The Ọ̀ọ̀ni, although separate from political competition himself, was shrewd enough to back the right horse at the right time, just as the Aláàfin had done a century ago.

I went to Ọ̀yọ́ with Bayo, because I thought it would be a good idea to appear at the Aláàfin's court with an entourage, to make me look important. I wore my Brooks Brothers seersucker suit and a tie, and carried pretentious business cards imprinted with my name and the word AUTHOR underneath.

In the palace office, a listless secretary sat with her head cradled on the desk on her folded arms. Bayo handed my letters of introduction to her more alert colleague, a youth of about twenty with his shirt not tucked in. He nodded, surveyed my papers and said, 'Come back next week, and then we will give you an appointment.'

We made the four-hour journey back to Ifẹ̀.

A week passed. We went back again to Ọ̀yọ́ as directed. Again

I wore my Brooks Brothers suit and tie. This time we were shown to deep armchairs in an antechamber to the Aláàfin's throne room. At the end of the room was a curtain, behind which lay his radiant inner sanctum.

The great Yoruba historian the Revd Samuel Johnson wrote in his *The History of the Yorubas* (1921), that the Aláàfin 'is more dreaded than even the gods.' Before I came I was told that one must bring the Aláàfin a present, not as a courtesy but to *propitiate* him. One should be jolly grateful to leave his presence alive. For this purpose I was equipped with a bottle of Johnnie Walker Black Label and a fistful of extra-large kola nuts, the traditional gifts for an *oba*.

While we awaited word of the Aláàfin's pleasure, I surveyed the room with a critical eye, assessing the other people in it, each of whom was, like me, an anxious supplicant for the Aláàfin's attention and, as such, my rival at court. Where did I stand in order of importance? It was vital not to be seen to be making this observation, for this would suggest a lack of confidence on my part and an acknowledgement of the superior status of someone with whom I was in competition. This could work to my own disadvantage in the mind of the Aláàfin, I reasoned, if it were to come to his notice.

We waited in the room from 10.00 a.m. until 4.00 p.m. Bayo abandoned ship and headed back to Ifẹ̀. 'In the time we have been waiting, we could have drunk that bottle,' he said in disgust as he rose to go. Now I was without my entourage. My case looked hopeless.

The elderly couple sitting opposite me were both asleep. They hadn't been chosen. Nor had anyone else. Some policemen were sitting with their shoes off, chatting, and rolling their heels from side to side on the thick carpet. As I was contemplating leaving myself, the secretary emerged from behind the curtain. Everyone woke up. He was approaching me! I was the only one favoured with a message from the reincarnation of the thunder-god! The secretary spoke in a low, confiding voice.

'Come back next week.'

On the night before my appointment with the Aláàfin, I checked into an abominable hotel in Ọ̀yọ́.

'I am looking for a room,' I said.

'There is no one here by that name,' the desk clerk replied.

I was in a linguistic wilderness. I didn't understand their version of English, and they didn't understand mine. And even the simplest communication in Yoruba was out of the question. For example, in the Yoruba language a word's meaning depends on the pitch and intonation with which it is pronounced. When I wanted to go to the palace, I would say to the taxi-driver 'Af-EE' when I should have been saying 'AH-fee'. Instead of saying the word for 'palace', as I was intending, I was saying 'albino'.

Staying in the hotel was a group of 'Ifa traditionalists'. They were a strange crew. Their leader was a flamboyant Curaçaoan who lived in Amsterdam and styled himself a Yoruba *oba* and a priest of Ifa. He wore red robes and carried a flywhisk, and was accompanied by an entourage of young, earnest, starry-eyed Dutchmen, who had converted to the Yoruba religion.

The desk clerk drew my attention to them. She said, 'There are people of your tribe here.'

'The white tribe?'

'Yes.'

I considered them spiritual tourists and accordingly kept my distance, although I kept running into them at the palace.

'I am a king,' the Curaçaoan said to me, as we stood in the palace courtyard surrounded by a hundred curious children. 'If I walk this way, and you walk that way, who do you think they will follow?' I was quite happy to let the mass of children follow him.

What was so embarrassing about this *soi-disant* king was that he seemed to think that Yoruba religion was fixed. In his mind it had been transformed to resemble Christianity in its schematic cosmic certainty. 'Ifa is God,' he would say. 'Ifa guides me in everything I do.' For a Yoruba of Ifẹ̀, Ifa is a fickle and greedy god, demanding sacrifices and only maybe giving something in return. The Curaçaoan also thought the Aláàfin wasn't a proper *oba*, unlike himself, because the Aláàfin had no spiritual power, he said.

I spent the whole of the following day in the Aláàfin's antechamber. The Aláàfin wasn't yet back from Lagos, but he was expected shortly.

Others were waiting in the room. God knows what they wanted. A drunken Yoruba courtier slouched towards me in his armchair, and breathed bad booze all over me. 'What is your mission? What is the nature of your m-mission in Nigeria?' Conceiving myself to be a far more important person at court than this person, I ignored him.

At the end of the day, the Aláàfin's son emerged from behind the curtain and approached me! The Aláàfin has a headache, he said. 'Come back Thursday.'

I've wasted a whole week waiting for that damn king, I thought.

That afternoon, despite his headache, and two hours late, the Aláàfin appeared on the palace porch because it was a holiday: the festival of Oru, the bullroarer god. The priests lay prone in front of the Aláàfin's chair, sprinkling earth on their bald occiputs in token of submission. Only they can interpret the voice of the god as it murmurs from the bullroarers that the boys of the town whirl around their heads. No woman may come outdoors on this day.

The next morning at breakfast, the King of the Dutch Antilles made an announcement. 'I am getting married,' he said, his heart brimming with joy. I thought he might break into an aria – *I promessi sposi*.

He had found an Ọ̀yọ́ bride with help of the *Babalawo* of Ọ̀yọ́, who chose her by divination. Although she didn't speak English or Dutch, and he didn't speak Yoruba, he intended to take her back to Amsterdam with him, if the palace could help him get her a passport.

On Thursday I returned to the palace office. My presence was a matter of complete indifference to the girl who was snoozing at her typewriter. No one knew anything about my appointment with the Aláàfin. Besides, she said, 'He is not around.' He was in Lagos, having been summoned there by President Babangida.

I could have telephoned in advance, of course, if there had been a working telephone in Ọ̀yọ́ State. A telephone in Nigeria is like a relic of some lost civilization about whose former use one can only speculate. 'Possibly a gaming piece, or an implement used in religious ceremonies.'

The palace of the Aláàfin is the largest in Yorubaland, and still has over a hundred 'slaves' and officials. His slaves, called *ilari*, carry names that reflect his attributes and epithets: The *Oba* Goes Around The World, The Town Worships Me, The *Oba* Leads, The *Oba* Prevents The World From Falling Apart, The *Oba* Sits Gorgeously (in his Mercedes Benz, presumably), The *Oba* Stops The Enemy, The Head Enables The *Oba* To Be Crowned, The *Oba* Is Gainful, The *Oba* Clears The Earth, The Mouth Likes The *Oba*, The *Oba* Has Good Luck, Tell The *Oba* (the *oba*'s stand-in when the *oba* is indisposed) and Don't Bother The *Oba*.

During the time of the Ọ̀yọ́ empire, the Aláàfin conducted diplomacy by sending *ilari* whose names corresponded with the message he wanted to convey, like The *Oba* Is Inflexible, and The *Oba* Is Not Ready.

By this time I had retreated to Ibadan, where I had checked into a more comfortable hotel, and was suffering from malaria. The telephones worked there and I spoke to the Aláàfin. He was very cordial, and invited me to join his entourage the following morning: he was going to attend a coronation at a place called Odeomu. I was to be at the palace at eight o'clock.

After a night of sweating and shivering in a hotel with no water, I felt like a wrung-out rag. I waited in the palace courtyard until nine, when someone said, 'The father is coming out now.'

Everyone waiting in the palace courtyard sprang to their feet: the Aláàfin was emerging from the palace. A panegyric was sung, a royal brolly was unfurled, and a trumpet blast sounded. The Aláàfin wore a splendid outfit of glittering lilac-and-silver cloth. From head to foot he was dressed in this cloth, even to the narrow pointed pumps on his feet. The door of the Mercedes Benz was held open. The reincarnation of Shango the thunder-god, His Royal Highness al-Hajji the Aláàfin, stepped into the cream-coloured automobile. His licence plate read

ALAAFIN OF OYO
IKU BABA YEYE

which is Yoruba for 'Master of Life and Death'.

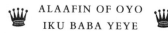

A police car's red and blue lights blazed and revolved, its siren whooped, and the cars moved out of the courtyard. A trumpeter in the front passenger seat of the police car held his instrument out the window and blew a fanfare. With the Aláàfin sitting gorgeously, we set off through the squalid streets of Ọ̀yọ́.

There were five cars in the motorcade. I sat with some chiefs in a Peugeot bringing up the rear.

Odeomu had been established in the early part of the twentieth century by migrants from a quarter of the town of Ifẹ̀ called Modakake, who themselves were migrants from Ọ̀yọ́, driven out of their ancestral kingdom after the destruction of Ọ̀yọ́ in the last century. Until now, they had not had their own *oba*, but only a *bale*, or mayor. They were loyal to the Aláàfin of Ọ̀yọ́.

The inhabitants of Modakake were called 'settlers' by everyone else in Ifẹ̀. Some people have very long memories. After the breakup of the Ọ̀yọ́ empire, they settled in Ifẹ̀, under the nominal protection of the Ọ̀ọ̀ni. Ever since then, the Modakakes and the Ifẹ̀s have been at war with each other. The Ọ̀ọ̀ni treated the Modakakes as vassals of war. They rebelled, and in the early part of this century overthrew the Ọ̀ọ̀ni, and the stool of Ifẹ̀ was vacant for twenty years. At the time of my visit, the Egungun 'masquerade' festival, in which men dress in hideous disguises in embodiment of the spirits of departed ancestors, ended in a brawl in which the Modakakes vandalized Ifẹ̀ property, sang war songs, and attacked anyone suspected of being from Ifẹ̀.

They're a rough bunch, the people of Modakake: they say the self-styled *oba* (i.e. the *bale*) charges foreigners twenty naira minimum just to say hello. Now I was witnessing the creation of a Modakake kingdom, something the Ọ̀ọ̀ni would never allow under his very nose.

The new *oba*, the Aleyegun, was a sour-looking, shrivelled old character. He sat on the canopied platform with the Aláàfin and other dignitaries. He wore a grotesque conical beaded crown with spiky protuberances and a bird on top (like a star on a Christmas tree, to symbolize his link with heaven) and a veil of beads covering his face.

After he had been handed his staff of office, he waved a document at the crowd. It had a big red seal.

May the crown stay long on his head!
May the sandals stay long on his feet!
May the authority of kingship stay long in his mouth!

My malaria passed, and I returned to the palace at Ọ̀yọ́, where I was at last allowed an audience with the Master of Life and Death. I passed beyond the curtain and into the Aláàfin's throne room. He sat in a deep armchair on a high platform reached by four carpeted steps. He wore a cream-coloured outfit and a matching cap with a central ridge and two pointed wings on either side. He had three short scars cut on to each cheek. His right foot rested on his left knee, and he rubbed the sole as he spoke.

I opened my notebook and he started talking: he knew what he wanted to say. Everything he said was on one theme: the primacy of Ọ̀yọ́ in Yoruba affairs and the relative insignificance of Ifẹ̀. He even paused until he had seen that I had written down every word.

'The kingdom of Dahomey used to pay the Aláàfin forty oxen and 400 loops of cowrie shells as tribute, in acknowledgement of the suzerainty of Ọ̀yọ́,' he said. 'The Ọ̀yó dialect is the standard dialect of the Yoruba language. All Yoruba sayings come from Ọ̀yó. Everyone copies Ọ̀yọ́; Ọ̀yọ́ copies nothing. The culture at the top is the superior culture.'

At one point he bounded down the steps and paced the room as he enthusiastically explained the administrative system of the Ọ̀yọ́ empire. 'When the Europeans came to Africa they marvelled at the wonderfully developed political system they met in this part of the world. There was a constitution that was monarchical and absolute, but democratic in practice because of checks and balances. The emperor cannot be a law unto himself . . .'

The Aláàfin crackled with the sense of his own prestige. 'People reverence the Aláàfin wherever he goes,' he said. 'You will marvel at how people rush out to greet the Aláàfin. No other *oba* is greeted in that way: they have said so to me. People surround the car: if I take my car out today, you will see what will happen. No palace in Yorubaland has the number of palace officials the Aláàfin has – more than one hundred.

'Now, if you will excuse me, I have someone else to see.'

I was bundled out of the room before I could give him his bottle of Johnnie Walker. It had been a dazzling performance, if brief. He came across like an American boxer at a pre-match press conference, practising psychological warfare against his opponent (in this case the Ọ̀ọ̀ni) through the press. One night on the beer terrace, a week later, one of the professors told me that the Aláàfin had indeed been a successful boxer in his youth, and had been chosen to represent Nigeria in the Commonwealth Games.

I went to the Nitel office as soon as I heard about this and put a call through to Ọ̀yọ́ to ask the Aláàfin about his sporting past. Once I managed to get through, it was hard to get him to stop talking.

He had indeed been selected to represent Nigeria, in the 1956 Commonwealth Games, as a bantamweight, but had had to withdraw because he had to sit some examinations at school. 'When I left school, I didn't want to make a career of it – I did it purely for the love of the game. I still do a lot of roadwork and exercises. I would have shown you some videotapes of my exercises while you were here.'

He was an admirer of Joe Louis, 'The Brown Bomber' – 'He was the best, for artistry, footwork, superb boxing and athletic display' – and of the English champion Henry Cooper – 'He had a perfect left hook that could put a man out with a single blow. He dropped Muhammad Ali with that left hook.' There's nothing a *vieux sportif* likes to talk about more than former glories.

The *Babalawo* of Ifẹ̀ had told me that Ifa would guide me when I found myself at a crossroads. Now I needed his help again to guide me to the greatest of all the Yoruba kings, the Ọ̀ọ̀ni of Ifẹ̀, whose full title was Alaiyeluwa Oba Okunade Sijuwade Olubuse II, the Oluaiye and the Ọ̀ọ̀ni of Ifẹ̀. For months I had been waiting for an introduction to Ọ̀ọ̀ni Sijuwade through an important palace chief, the Apena of Ifẹ̀, who was the head of a secret fraternity of chiefs who had the power to create and destroy in Ifẹ̀. He was a professor at the university, but spent little time at his post, as far as I could tell, being continually in transit around the globe on missions for the Ọ̀ọ̀ni. He was never in his office, because he was always in Lagos or Brazil or Iran. I was running out of time.

Ifa appeared to me as a formless body in a flashing ziggurat of red and green light. He said, 'To hell with the Apena of Ifẹ̀. Go straight to the palace. The security guards will melt away at your approach.' And so they did.

The following morning, I passed through the palace gates and entered the office of the Ọ̀ọ̀ni's elderly traditional secretary. Here I forlornly waited with half a dozen other supplicants for an audience with the Ọ̀ọ̀ni.

The silence was broken when some drumming and singing started up outside. I asked a fellow supplicant what the singers were saying. 'They are singing to wake up the Ọ̀ọ̀ni, and to praise him and his ancestors.' It was 9.00 a.m., and the Ọ̀ọ̀ni was already awake. At that instant he was having a meeting with his palace chiefs, I learned later.

The *oba* is asleep. The *oba* is waking up. 'The magnitude of his rule was reflected by his domestic functions,' the sociologist Norbert Elias wrote of Louis XIV. Queen Salote of Tonga was woken every morning by musicians playing the nose-flute under her window. The Yoruba have their own traditions of the royal levee. Clapperton records that it was, at the time of his visit, 'the etiquette of Yourriba to hold a levée twice a day, at six in the morning and at two in the afternoon'. The *obas* of Lagos, Ondo and Oshogbo were all asleep when I called at their palaces. In anyone else it would be considered slothful: in a king it's one of the rhythms of an ordered universe, and a sign of his power that he is unavailable to callers. The more powerful he is, the less he has to do, and the more time he can spend in bed. This is a waking-up song for the Timi of Ede:

> O man of prestige, you have woken well;
> Timi, you have woken well.
> The guinea-pig has woken well at the housepost;
> The aferebojo has woken well in its burrow.
> The waking of a chief, the waking of a man learned in holy mysteries,

The waking of the king-at-the-market who fills himself with shea-butter!
Adetoyese, Akanji, the elephant!
As long as you have woken well, all is well.
Arise and put on your trousers:
One does not send a messenger to defecate on one's behalf.

After four hours' wait, I was shown into the Ọ̀ọ̀ni's sitting-room, and before long I found myself prostrate before him, petitioning him for a royal interview for my unfinishable encyclopaedia of Yoruba kings.

'But I am going to Kano,' he said. Then, after a moment's thought, 'You can join my entourage. Collect your things and be back here in half an hour. I will send a car to take you. We leave at three.'

The Ọ̀ọ̀ni of Ifẹ̀ was going to Kano with his court to offer his condolences to the Emir of Kano, whose mother had died. The Ọ̀ọ̀ni and the Emir were old friends. In 1984 they had been suspended from their offices and confined to their homes by the military government for making a trip to Israel.

The Ọ̀ọ̀ni sat in a chair upholstered in artificial leopard skin and commanded his servants in preparation for the journey to Kano. They were supposed to have left at eight o'clock that morning, but as usual the Ọ̀ọ̀ni was conducting all of his important business at the last minute. On top of that, the Ambassador from Benin, a Francophone Yoruba, had to be received, which involved half an hour's leisurely diplomatic small talk and sedate fraternal bilateral sitting.

The room had no windows and could have been the interior of the flat of some rich foreigner in Kensington, opulently kitschy. On a glass coffee-table there was a square-rigger made of glass, some wooden carvings and a brass elephant. Before the Ọ̀ọ̀ni's chair was a leopard-skin rug, with the head baring its fangs. Through a doorway I could see into a zone of greater intimacy: a bijou sitting-room with Louis-style furniture and a coffee-table supporting a tasteful pile of illustrated books.

The palace at Ifẹ̀ was a jumble of buildings, none of them more than about seventy years old, inside a large walled compound. For the purposes of contact between the Ọọ̀ni and his subjects, there was a variety of rooms, public and private, with several grades in between. These reception rooms represent points on concentric rings of graduated proximity to the Ọọ̀ni himself. The inner sanctum was the swimming-pool, said to be as luxurious and Hockneyesque a spot as any in Beverly Hills. Radiating from that was a series of throne rooms of increasing size and decreasing intimacy, culminating in a large porch near the main gate where the people of the town could be met.

The Ọọ̀ni (correctly pronounced as three syllables: 'aw-aw-ni') is a paunchy, fiftyish man with a round, friendly face and slightly bulbous eyes that point in two different directions, which gives the impression that he's deep in abstruse thought when he's merely staring into space. He purses his lips and raises his small chin when he's on display and trying to look his most regal. Otherwise his manner is relaxed and unassuming: when he entered the room for the first time, I barely noticed him. This is the divine king who is the descendant of the god who created the earth. He is also a millionaire businessman with a house in Belgravia and business interests around the world. He is a Christian, and has been Ọọ̀ni since 1980.

Sijuwade thaumaturge! Some years ago, the story goes, his followers in Cuba petitioned him for help after years of drought which had ruined their crops. He said some prayers over a bucket of water and commanded the heavens to provide rain. The heavens obeyed immediately and the crops flourished.

He has political as well as supernatural influence. In 1989, after the government closed down the country's main universities because of riots over a rise in the price of petrol, the Ọọ̀ni and other traditional rulers were able to persuade the authorities to allow them to reopen. He successfully campaigned for the creation of a new state in the Nigerian federation, Oshun State, of which Ifẹ̀ is now the capital.

The Ọọ̀ni called for his chief driver. The driver wore a sober brown suit of lightweight polyester and lay prone in the crowded doorway to listen to the instructions the Ọọ̀ni rattled off to him.

The Ọ̀ọ̀ni spends much of his time travelling. His court is perpetually on the move. His vehicles are his horses, his drivers his soldiers, his journeys his campaigns, and thus he subdues his dominions. He has twelve Mercedes Benzes, a Rolls-Royce (then undergoing repair in London), a bus and a multitude of other vehicles, right down to the shell of a taxi rusting in the palace yard. The Ọ̀ọ̀ni's principal Mercedes (OY I FE) is silver and has tinted windows, which are illegal for mortals in Nigeria.

The Ọ̀ọ̀ni miraculously withdrew from the folds of his robes a wad of twenty-naira notes an inch thick and gave it to his secretary, who gave it to the driver. It was probably two thousand naira – about two hundred dollars on the free greenback market. Pocket change; lunch in Belgravia. This was for the expenses of the party travelling by road. 'I am lending it to you,' the humorous god-king jested. It was as if he radiated money. It emanated from him as easily as light from the sun.

'For thus said the Holy Spirit, "If the late Oba Adesoji Aderemi had brought to Ile-Ife a golden era, your own reign will bring to Ile-Ife a diamond era!"' Thus spake the Most Revd apostle, Dr E. O. A. Adejobi, Pastor of the Church of the Lord Aladura Throughout the World – 'Cables and Telegrams HALLELUYAH, Lagos' – to HRH the Ọ̀ọ̀ni on the occasion of his accession and coronation at Ile-Ifẹ̀ on 6 December 1980.

We set off at three: the Ọ̀ọ̀ni and his entourage to Lagos, where they would board a plane; the lesser court functionaries, his panegyrist, trumpeter, drivers and police escort, travelling the whole way by road. A gigantic brolly was opened to shade the Ọ̀ọ̀ni as he walked the few steps from the palace to his car.

The Ọ̀ọ̀ni had a young English secretary – a small, plump, blonde English rose from Surrey, twenty-one years old, who had answered an advertisement for a secretary to 'an African dignitary'. Before that she had been temping in London. Now she was part of the court of a divine king. She was going by plane, so the Ọ̀ọ̀ni could dictate letters.

The Ọ̀ọ̀ni's letters were typed in purple capital letters on flamboyant stationery (embossed at the top with a gold crown surrounded by laurels and flywhisks) and ended with the formula WISHING YOU AND YOUR COMPANY A CONTINUED GLORIOUS YEAR.

The supernatural status of the Ọ̀ọ̀ni extends to his vehicles, which travel in awesome disregard for the laws and conventions that govern sublunar road traffic. They scream, they screech, and they drive in the middle of the road. I was in the group that went by car. There were five vehicles in our non-royal convoy of chiefs and servants. My driver drove with the horn blaring, with the headlights on full beam to dazzle the eyes of mortal motorists. He waved the cars and buses aside, and shouted curses and threats at those who didn't respond quickly enough. We were fast, we were spectacular. We were led by a police car with spinning red and blue lights. Inside it were men bearing trumpets and machine-guns. Nothing must stand in the way of the Ọ̀ọ̀ni's wish and its fulfilment. If the Ọ̀ọ̀ni commands that the cars be in Kano, they must be there instantly – as if by magic.

The Ọ̀ọ̀ni is rich because he is a god. The economic injustice of his wealth amid terrible poverty reflects the cosmic order: his wealth fills us with awe. In a place like Ifẹ̀, such wealth as the Ọ̀ọ̀ni possesses is magical. The Mercedes Benz star, three-pointed and encircled in unearthly shininess, is the token of this relationship between heaven and earth, an awful talisman of power. The people in the street bow when they see it streaking past them like a comet. A dozen of these sleek vehicles is like a vision of the four horsemen of the apocalypse.

'He has nothing smaller than a Peugeot, and he only has one of those,' our driver said.

The *oba*'s head is encircled by speeding Mercedes Benzes!

We drove for ten hours, through scenery that gradually changed from tropical forest to open savannah, and arrived at Kaduna at 1.30 a.m., where we slept in a fleabag hotel. Five hours later we were on the road again. Sunrise revealed a prosperous country very different from dirt-poor southern Nigeria.

At 9.00 a.m. we arrived before the great gates of Kano. Compared to the shanty towns of southern Nigeria, the city was like one of the rich petrocities of the Persian Gulf, with tall bank buildings, roundabouts with abstract sculptures in the middle, and new buildings in a daring modern-Islamic style of architecture. In Nigeria, wealth and power stay in the north.

The vast mud-brick palace of the Emir of Kano was a superb example of Saharan Islamic architecture, and a forceful display of the Fulani dynasty's past military power. Within its thick defensive walls was a labyrinth of alleys and courtyards and buildings, housing hundreds of people.

In an inner courtyard, palace guards called *dogari* strode about in red-and-green robes and turbans, looking like PhD candidates. Kano grandees wore huge turbans of a fine, white, gauze-like cloth, tied at the top in a big bow like rabbit ears.

The Emir of Kano's palace is the most splendid in the northern emirates. Because the Sultan of Sokoto, the most important northern ruler, is the leader of Nigeria's Muslims, a modesty becoming a religious leader is observed in his palace and ceremonial. The Emir of Kano, by contrast, is famous for his court musicians and his spectacular durbars, equestrian displays which are held on special occasions on the broad open space in front of the palace, while he watches from a covered enclosure atop the palace walls. Every morning he rides a richly panoplied horse a hundred metres from his quarters in the palace to the council chamber, accompanied by trumpeters and guards armed with clubs, to preside over the deliberations of an essentially powerless body. For the Ọọni's visit, the ceremonial was toned down because of the sombre nature of the occasion.

The Yoruba delegation made its presence known to officials of the Emir's palace. A minor rebellion broke out among the Yoruba chiefs and drivers against the Kano officials who wanted us to go straight to the airport to wait for the Ọọni, whose flight wasn't due until noon. We wanted 'chop' – food. I certainly did.

We all bundled into our cars and set off for an appalling joint where we had some really awful food. The price of every lump of gristly meat was haggled over as we crowded around the cook's open pots waving our dishes.

SONG

I want antelope stew and pangolin,
Chicken in a pot with the head thrown in,
Slippery okra and hot pepper soup,

Glutinous *eba* to scoop it all up;
Onions, tomatoes and chillies for heat,
Simmered with big cubes of giant snail meat.
And *amala* cake is a favourite of mine,
Drunk with a calabash of fresh palm wine.
Damn raw vegetables, bean sprouts and tofu:
Give me goat offal, bush meat and foufou.

Having eaten, we went up to the airport, where we resumed our waiting, this time in a parking-lot in the hot sun, until one of the Ọ̀ọ̀ni's aides ran out of the terminal announcing excitedly that the plane had landed. We scrambled to our vehicles. Our cars fell into place in front of the long black Mercedes the Emir had sent for him. The Ọ̀ọ̀ni was among us again! Meeting him was the object of our entire morning's efforts. The trumpeter in the police car leading the way put his trumpet out the window and blasted. The panegyrist thrust out his head and bellowed.

'Sijuwade! We fear you as a poor man fears a rich man! We flee before you as from a rampaging lion!'

There were nine vehicles in the Ọ̀ọ̀ni's motorcade. The Aláàfin had had only five. I was sitting in the front passenger seat of the fifth Mercedes, licence plate OY 6 FE. The other passengers were the Ọ̀ọ̀ni's secretary and an elderly palace chief called the Agroo of Ifẹ̀. I would call him '*baba*', meaning father, because in Yoruba etiquette it is impolite to address a senior person by his personal name. The Ataoja of Oshogbo had explained to me the Yoruba use of kinship titles. 'The chiefs' wives, who come to greet me, are the wives of my cousins, my nephews, my brothers, my uncles. Your aunt is your mother; you have a big mother and a small mother. Your uncle in New York is your father. Sometimes it's difficult to know who your father is!' If you want to attract a woman's attention politely, you address her as 'auntie', and so on.

In the Emir's palace, the Ọ̀ọ̀ni and the Emir sat on gold chairs at the far end of a long room, with a gold curtain behind them, and faced a multitude of men in white robes and turbans, kneeling and sitting on the carpet. The Emir was dressed in white, and wore a big, round, white turban wrapped around his head like a bandage. He formally welcomed the Ọọ̀ni to Kano, speaking in Hausa. His words were translated by an interpreter.

'His Highness welcomes you to Kano, and welcomes you to his palace. His Highness is very happy that you have come personally to express your concern over the death of his mother, and thanks you. Your coming here shows the exemplary relationship that exists between Ifẹ̀ and the people of Kano. He hopes the people of your dominion will be happy. He hopes all your people will emulate the good example you are showing. His Highness is very much aware of your efforts to unite Nigerians. By paying this visit, you show ways and means of uniting people, so the people of Nigeria can be one. His Highness once more would like to express his gratitude for coming here to offer condolences, and for this sign of brotherhood. His Highness gives you the blessing of God, and hopes each and every one of you will reach your destination safely.' The chief *qadi* of Kano then offered prayers.

Among the public stood a *dogari* with a pike, who called out a loud blessing at intervals, which caused a murmur of prayer to surge up from the well-wishers, creating a tide of sound in the hall.

'May God bless the soul of the late one! in the name of the Holy Prophet, the messenger of GOD.'

The visitors came, kneeled, murmured and left, to be replaced by others at a brisk rate of turnover. After half an hour, sufficient condolences having been offered, the two rulers rose and swept out of the room with their attendants.

It took about a hundred people, who all had to be fed and lodged, a whole week, travelling a thousand kilometres each way, in a string of vehicles that had to be looked after and filled with petrol, for the Ọọ̀ni to be able to spend half an hour sitting in silence with the Emir.

Work.

For most of the members of the Ọọ̀ni's entourage, most of the time before and after this half hour was spent waiting for the Ọọ̀ni. They were content to wait for hours at the pleasure of the Ọọ̀ni, just to be near him and to see him occasionally, while the Ọọ̀ni derived prestige from having so many people around him, living tokens of his importance. The Ọọ̀ni was the only Yoruba king who travelled with such a retinue.

People in royal entourages do a lot of waiting. This is one of the universal features of court life anywhere in the world, at any time in history. The first lines of Racine's *Britannicus* reveal the Emperor Nero's mother, Agrippine, waiting outside her son's chambers:

> ALBINE:
> *Quoi! tandis que Néron s'abandonne au sommeil,*
> *Faut-il que vous veniez attendre son réveil?*
> *Qu'errant dans le palais sans suite et sans escorte,*
> *La mère de César veille seule à sa porte?*

Albine is shocked because the Emperor keeps his mother, Agrippine, waiting outside his chamber, while he remains in bed. He is treating her like a courtier, and, moreover, one who has fallen out of favour. To her, he is 'in a meeting'. It prepares the audience for worse outrages to follow.

Every aspect of this play concerns court intrigue and competition. It was written not as a mirror of court life, but as an act of participation in it: it was written, indeed, to promote Racine ahead of his rival, Corneille. Racine's plays were not diversions: they existed in order to be seen by the court, and to advance Racine's position within it before the King. During the first performance of *Britannicus*, in the Hôtel de Bourgogne, Corneille sat alone in a box, frowning throughout the performance. Even the vocabulary reflects the tension of court life, it seems: Racine keeps it austerely simple, lest any highfalutin words (which Racine had in plenty) open him to charges of attempting to browbeat his slackly educated aristocratic audience and cause his downfall.

Eventually, once Racine had succeeded at court to the extent of being appointed Royal Historiographer (an appointment which caused much huffing and puffing among better-born candidates), he turned his back on courtly ambition and devoted the rest of his life to piety, ending his life in a state of spiritual peace and royal disfavour. I have always admired Racine for this, and had no feeling of loss when I read that his royally commissioned history of the reign of Louis XIV was destroyed in a fire.

The courtiers and servants in the Ọ̀ọ̀ni's entourage never knew where they were going to sleep, or when, or when they were going to eat, or if. Plans were always changing at the will of the king. He was the only one allowed to have any preference about anything, and he was supported in his movements through the day by a cushion of loyal individuals whose only interest was to be with him and to observe his wishes. These palace people had endless patience and never complained; all egos were subordinated to the will of the ruler.

The waiting is part of court culture. The courtiers enjoy it. A group of chiefs waiting for the Ọ̀ọ̀ni all day pass the time enjoying each other's society, exchanging jokes and offering each other elaborate courtesies. Waiting is a natural part of the stately rhythm of court life. Unlike our kind of waiting, it does not involve a sense of anxiety for the eventual fulfilment of an expected event or outcome with the shortest possible expense of time. No one looks at his watch wondering when the Ọ̀ọ̀ni is finally going to arrive.

The Ọ̀ọ̀ni must not wait for the fulfilment of his wishes, but everyone must wait for the Ọ̀ọ̀ni.

By the end of the day, short on sleep, weak with hunger, and frazzled by travel and contending with Nigerians, I was a wreck.

I never knew what was going on, partly because no one spoke good enough English to tell me. I hovered in one of the outer circles of proximity to the royal presence. Word only percolated out to me late and in a form that was either wrong or highly simplified.

We were in Kano for five days. We left by plane, a hundred and fifty of us in an aircraft chartered by the Ọ̀ọ̀ni for the purpose. The Ọ̀ọ̀ni was to spend the night in his house in Lagos, and drive from there to Ifẹ̀.

As we drove to the airport, the Yoruba grandees in my car gasped at the sight of the tall buildings of Kano, the roundabouts with abstract sculptures in the middle, the daring modern-Islamic architecture, the likes of which are nowhere to be seen in Ifẹ̀. For many it was their first trip to the north. But when I asked them what they thought about it, they claimed to be unimpressed. 'Too many flies in Kano,' they said. 'Too many beggars.'

I wrote to a friend: The Ọ̀ọ̀ni liked having me along, I think, because I added variety to the party. As we waited in the VIP lounge at the domestic air terminal at Lagos, the Ọ̀ọ̀ni, sitting some distance away with his group of accompanying *obas*, summoned me forward. The *obas* stared at me.

'What impression have you formed of the trip?' he said.

'Very good, Kabiyesi, thank you.'

'He is writing a book about kings,' the Ọ̀ọ̀ni told the other *obas*.

It was as if I was being exhibited as a court curiosity, like a giraffe or a trained elephant brought in to entertain their royal highnesses during a quiet moment, as they waited for their cars.

When the cars arrived, I sat, according to the status that had been allocated to me in the precedence of the Ọ̀ọ̀ni's motorcade, in the front seat of the fifth Mercedes, and we set off for Ifẹ̀. The traffic shrank away before his terrible speeding vehicles.

At a tollbooth on the Lagos–Ibadan Expressway, the Ọ̀ọ̀ni gave 300 naira to a group of delighted policemen who flung themselves on to the tarmac in greeting.

We reached Ifẹ̀, and pulled into the inner courtyard of the palace. As I sat in the car, wondering, as always, what was going to happen next, his young English secretary emerged and summoned me into the throne room with a little wave. 'Kabiyesi wants to play the organ for you,' she said.

I beheld the reincarnation of the creator-god in his throne room, jamming on a Yamaha Electone organ. From the range of pre-programmed electronic rhythms, he had selected a brisk bossa nova and was playing a noodling improvisation over it, as absorbed as a child finger-painting. Somehow he was managing to produce a weird Yoruba electronic undertow as well. He didn't look up when I entered, but continued to play. The secretary told me to sit right by him. Eventually he looked up and said dreamily, 'I want to know something about you.' We talked about my book, which I described as an encyclopaedia of kings. He asked me if I had enough money, which was sweet of him. I lied and said that I had.

His attention was distracted when he found that he could conjure up the tune of 'God Save the Queen' from the fathomless electronic depths of the instrument. He was delighted by the discovery. It was rendered in a minor key, with the bossa-nova rhythm and the strange electronic undercurrent bubbling in the background. 'Do you recognize that?' he said. I did, but the English secretary didn't.

He continued to play, the stream of his musical imagination drifting on to another formless improvisation. Then he said, 'Is there anything you want to ask me? Anything I can do for you?' I felt as if I was speaking to Aladdin's genie. The secretary prodded me from behind and whispered loudly, '*Ask him something!*'

The *oba*'s crown is made of money!

This is a traditional moment in African travel, where the traveller asks the ruler for help in passing on to his next destination. In his *Journal of a Second Expedition into the Interior of Africa* (1829), the luckless Captain Hugh Clapperton reports what he said to the Shehu of Bornu at the same juncture:

> I then told him that I had been sent by the King of England to visit Bornou; that I was the King of England's servant, and hoped he would assist me in proceeding on my journey; and that I intended to make him a suitable present; that I wanted thirty-six men to carry my baggage, and two horses for my servants to ride; and that I wished to stay as short a time as possible, as the rains were near at hand, which, if overtaken by them, would prevent my travelling; that the season of the rains was very sickly, and fatal to white men; that three of the white men who had left England with me had died in Yourriba; that it was more than probable that I should die also, if exposed in any of these countries to the rains.

I told him I needed help getting a re-entry visa into Nigeria, as I was planning to go to Niger to see the Sultan of Zinder. 'Not only will I help you with that, I will give you a letter to take to the Sultan,' he said, in a flourish of generosity. In the end I got neither, and anyway never went to Niger.

'When he's in that kind of mood, you can ask him anything,' the secretary said.

The Ọọ̀ni had one more engagement that week: his vehicles hit the road again the next day to attend a memorial service for the chief of a royal house in the Middle Belt of Nigeria, where people speak Yoruba but are Muslims.

By the time it ended it had been a typical week for the Ọ̀ọ̀ni: travelling, visiting, dictating letters, looking after his overseas business interests by long-distance telephone (when he could get through: even the Ọ̀ọ̀ni of Ifẹ̀ is at the mercy of Nigeria's terrible telephone system), sitting for hours with other traditional rulers in an endless round of protocol visits.

When I last saw the Ọ̀ọ̀ni, he was sitting in his throne room with his Asprey briefcase on his lap, giving orders and instructions and saying goodbye to the Aleoku of Abeokuta. 'I like your outfit,' the Ọ̀ọ̀ni said, snapping open the locks of the briefcase. The Ọ̀ọ̀ni wasn't too badly turned out himself: he was dressed in white and turquoise and wore slippers decorated with the jewel-like tips of peacocks' tails, a gold ring with a chunky pearl, and a gold watch whose face glittered with diamonds. All that week I never saw him wear the same costume twice.

From the open briefcase, he doled out wads of naira to palace servants who tremblingly stepped forward to receive them.

The Agroo of Ifẹ̀ came in to pay his respects. He slowly lowered himself into a prone position in the doorway. The sight made me think of the technical problems that one might encounter in felling a tall and ancient oak tree in the forest. I worried that he would never get up again: when one sees a man of eighty lying in a prone position one assumes something is wrong. But his frame had proven itself resilient enough to deal with the exertions and stresses of the past week.

As the Ọ̀ọ̀ni spoke to the Agroo, he was interrupted by the panegyrist in the doorway, whose delivery was so loud it hurt the eardrums. The Ọ̀ọ̀ni winced. He turned to me and said, by way of explanation, or excuse, 'He's come two hundred miles to sing encomiums to me.'

The *oyinbo* secretary tried to get a word in above these distractions. 'Don't forget that there is a visitor coming tomorrow.'

'What visitor? There is no visitor.'

'The Jegun of Ile Oliyi.'

'Oh. I forgot! What time is he coming?'

She told him.

I went back to the OAU guest-house, packed and left Ifẹ̀ for the last time. But I had one final task in Nigeria. This was to return to Kano to learn about a Hausa 'mirror for princes': *The Crown of Religion Concerning the Obligations of Princes* of Sheikh Abu 'Abd Allah Muhammad ibn 'Abd al-Karim al-Maghili al-Tilimsani – an Arabic text written in 1492 for the ruler of Kano, Sarkin Muhammadu Rumfa. Not only did this text serve as the blueprint for Kano's establishment as an Islamic state, it was the first important literary work produced in the western Sudan. Al-Maghili is described by the explorer Heinrich Barth as 'the man who introduced Islam into central Negroland'.

The Emir of Kano, Alhaji Ado Bayero, was Nigeria's Ambassador to Senegal in the 1960s, and has been Emir since 1964. He is the thirteenth Emir of the Fulani dynasty, which assumed power in Kano by conquest in 1806 in the jihad of Uthman Dan Fodio. From its base in Sokoto, it then swept Nigeria and was indirectly responsible for the destruction of the Ọ̀yọ́ empire.

I called on the Emir in his palace. He wore his big gauzy turban, which covered the sides of his face and his chin, leaving only his eyes, nose and mouth visible, and sat in a stiff-backed chair. His eyes were gentle, and he spoke quietly and precisely. He told me that a dissertation on al-Maghili had been written by the late Grand *Qadi* of Kano, Dr Hassan Gwarza.

Al-Maghili was a travelling preacher and political agitator. He came to Kano in 1492 at Sarkin Rumfa's invitation. Gwarza records that he already had a considerable reputation before he came to Kano, for the severity of his doctrine and for miracles. On a pilgrimage to Mecca, he caused the window of the tomb of the Prophet to open automatically before him. When asked once to find the *qibla*, the direction of Mecca, a matter of disagreement among the learned, he pointed with his staff toward the Ka'ba, and a radiant vision of the House of God appeared on the horizon.

On Friday mornings before midday prayers the Emir's ministers come to report to him and greet him. It is an empty ritual: his law goes no further than the palace gates. The only real powers the Emir has left, apart from those connected with his private business interests, are advising local government and the appointment of imams to mosques. Nevertheless, the ceremony is like a furnace in which order is forged in the bright fire of absolute power. The Emir's real power has gone, but the drama of power, its light or emanation, continues.

When the civilian Governor of Kano State tried in 1981 to challenge what he saw as the royal family's 'feudal' privileges, there were riots in Kano. Governments come and go in Nigeria, in a dismaying cycle of *coup d'état* and corruption, but traditional rulers remain with a glorious and untainted persistence.

The Friday ceremony took place in the room where the Emir and the Ọ̀ọ̀ni had sat. The Emir sat motionless on a carpeted platform, his face covered in a green gauze veil, his feet in slippers decorated with black ostrich feathers. His ministers sat on the floor in two rows facing each other, forming a corridor towards the Emir's platform. Behind the ministers stood *dogaris*, who maintained the intensity of the occasion by shouting slogans.

'Be cool! Be steady.'

'Live long! Live well.'

'The Emir salutes you.'

One by one his ministers reported to him. The night before, Thursday night, I had made a recording of the palace musicians in a courtyard behind the palace. Afterwards I had given them some money. The head of the musicians, the *sarkin busa*, came forward and stood as stiff as a poker before the Emir. He reported, according to the translation whispered to me by Waziri, the Emir's secretary, 'A white man came and we played music for him and he gave us 200 naira.'

After the ministers and 'district heads' had reported, petitions from the Emir's subjects were heard. A frail, bearded old man in white entered and fell on his knees and began to supplicate the Emir with upraised hands.

'What's he saying?' I whispered to Waziri.

'He is saying that somebody stole his car. He is asking the Emir to pray for him and to give him some money.'

'Will he give him some?'

'Maybe.'

At noon, the Emir processed from the palace to the adjacent Grand Mosque for prayers, a distance of about fifty metres. He rode out on horseback, accompanied by a throng of club-wielding *dogaris*. His face was veiled, but his eyes were uncovered and darted threateningly over the crowd. They greeted him with a clenched-fist salute, which he returned.

About a hundred thousand people in orderly rows filled the grounds of the mosque and the dusty streets around it, standing and kneeling in the hot sun to perform their prayers.

The Emir's appearance and comportment in the ceremony matched remarkably closely the recommendations of al-Maghili:

> It is an obligation for every Emir to clothe himself in a cloak of dignity, whether he is among his councillors or alone . . . You may adorn your body and sweeten your odour, and embellish your clothes as far as (Muslim law) permits the adornment of men, without the imitation of women or bankrupting the public treasury. Do not adorn yourself in gold, silver or silk.
>
> If you sit, sit cross-legged and be calm whenever possible, and do not fidget, even with your hands. Let your glance be a scrutiny, and let the lowering of your head be for meditation . . . And do not open your mouth, even if it is to yawn. If a yawn is about to overcome you, then remember your Lord and it will leave you. And if you forget, until you are overcome, then cover your mouth with the back of one of your hands.

Al-Maghili's main point, repeated throughout the treatise, is 'The height of affliction is the isolation of the ruler from his subjects.' The royal body must be always on display.

He advises the establishment of a strong army of courageous men, the building of fortresses and the maintenance of armouries of 'powerful implements of war'. Spies should be sent into neighbouring kingdoms bearing gifts and gathering intelligence.

To strengthen his authority, al-Maghili advised, the ruler should engage in continuous military campaigns, and avoid court culture. 'The residence of the ruler in the capital is the root of all manner of calamity and harm.' He emphasizes the point with a poem: 'The domain of the eagle is flying through the sky and open countryside, while even the most energetic rooster is limited to wandering around the house. And there is no authority unless the king resolves to be like the eagle. For the command of a rooster is effective only upon chickens.'

The horses of resolution are ridden on saddles of determination: 'Uplift the country from the bareness of corruption. [Purge it] with winds of battle, and clouds of dust [of armies] and the thunder of neighing [of cavalry] and the lightning flashes of swords and the thunderous noises of sabres and endless waves of soldiers. For indeed, sovereignty is [won] by the sword and not by procrastination.'

He advised Rumfa to increase the security of the town, to have plenty of spare horses, and to take special care of his own personal security: 'He should be afraid of a rope so that he may not be stung by a snake.'

The personal belongings of al-Maghili are still in the possession of his descendants in Kano: his Qur'an, rosary, sword, walking-stick and pair of scales.

Such are the differences between the Yoruba and the Hausa: while the Yoruba 'mirror for princes', in the case of the Akirun of Ikirun, was a body of unwritten and localized traditional knowledge, transmitted orally during a three-month period of secluded initiation, the Hausa 'mirror' is written in Arabic and supplies the model of an Islamic state which would be recognizable anywhere in the Islamic world.

Royal knowledge in Kano had another dimension. Through Nasr Ado Bayero, a son of the Emir whom I had met on the Ọọ̀ni's plane from Kano to Lagos, I was put in touch with Tanko, a primary-school teacher, who told me the following.

'There is a secret library in the palace which only the Emir can enter. It contains books inherited from past Emirs on the government of the state. Whoever possesses that library becomes the Emir.'

I was stunned by this idea, and determined to find out more about the secret library before I left Kano.

Tanko lived in the quarters at the rear of the palace, along with hundreds of 'inherited families': the families of palace slaves and servants and their descendants.

My request for a tour of this inner region of the palace received a blank stare from Waziri. The royal household is said to be dominated by two chief concubines, titled Venus and Mercury, and they run the palace. The Emir has fifty-seven children by four wives and an unknown number of concubines. The previous Emir had over three hundred. The power of the concubines is such that no son of the wife of an Emir has ever become Emir: Emirs have always been the sons of concubines.

One night, Tanko took me to a traditional Hausa healing ceremony, called *bori*, in a village some distance outside the city walls. It was the kind of pagan practice that both al-Maghili and later the Fulani dynasty tried to stamp out, but the point Tanko was making to me was that Kano was the conjunction of two distinct cultures: one Islamic (Fulani), the other African (Hausa).

A 'doctor' – the *sarkin bori* – cured 'mentally ill' people by driving 'jinns' or demons out of them. The patient was kept in seclusion in a room for several weeks. Then contact was established with the jinn that was possessing the patient through singing and music performed on a *garaya*, a two-stringed gourd-bodied instrument, and drums. Once the identity of the jinn had been determined, the jinn would be purged and enter the body of an assistant, who would act out its personality. It was an intensely theatrical ritual, which culminated in a display of fire-eating by one of the *sarkin bori*'s assistants.

While we waited for the *bori* to start, the driver of our taxi told me how to recognize a jinn. 'If you see a snake with a ring in its ear, it's not a normal snake, it's a jinn. A jinn can make the road split in two before your eyes, and force you off the road.'

'Everyone here was crazy until the doctor cured them,' Tanko told me. 'He used to be crazy himself.'

At the palace the next day, a lanky *dogari* turned smilingly to me and said, 'I saw you last night at the *bori*.'

In my last dismal days in Kano, I was running out of money, and running out of time. The university was closed for the summer, and my contacts there had all gone on leave. The secret library was to keep its secrets. Its inscrutable image smirked at me.

On my last full day, as I sat hopelessly in an outer waiting-room of the palace, vainly hoping to see the Emir again to ask him about the secret library, with only a whining electric fan for company, a young man emerged who introduced himself as Mahmoud Ado Bayero, another one of the Emir's sons. I said I had come to see the Emir. 'My father is asleep,' he said. (Well, naturally, I thought, in the irresponsible exasperation one feels with a place one is about to leave. These kings were like disappointing zoo animals – always asleep when you wanted to see them.) I told him that there was one thing I wanted to know before I left Nigeria: Was there a secret library in the palace, to which only the Emir has access? A repository of royal knowledge, whoever has custody of which becomes the Emir?

'Yes.'

Could I see it?

'It's a secret.'

A week later, back in London, in the clamorous surroundings of the underground bar of the School of Oriental and African Studies, Dr John Lavers of Ahmadu Bello University revealed to me the secret of the secret library.

'Oh yes,' he said jovially, over his pint. 'There's nothing in it but detective novels, and some Arabic books published in Egypt, probably bought by someone on pilgrimage. All the manuscripts were given to the university years ago by the previous Emir.'

CHAPTER 4

Invisible Kingdom – Swaziland

SWOLLEN WITH CONFIDENCE as a result of my success with the Nigerian rulers, I then set about investigating an African monarchy – a kingdom where the King was the ruler of the state. There was one functioning monarchy left in sub-Saharan Africa, Swaziland. It had a population about the same as Tonga's, so I assumed that it would be as easy to see the King, Mswati III, as it had been to see Taufa'ahau Tupou IV. I consulted some American academics that I knew who had lived in Swaziland for many years. The time was just after Christmas.

'It's a pity you're not there now,' they said. It was the time of the *incwala*, the annual ritual of Swazi kingship. The *incwala* was a kind of drama in which the King, the Ngwenyama, was the central character. Now the King was in ritual seclusion, being treated by his doctors with magical ointments. He would soon emerge in the role of a supernatural hero, to perform a dance in which he would command the forces of nature to obey him and to give him power for the coming year. The unity of the nation and the fruitfulness of the land depended on it. The slightest error in the performance of the ritual could have grave consequences.

The *incwala* begins with the waxing of the first moon after the winter solstice. Astronomical conditions were such that I had only a few days to arrange my trip. I might just get there in time. I knew that if I didn't see the King at the *incwala*, I would probably never see him at all.

The King of Swaziland, Mswati III, had been King for nearly five years, but he was only twenty-two, and he did not have the mystical charisma and the practical experience of kingship the Swazis call 'shadow'. He was surrounded by an extensive and invisible web of advisers and minders who made sure their captive

King wasn't allowed to put a foot wrong. The King was young, and there was popular clamour for reform, so, politically, the monarchy was vulnerable: it was existing only to defend itself. This was only one of the facts that in my Nigerian-induced *folie de grandeur* I had not adequately considered. I sent off a letter to the palace and, without waiting for a reply, made preparations to go.

I arrived in Johannesburg on New Year's Day and boarded an early-morning bus to Swaziland that slowly chugged and wheezed through the plains of the eastern Transvaal. It was a 'black bus': it stopped mainly in the ramshackle black townships that coexisted beside the neat white suburbs. Most of my fellow passengers were Swazis on their way home from their jobs in South Africa.

The towns were depressingly familiar close cousins of the featureless and charmless small towns of middle America, but set in a vast and beautiful landscape. The earth was terracotta red, and under the broad, blazing sky seemed to vibrate with the power of life, thrusting up proud, towering trees and sleek fields of grain. The tribes of South Africa, white and black, had been fighting over this rich, potent land for two centuries.

By afternoon the air was growing cool and the geography was greener and rockier than it had been in the heart of the Transvaal. We were climbing the hill that forms the natural gateway into Swaziland: beyond it the country slopes gradually downward toward Mozambique, evolving as it does so from high forest, to rich green hills, and finally flattening out into parched bush veld.

The bus descended into Mbabane, where I disembarked. My American friends had lent me a house outside the town. The house overlooked a misty green valley and had a corrugated-metal roof. It had a housekeeper and a half-wild guard dog. 'Don't pick up the telephone during a thunderstorm, or you'll be electrocuted,' they warned.

It was here that I hovered for a month on the margin of Swazi society, an outsider looking in, straining to see, through thick veils of secrecy, suspicion, fear and deceptiveness, the true form of Swazi kingship.

The *incwala* was being performed at a place called Ludzidzini royal kraal. Ludzidzini was the Queen Mother's compound. The

Queen Mother – the *Indlovukazi*, the Great She Elephant – was nearly as important as the King, but much less visible. The Swazi monarchy is often described as a 'dual monarchy' because her authority balances the King's.

The Queen Mother's kraal was located in the middle of an area called Ezulwini, the sacred valley of Swazi kingship, a beautiful setting overlooking a serene green plain with hills a darker shade of green in the distance. In 1820 Sobhuza I chose the site of Ezulwini as his capital when he was retreating from the enemy Ndandwe tribe. Sobhuza II established his ritual capital and the parliament building at nearby Lobamba. Ezulwini is a few miles out of Mbabane, beside the country's main highway which runs through the valley. Besides being the sacred valley of Swazi kingship, it is also the metropolitan area's main drag, the centre of the white tourist trade, with hotels and casinos and roadside stands selling kitschy handicrafts.

I left the road and approached the royal kraal by a narrow path through a field of grazing cows. From a distance it looked like a military encampment: a cluster of dome-shaped huts inside a circular fence of long sticks. The huts were made of woven branches, and were fragile, temporary-looking structures that might have belonged to a campaigning army, ready to set off the next day to fight the Zulus. The military *gloire* of Swazi society, a kingdom held together in the past by a warrior king, is an important part of the Swazi monarchy's official idea of itself: men still belong to regiments and must carry shields for certain royal duties, as if they are going to war. Lightning rods rose among the huts of the kraal like battle standards.

Talking my way through the military checkpoint guarding the kraal's outer perimeter involved half an hour's pleading with a soldier. Around the kraal's high fence, men in traditional warrior's attire – bare-chested, wearing skirts, animal skins around their loins, beads around their necks, with feathers in their hair, and carrying cowhide shields – strolled about and sat in the fence's sparse shade, waiting for the ceremony to begin and the King to appear.

Huge cattle freely mingled among the gathered warriors, signalling their approach by the munching sound they made as they cropped the grass. The big dark spots on their hides were like continents on a map of an imaginary world, or the clouds that scudded across the sky. Their bones formed elegant parallelograms as they moved. All the beasts were different, yet perfect, like snowflakes. Like snowflakes, they were innumerable. These were the cattle of the royal herd, the largest in the country. Most of the cattle were gifts to the king, as indicated by the variety of their brands and earclips.

It's hard to think of anything more important to the Swazis than cattle: they are life and death and everything in between that matters – namely wealth and prestige. The whole country exists for their sake: it is a cattle ranch from border to border. There are few wild animals in Swaziland, because a Swazi's first impulse is to kill anything that might threaten cattle. When a man kills a leopard, the King gives him a cow as a reward. The King's herds are the most visible sign of his temporal power. The body of the late King Sobhuza II was entombed wrapped in the hide of a black cow.

The Swazis despise sheep. If a member of the Dlamini clan (the dominant and most numerous in Swaziland, from which the King is always chosen) eats a black sheep, he will go mad. Better for a Dlamini not to eat lamb or mutton at all, since he can't tell the colour of the sheep it came from. As a large proportion of the population is called Dlamini, this means that lamb and mutton consumption in Swaziland is low.

My plans originally included purchasing a cow and giving it to the King as *kwetfulu*, as tribute. I studied a book called *Animal Husbandry in the Tropics* for advice on how to buy one. (From this book I learned that the majority of Swazi cattle are a cross between the long-horned African zebu cattle, with a hump and loose skin, and fatter and higher-yielding European breeds.) I found out that calf prices start at about four hundred dollars and that, although the King is frequently presented with cattle, he never receives them personally, so I abandoned the idea.

Around the royal kraal, one must take off one's hat. It is bad form to shield one's eyes from the sun with one's hand. It is forbidden to point at the King's hut. This is Swazi etiquette.

Within the hut, the King was washing himself with sea water and sacred ointments and other magical treatments called *mutis*. I discovered that I had got there in time for the last day of the *incwala*.

I sought permission to enter the enclosure. A plain-clothes security man was frankly opposed to my presence. 'What is your mission here?' he said.

'I am writing a book about kingdoms.'

'But what is your mission?'

The Governor of Ludzidzini, a man with a huge head-dress of glossy black ostrich feathers, emerged from the enclosure and, towering over me, asked me to state my business. He had flaring nostrils and an imperious manner, and wore long chains of beads around his neck. I was surrounded by soldiers and officials. After giving me a long stare he allowed me to pass inside. 'In Swaziland, we do things with *permission*,' he said sternly.

Inside the circular enclosure, about two hundred warriors formed a crescent, facing the opening through which the King would enter. In the centre, a smouldering heap of wood gave off a thin ribbon of smoke. On this fire, personal objects of the King were being burned, to dramatize the destruction of the things of the old year: a sleeping-mat, the paraphernalia he used in the previous days' ceremonies, and earth from different parts of the country. This ritual of completion and purification is traditionally concluded by a heavy shower of rain, which extinguishes the fire. As the *incwala* takes place during the rainy season, this can usually be counted on, although today the skies were clear.

Although the *incwala* looks as if it has been performed since time immemorial, it was introduced only in the middle of the last century, developed from a type of rain ritual common throughout the region. King Mswati II had greatly expanded the Swazi kingdom by conquest. He absorbed the conquered tribes into an expanded Swazi polity by organizing their men into centralized regiments, and by introducing a ritual which placed the King at the fulcrum of heaven and earth, and gave him an indispensable role in keeping the two in balance. In the *incwala*, the King acts out this supernatural role, as rain-maker and protector of cosmic harmony. He brings into being rain, the year's agricultural cycle and political harmony. When it was smaller, the Dlamini monarchy could be governed as a single huge family. After Mswati's conquests, something less personal, more indirect – yet effective – was called for. In this way, government through symbolism and drama – one of the universal techniques of monarchy – came to Swaziland.

The warriors were chanting in low, sonorous voices, and swaying from side to side. A group of women stood apart from them, dancing the same way. The women wore long gowns, and their hair was coiffed into neat, round buns, encircled by a narrow band. Their stylized appearance recalled the queens in a pack of playing-cards.

Eventually the King appeared. He marched into the kraal dressed like the warriors, but wearing an enormous head-dress of black feathers, distinguished from those of the other senior figures by three white feathers at nine, twelve and three o'clock around his head. He was young and sturdily built and good-looking. Leading a group of senior warriors, he crossed the open space and stood facing the regiments, who surged forward in an orderly, swinging motion, still chanting in a low, monotonous rhythm. After some time he joined their ranks, occupying the central position. It is believed that, in this position of first among equals, dressed the same as his warriors, the King stands out by the sheer magnetism of his personality, his charisma. In fact, if you didn't know what he looked like, you would wonder, looking at those swaying ranks, which one was the King.

The pace of the ceremony was slow and tedious. Deviations in ritual practice are said to be dangerous for the kingdom, and to throw it off balance, but this warriors' turnout, with sticks and shields, smacked more of military than of ritual precision. Towards the end, after the few of us who were spectators had stood through more than two hours of very monotonous singing, the security man who had questioned me earlier turned around and said, 'Take your hands out of your pockets and stand still!'

When the ceremony was over, the King paraded out of the enclosure. As he walked towards the wooden platform where we stood, he stared at me, the only white man present, and I lowered my gaze in deference. One must never look kings in the eye, I instinctively felt: something to do with the gaze of power.

Your Majesty, in so far as I am under your gaze, I no longer see the eye that looks at me. For if I see your eye, the gaze disappears.

After this, the King and his warriors had a feast of grilled royal beef and beer, to which I was pointedly not invited, so I left.

For the next two weeks, the countryside around the royal residences would be full of men weeding the king's millet fields. The Swazis call it their form of national service. You can be fined a cow by your local chief for not showing up. When this tribute labour had accomplished its task (trampling half the millet plants in the process), about two weeks later, the King would dismiss the men with a speech that usually included an important policy statement.

My next step was to approach the palace to ask to see the King. I put on my traditional regalia (Brooks Brothers seersucker suit and tie) and drove out to Lozitha Palace, where I was to put my request for an audience before Elias Mkhonta, the King's private secretary.

Lozitha Palace stands on a gentle hill overlooking the broad green expanse of the Ezulwini valley. It is a modern palace, built by Sobhuza II. Its rural setting dramatizes the relationship between Swazi kingship and the land. It is a modest palace, architecturally unexceptional. It could be an agricultural college somewhere in the United States. There is even a cattle-grid at the head of the long road that leads up to it. Sobhuza insisted on placing the centres of Swazi political power, including the parliament building, in this rural setting, in the sacred valley of Swazi kingship, and at a distance from Mbabane, the colonial and administrative capital. The only token of royal splendour is the peacocks that roam about the grounds.

The King's palace office had been reformed since Mswati came to power, under British guidance. A Foreign Office appointee, a former officer of the Ghurkhas and ADC to the governor of Hong Kong named George Lys, had been installed as 'Tutor/

Coordinator' and been given the jobs of organizing the King's schedule, seeing that he got to his appointments on time and supervising his education. The King received twelve hours' instruction a week in history, economics, computers and politics, and the Foreign Office in London also sent regular packages of reading matter, which, it was rumoured, he never read. It was a classic example of the British practice of providing tutors for young kings. The elders were said not to be at all happy with the permanent presence of a white man so close to the Ngwenyama. Others said that in his role as tutor Lys had little to offer the King besides the precepts of jungle warfare.

Elias Mkhonta responded to my request as if I was a goat requesting permission to browse in the royal flowerbeds.

At first he was mild and apologetic and polite. He was a small, serious man, tweedy in dress and pedagogical in manner. He advised me to read J. S. M. Matsebula's *A History of Swaziland*, a book that was available to me in libraries in London.

'The King is young, and he cannot explain things . . . He is busy all day with official matters . . . When I recommend someone for an audience, His Majesty asks me if it is in the interests of Swaziland for him to see that person . . . I could not recommend that he see someone just for the sake of a *book*.' He spat out the word 'book' as if it had been ashes and wormwood.

Then his tone grew heated. 'I have just been in England. I didn't see the Queen Mother. Do you think I could have seen the Queen Mother just like that? If I went to America, do you think I could have seen George Bush, just by asking? I don't know why you came here. It is not easy to see heads of state. And now, if you don't mind, I have work to do.'

The portcullis slammed down behind me. My mind smarted with the verbal hiding I had been given.

I retreated, wounded, to the house on the ridge to lick my wounds and consider my position. I had made the mistake of thinking that the Swazis would be just as open and gregarious as the Nigerians had been. The Yoruba were a roaring, hydra-headed monster of a culture, free and unconscious of itself, engorging everything that approached it. No two peoples could have been more different! The Swazis were the Japanese of Africa, inscrutable, and their court impenetrable. To them, there were two types of white man: those of the past – the swindling concessionaires and insincere imperial officials – and those of the present – the half-naked South African tourists, down for the weekend to booze and gamble in the Ezulwini casinos.

I was going about the business of asking to see the King in quite the wrong way. You couldn't just march up to the palace and ask to see the King, as I had done in Nigeria. In his memoir of serving as the King's private secretary, *The King's Eye*, J. S. M. Matsebula writes, 'Usually before being ushered into the presence of a king, you have to wait: for a few minutes, for an hour, for a day, for a month, for months, for a year, or even indefinitely.'

To cut through this, one needs a *lincusa*. A *lincusa* is an advocate, go-between or pleader. In Swaziland you cannot approach someone out of the blue, especially someone important: you must have a third party to state your business for you and arrange a meeting. So I changed my strategy, and sought a *lincusa*. This would take time. In the meantime, the final episode of the *incwala* drama was about to take place, in which the King dismisses the regiments who had been weeding his millet fields. I tried to discover when and where this would happen. Discovering anything in Swaziland was a matter of considerable difficulty, but one day, as I was emerging from the Swaziland national museum, a minor breakthrough occurred.

A traditional Swazi beehive hut had been erected beside the museum for educational purposes, and a man and woman in Swazi costume were sitting inside. The man beckoned me in. The hut had a smooth mud floor. Like an oracle, this anonymous Swazi, whose face I could barely see, sat in the darkness and spoke of secrets. The woman sewed, and remained silent.

He began by talking about the Gulf War, which had just started.

'Every culture is based on belief: Islam, Judaism, Christianity, African culture. And every culture has a secret core which is kept secret by a few individuals. That is why no culture can really understand another culture. That is the reason for this war,' he said. He might have been talking about Swaziland: its sense of national identity and cohesion depended on the defence of a secret core which it was quixotic folly to attempt to penetrate.

'All these people who are asking for change want to preserve everything else,' he went on. 'They want to preserve the trees, they want to preserve the animals; but they don't want to preserve the most important thing in their life, which is their culture. It is our culture which holds us together. They ask for *glasnost* and *perestroika*, but do they want to throw their culture away? They want every man to get along as best he can, any which way he can. What good is that?'

And then he added, to my amazement, 'Aren't you going to see the King dismissing the regiments?'

'That's today? I thought it was this Saturday!' I had been misinformed by a previous informant. This seemed to happen a lot in Swaziland.

I left the oracle in the beehive hut and went up to Lozitha Palace to check. At the police booth at the palace gate, I asked where the ceremony was taking place.

'Show me your documents,' the policeman said. I showed him.

'Will you do me a favour?'

'Certainly.'

'Give me two rand fifty for a drink.'

I declined this request, but still wanted to know where the ceremony was happening.

'OK, go down to the main road, turn right, and then turn right again.'

I could see the royal homestead from this position on the brow of a hill, and could tell that he was sending me in exactly the wrong direction.

I got there without his help. The kraal stood in the middle of a broad, flat plain, baking under a hot white sun. Its name was Engabezweni. I parked at a distance and plunged into the crowd of Swazi warriors, conspicuous in my Western dress. Among them, women sat under umbrellas selling food and beer.

A group of Swazis sitting in the shade of a pick-up truck called me over and handed me a half-gallon tin they were drinking from. An old man with the single red lourie feather of the Dlamini clan in his hair passed by. His build was small and delicate; he had fine, aristocratic features. He looked at me with that severe, suspicious squint that Swazis employ when sizing up a white man. 'He is offering you traditional brew, man. Swazi beer, in other words. Drink it.'

It was sour and yeasty and had a metallic tang from the vessel it was in. I passed it back. The old man then spoke to me in an eccentric, mock-archaic English.

'Art thou a practitioner of the photographic art, sir?' he said.

'Sometimes,' I said.

'Dost thou have the permission of the appropriate authorities?'

I said I didn't.

'Whence dost thou come?'

I said I was from New York.

'I have been there several times, to attend the Security Council of the United Nations.' (Mswati addressed it in 1989.) Then he jerked his grey head aside in peremptory conclusion and walked enigmatically away.

'That is one of our elders,' one of the youths sitting on the ground said.

The elder was one of the men who run the country, who rule the King. Diplomats call them 'the men in skins', because they seldom wear Western dress. Here his role seemed to be maintaining discipline. I never found out his name. J. S. M. Matsebula was once asked by a foreign journalist who the elders were. 'They are men,' he replied, 'and they are everywhere.'

Baden-Powell is said to have had the inspiration for the Boy Scout movement from the example of the Swazi regiments. Like samurai, they are held together by military discipline and a code of high conduct – one might almost say of chivalry. They displayed the most courtly of manners to me. Standing in a circle, sharing a large bottle of beer on terms of the strictest fairness, we were approached by a drunk. He bawled at me in siSwati, demanding money. My companions sent him about his business.

'We told him not to interrupt us, and that if he wants to talk to you he must first approach us, and we will make an introduction.'

Beneath the Swazi warrior's wild appearance lay a highly fastidious personality. We took a collection for another bottle of beer, as they wouldn't stand for my being the only one to pay.

At noon, the regiments formed into ranks at a trombone's call and marched to the royal enclosure.

I had extracted myself from the beer-drinkers by this point and was leaning on the roof of my rented car when a slender young man sidled up to me. I asked him why he wasn't marching with the regiments: most Swazis belong to one. 'I am not marching today because I was with the King,' he said. I didn't understand this, but I accepted it. He pointed out the Prime Minister, Obed Dlamini, who was marching with his regiment and displaying his official's pot-belly. He identified Dlamini royals, wearing single red lourie feathers in their hair. He seemed to know a lot, and he was willing to talk to me.

'When is the King coming?' I said.

'He is coming soon. Do you want to meet him?'

I was amazed by this. I said I did. Was this the *lincusa* I was looking for?

'What is the King doing these days? Is he busy?' I said, trying to make the most of this golden opportunity.

'No. He's not doing anything. Just dancing.' This account differed starkly from Elias Mkhonta's description of the King being very busy with official matters.

But why was this young man interested in helping me? I reckoned him for a palace hanger-on of some sort, but a poor one. While the front door of the palace was as if bolted shut against the likes of me, there were back doors, it seemed, flying on their hinges to admit people like him, 'palace insignificants'. He wrote down his name, Validlela, and gave his address as Lozitha Palace. Then he asked me for five rand. I had finally found a *lincusa*! I arranged to meet him the next day.

The King emerged from his dome-shaped hut. A blue Mercedes was parked outside. A retinue of warriors led him into the enclosure. I stood among the *bokholo*, those who were not wearing traditional attire, thinking I would blend in that way, and looked over the heads of those in front of me at the King.

The King wore a leopard loin skin and red feathers in his hair, and spoke from a note in his hand that he glanced at after each point. He spoke confidently in siSwati, rocking slightly from one foot to the other as he got into his stride. About a thousand men gathered in a circle around him. They loved him, and you could feel it. At every pause in his speech, they whistled and cried out the royal salute: 'Ba-ye-the!'

Sometimes an individual would rush forward and slam his cowhide shield on to the ground – a gesture of loyalty.

'The last time I addressed you, the sun was very hot,' he said, and everyone laughed drily. The last time he addressed this gathering, a year previously, he had made an intemperate speech blasting the country's teachers, who were on strike. He had abused them and called them thieves: it was most 'unSwazi'. People said he was drunk, or worse. He later subtly apologized, but it was one of his worst mistakes. The reference to a hot sun was a cunning Swazi euphemism.

This time strikes were again his theme. He exhorted his subjects to follow the line of King Sobhuza II, who believed in peace through negotiation. He made yet another promise of electoral reform, promising a new system by the end of the year. The purpose of the speech was simply to keep a lid on things. The monarchy would do that for as long as it could.

I drove back to Engabezweni the next day to find my new friend. The weather was misty, drizzly and cold. I spotted him trudging through a muddy field with a stick and a gourd filled with *mahewu*, millet beer. He wore a wool sweater and a Swazi skirt and loin skin.

He had a friend with him, and they both got into the car. His friend was carrying in two hands a large bundle wrapped in newspaper. The paper was stained red with wet, glistening blood. He sat in the back seat with this grisly parcel; it dripped blood on to the upholstery. They told me that thirty-two of the king's cattle had been slaughtered that morning and distributed to men of the regiments, according to custom.

Validlela asked me to drive him to his grandmother's homestead, which I did. After a while I realized that Validlela couldn't really bring me to the King. He was wasting my time and my money, and he made me nervous. It was hard to get him out of the car. I cut my next appointment with him.

I saw him later, walking down the street in Mbabane, and he walked right by me as if I were someone else, as if he were invisible.

In the Lourenço Marques Restaurant, I gloomily picked at my Mozambique prawns. They had obviously come under heavy RENAMO fire during the rail journey from Maputo. I counted the days I had left in Swaziland.

The Validlela strategy having failed, I went to see Percy Mngomezulu, Principal Secretary at the Ministry of Justice, to see if he would be my *lincusa*. He told me that if I wanted to see the King I needed a *lincusa* inside the palace. He didn't offer to help, but there were two official *lincusas* inside the palace for the purpose.

'How do I get to them?'

'The Governor of Ludzidzini should act as your *lincusa* to get to them.'

'How do I get to him?'

'You need a *lincusa*.'

An infinite series of go-betweens stretched out before me, towards a vanishing-point that coincided somewhere in space with the boy-king himself, whom I imagined subsisting in a timeless plasma of omniscient self-contemplation, veiled and terrible, but was more likely lounging in an armchair in the palace watching a video.

I passed days in the house I had been lent, when the valley was veiled in mist, hovering in a void of uncertainty, despondently pondering tactics to break out of the paralysis in which Swazi reticence had confined me. The King's powerful magic – the strongest in Swaziland – was keeping me away from him.

The fluttering of moths' wings against the windows carried on all night. During the day, birds flew into the glass doors and lay stunned or dead on the concrete. Some of them were quite rare ornithological specimens. At night the dog barked into the cold valley at an invisible enemy.

I went to see J. S. M. Matsebula, author of *A History of Swaziland*. Perhaps he would be my *lincusa*. His secretary asked for my business card, which came back with a single word written on the back: 'Subject?' I sent in a note and my letters of introduction. Another note came back: 'I am not available.'

I called a Swazi anthropologist, an expert on tradition, who had been recommended to me. After hearing my request, she said, 'It's not working,' and wouldn't agree to meet me this week, next week, this month or next month. I didn't know what she meant by 'It's not working,' until I realized she was speaking of my entreaties: my desperate, courtierish posturings weren't working. Indeed they were not.

Day after day passed like this. Name after name on my list of contacts drew a blank. I called George Lys, the Gurkha, Mswati's private tutor. His answering-machine message said, 'Oh, all right, if you must, leave a message after the beep.' I must have called him twenty times. He never called back.

I tried to make sense of my position and to figure out why everyone was avoiding me, so I sought consolation in history.

The kingdom of Swaziland has survived up to now through a combination of luck, shrewd diplomacy and, in military affairs, knowing when it is safe to attack an enemy and when prudent to run away.

Sobhuza I established the principle that it was only safe to attack an enemy you were sure of defeating. Sobhuza, who ruled from 1816 to 1836, never took on Shaka, the great Zulu leader, which was prudent, and was never attacked by him, which was good luck. (Shaka was killed in battle before he got the chance.)

Sobhuza I was followed by Mswati II, the greatest Swazi warrior king. He increased his father's conquests, adding land and non-Swazi tribes to his dominions. At its furthest extent, the Swazi kingdom extended well into the lands north and south of the present Swazi border, and raids were being made as far north as southern Zimbabwe.

Never fighting an enemy you weren't sure of defeating also meant never fighting the white man – on the battlefield, at least. This second important principle of Swazi survival came to Sobhuza I in a dream, before he had ever seen a white man. He told his councillors the next day that he had had a vision of white-skinned people 'with hair like tassels of cattle' who came bringing with them two things. One was a book (some say the Bible); the other was money. They should accept the book, but be careful about taking the money. The Swazis must never spill a drop of white man's blood, for to do so would lead to the destruction of the country and the disappearance of the Swazi nation. The Zulus fought the white man, and for this they were beaten and subjugated.

In diplomacy, the Swazis knew how to play the Boer and the British off against one another. Neither wanted the other to gain complete control of the country. Consequently Swaziland enjoyed a kind of independence throughout the nineteenth century, until the British finally prevailed over South Africa in the Boer War of 1899–1902 and took over the administration of Swaziland.

The Swazis always preferred the British, because they could see how tribes like the Zulus fared under South African rule, but also because of a mysterious cultural empathy between the two peoples. They saw a bit of themselves in each other. Each had a culture of clenched good manners, restraint, discipline, understatement and secrecy, arranged into a strict social hierarchy with a King at the top. A Swazi saying expresses exactly the relationship that developed between the two cultures: '*Liswati Nalingisi, Zulu Nelibhunu.*' It means, 'Let the Swazi and the English deceive each other with politeness, and the Zulu and the Boer have it out with clubs.'

King Mbandzeni (who reigned from 1875 to 1889) did not heed Sobhuza's warning about the white man's money, and sold most of the country to foreign concessionaires. Getting that land back was to become the focus of Swazi nationalism.

The official version of Swazi history puts it like this: white settlers came to Swaziland in the early nineteenth century. The King allowed them to settle on Swazi land as his subjects. The cattle they gave him was tribute for the right to use land temporarily, not payment for land to be alienated permanently, for Swazi land cannot be sold: it is held by the King in trust for the nation. But the Swazis could not read and did not understand the contracts. A royal counsellor said at the time, 'We hold the feather and sign. We take money, but we do not know what it is for.'

The other version (set out by the South African historian Phillip Bonner) suggests that the land sales were understood by both sides to be temporary agreements, made by the Swazi King to create white-occupied buffer zones between himself and his enemies. The military situation between whites and blacks was fluid in those days and did not invariably favour the whites.

The official version was of use in the struggle for independence, where the reacquisition of alienated land was of great symbolic importance. It shows Swaziland doing battle against the greater power and eventually prevailing; the other version shows Swazi nationalism undoing the work of an earlier Swazi King.

Swaziland as it is today is the creation of Sobhuza II, who reigned for sixty years until his death in 1982. He inherited from his mother, the Queen Regent Labotsibeni, a mission to buy back for the Swazi people alienated Swazi land from the foreign concessionaires. His crowning achievement was the independence of Swaziland from Britain in 1968.

He conducted the campaign for independence with diplomacy, subtlety and skill. His ideology was tradition: he saw to it that the independent state of Swaziland was based on the traditional institutions of the Swazi polity that existed before the arrival of the white man. The King would be a real King, not a figurehead. Swaziland would only take from the West ways that complemented its own. Sobhuza's biographer Hilda Kuper called this 'cultural nationalism'. It unified the homogeneous Swazi people through values and institutions that were familiar to all of them.

For all Swazis, whether their outlook is modern and progressive or conservative and traditional, the monarchy is the heart of national identity. When the country was under British administration, Sobhuza II was not recognized by the British as a 'king': he was merely, according to the terms of indirect rule, a 'paramount chief'. When the Swazi royal anthem was sung before the King and the British High Commissioner, the Swazis were singing it to Sobhuza, not to the representative of the British crown. The British didn't notice this stroke of Swazi subtlety.

The Swazi monarchy is legitimized by tradition – but what is tradition? Under Sobhuza II, it was whatever he said it was. He introduced a bizarre electoral system that was said to be based on traditional rural councils, but was in fact an invention. He reintroduced the reed dance, in which bare-breasted maidens dance before the King, a custom that had died out among the Zulus more than a century before.

Sobhuza accepted the Westminster-style constitution and parliament the British imposed as one of the terms of independence, but he didn't like it: the role it gave the King was 'untraditional'. It also allowed for political parties, which went against the principle that Swazis should be united under him. But it is not the Swazi style to oppose something directly. He tolerated the constitution for five years, and then abolished it. The King's Proclamation of April 1973 suspending the constitution and banning political parties remains the country's basic law: it was adjusted slightly to fit Mswati III when he became King in 1986. It firmly places all power in the hands of the King, and allows him to order anyone to be detained for two months without being charged – a temporary measure that became permanent. This provision has become the monarchy's main weapon against its opponents.

Sobhuza died at the age of eighty-three. On a moonless night after his state funeral, his embalmed body was carried on a wooden bier to a cave near Nhlangano in the south of the country and was placed beside those of his royal ancestors, with a live black goat and personal objects for his comfort in the afterlife. He was one of Africa's greatest independence leaders, and his death left a political vacuum which has never completely been filled.

Sobhuza ruled for so long that there were no ritual specialists alive at the palace who knew how to perform the traditional rites for the death of a King. Ritual errors were committed: certain personal objects of the King were buried not some distance outside, but inside the Lobamba royal homestead, thus polluting it. J. S. M. Matsebula – King Sobhuza's private secretary, Swaziland's official historian and the leading commissar of Swazi cultural nationalism post-Sobhuza – wrote in his *A History of Swaziland* that he felt at the time 'that this was such a ritual blunder that it might bring about serious ill omens to the nation. I am firmly convinced,' he concluded, 'that all the shocking episodes which followed one another during the period of crisis had their roots here.'

The cosmic gyroscope wobbled on its pivot, and a dark force arose in the form of the irrational and ambitious Prince Mfanasibili Dlamini. As head of the royal lineage that had been passed over when Sobhuza II had been chosen as King, at Sobhuza's death Mfanasibili felt that his time had come. While believing himself to be the defender of the royal tradition in Swaziland, in his struggle for power he did more than anyone to undermine it.

He was a member of the *Liqoqo*, the body that ruled Swaziland during the four-year interregnum between Sobhuza and Mswati, and for a while he dominated it. One of Sobhuza's last acts was to formalize the power of this small and traditional advisory body into the 'supreme council of state', perhaps intending it to serve as a collective presidency after his death. Parliament, by contrast, has never been sovereign in Swaziland; it has about as much legislative power as a city council.

The *Liqoqo* manœuvred the dismissal of the Prime Minister, Prince Mabandla, who was thought to favour political reform that would upset Dlamini hegemony. Towards the end of his term, Mabandla was sleeping in his office in case he should find himself unable to return to it.

When the Queen Regent, Dzeliwe, the acting head of state in the interregnum, refused to sign the order for Mabandla's dismissal, the *Liqoqo* overthrew her and installed in her place the more compliant Ntombi, mother of the Crown Prince, Makhosetive.

The government gazette in this period chronicles the purges that followed: a storm of sackings and bewildering appointments. There were public demonstrations to protest against the removal of Dzeliwe. There were roadblocks in the streets. People waited tensely for the announcement of a coup.

It is possible, as the official history claims, that Makhosetive was chosen by his father, Sobhuza II, before the trouble began, and that this choice was simply confirmed by the council of Dlamini princes after other candidates had been considered and rejected. As in most non-European royal traditions, there was no rule of primogeniture in Swaziland. Makhosetive was born in the year of Swaziland's independence, 1968, when Sobhuza was sixty-nine years old, and was the youngest of his sons.

It is Swazi tradition to choose a boy as King. It guarantees that he is a blank page, untainted by politics, a perfect, pure, virgin being. He must have no brothers and no son of his own who might rise up against him. His choice has nothing to do with any personal qualities. The idea of a boy as the father of his people, many of whom are old enough to be *his* father, is part of the superhuman mystique of Swazi kingship. To say that an eighteen-year-old is governing the state requires an amazing leap of faith.

Makhosetive's mother was a handmaiden to a senior queen, and low in the hierarchy of queens. It was expected that Makhosetive would be crowned when he was twenty-one. His mother would then become Queen Mother. But because Queen Regent Dzeliwe was being obstructive, Ntombi was installed prematurely.

Once enthroned, Ntombi swiftly turned against Mfanasibili, one of those who had installed her. They are rumoured to have been lovers. In 1986, under her order, Mfanasibili was arrested, held under the sixty-day detention law, and eventually jailed for 'obstructing the ends of justice'.

Mfanasibili was ambitious and Machiavellian, but his tactics were those of someone not fully in touch with reality. He was too fond of magic. He was shot while trying to break into the tomb of King Sobhuza, while attempting, it was said, to steal the late King's arm. Eating a part of the King would give him some of the King's power, and help him become King in turn.

Mfanasibili was a liability, and remained ever after on the margins of the court power struggle, fighting to get back into it. His subsequent activities were well covered by the *Times of*

Swaziland because their bizarreness made for good copy yet it was also politically safe to report them. In 1990, for example, after serving his jail term for 'obstructing the ends of justice', he was charged again with trying to plot the King's overthrow, from prison. His plot involved three co-prisoners, a handful of smuggled weapons and magic spells. He gave his co-conspirators *mutis*, magic preparations, that would make them invisible. They were apprehended by prison guards as they walked visibly towards the prison gate. He had a *muti* that would enable him to see what was going on inside the royal kraal. For use once he had escaped, he had another *muti* that would rob the King of his will and turn him into an obedient drone.

The case against Mfanasibili fell apart in court. The English judge said the prosecution 'had an air of fantasy and unreality', and his co-conspirators, who were witnesses against him, were 'unreliable hardcore criminals'. He was freed, and immediately rearrested outside the prison under the sixty-day detention law.

Makhosetive was 'presented to the nation' in 1983 at a private ceremony, soon after the death of Sobhuza. Then he was sent to Sherborne School in England for three years. Swazi traditionalists are still angry about this, because it was done without the usual discussion inside the royal family. King Sobhuza had also been sent away to school, in South Africa, but there was a consensus for this decision. Makhosetive, by contrast, was secretly whisked away, as much for his own protection as for his education. In England he would be safe from the plots of Mfanasibili.

Even there he was in danger. A witch-doctor in full ritual attire was found crouching in the bushes in the grounds of the school one moonless night, trying to kill the King by burying a *kuphosa*, a type of *muti* which, according to the available literature, 'exudes disaster . . . rendering the victim susceptible to misfortunes and death'.

Three years early, Makhosetive was crowned King and given the royal name Mswati III. It was hoped that a new King would stop the palace infighting.

His first actions – or the first actions taken in his name – were the abolition of the *Liqoqo* and the promulgation of decrees to strengthen his position while still an inexperienced ruler. King's Decree No. 1 of 1986 amended the King's Proclamation of 1973 by adding a provision allowing the King 'to delegate any of his powers and functions'. The King's Delegation of Powers Notice, 1986, gave the Queen Mother the right to exercise the King's powers 'after consultation with the King'.

King's Decree No. 2 established a secret 'star chamber' tribunal to try those believed by the Prime Minister somehow to have offended the King, the Queen Mother 'and/or Swazi Law and Custom'. Such offences are left undefined. No one appearing before it is allowed legal representation. The tribunal was empowered to send offenders to prison for up to twenty years. Its six members included the official historian, J. S. M. Matsebula.

There were purges of the royal family throughout 1987, to discipline those who had backed rival candidates for the throne. The *Times of Swaziland* reported the names of those arrested, but never gave reasons. There were also purges of ministers, and among the detainees was the former Prime Minister, Prince Bekhimpi. He was later charged with treason, though his sentence was commuted. His offence was that he had treated the young King like a *boy*, giving him orders. The boy was fighting back.

Apart from those early purges, it was difficult to tell whether Mswati had put any personal stamp on the monarchy or on Swazi politics. The King was young and lacked *shadow*, and innovation is not the Swazi way: the monarchy's legitimacy is based on an illusion of changelessness.

A Swazi King is not a tyrant. He must act in agreement with the wishes of his subjects and of his councillors. Mswati is controlled by a swarm of advisers who govern his every action. Until he matures, and is ready to fill the shoes he inherited, he is a palace prisoner.

The King is like the king in a game of chess: the most valuable piece, protected by all the others, but in itself almost powerless. The king exists only to be defended. When this piece is taken, the game is over.

As in chess, the Queen is the most powerful player. Queen Mother Ntombi appoints the members of the reconstituted *Liqoqo* and this body rules the country. Her motive is making sure her son remains King. She rarely leaves the capital, is rarely seen in public, and is said to have little sense of the world outside Swaziland.

The web of advisers around the King is informal, extensive and unstructured. The fortunes of individuals within it rise and fall according to the unpredictable and timeless mechanics of royal courts anywhere in the world, at any time in history.

By the time of my visit, this new *Liqoqo* had been formed. Its members all served under Sobhuza, and were collectively dedicated to a conservative policy which sought to maintain the power of the monarchy at the expense of the fewest possible concessions to political reform.

The *Liqoqo* was continuing the policy of fossilized authoritarianism that had begun after Sobhuza's death, resisting pressure for change. This pressure came from sections of the Swazi population that were growing in numbers: the educated middle-class town-dwellers with no links to the royal family or to the countryside. Because political parties were illegal, strikes were a common occurrence, as they were the only legal form of political expression. When students at the University of Swaziland demonstrated in November 1990, soldiers were sent in and many students were badly injured.

In Swaziland, the government was headed by ministers whose offices have no political role. Even the Prime Minister could not set policy: this was done in secret at Lobamba. The newspapers were forbidden to discuss such 'sacred national matters'. When the Justice Minister tried to defend the principle of the independence of the judiciary and the rule of law, he was sacked and replaced by a hardline traditionalist from the *Liqoqo* with little education and no legal training.

The motto of Swaziland is '*Siyinqaba*,' which means, 'We are the fortress.' In the post-Sobhuza era of Swazi history, change was the new enemy, because there was no one of his calibre to cope with it, to mediate and 'Swazi-ize' it. To defend themselves, the monarchists had drawn up the drawbridge against change. Defending the monarchy was the same as defending Swazi nationhood, society and culture, they said.

The King was really free only to do things that any other twenty-two-year-old might want (but never be able) to do. As 'the child of the nation', the King was expected to have a rich personal life. He was said to give frequent parties, at which he would act as disc jockey.

He was allowed to build a new palace, a temple to adolescent fantasy. The palace is a round, windowless pillbox larded with post-modern architectural ornamentation. It sits on a hill overlooking the road from South Africa into Mbabane, and is painted red, yellow and blue, the colours of the Swazi national flag. There is an enormous satellite dish beside it, and it is said to have several underground storeys. Its main feature is said to be a glass-bottomed swimming-pool above a disco dance floor. It also has a throne on a mechanical riser.

The King is obliged to respect the wishes of the Dlamini royal family, a multitude of anonymous princes and princesses, many of them sons and daughters of King Sobhuza. They are, like most Swazis, 'conservative': they want to protect traditional ways and the primacy of their business interests.

Shortly after he became King, Mswati fell in love with a girl called Sibole ('Poppy') Mngomezulu. She was beautiful in a glamorous, Western sort of way, and is the daughter of the Principal Secretary at the Ministry of Justice, Percy Mngomezulu, whom I had unsuccessfully visited in the hope of securing a *lincusa*. It is Swazi custom for the King to marry two ceremonial queens soon after his coronation; they take the titles La Motsa and La Matsebula, after the clans they represent. His third and subsequent wives are his own choice. La Mngomezulu, as she became, wanted to be The Queen in the European sense – the single (or at least the most important) consort of the King – and to appear as such with him in public. It is said that Mswati built the palace with the glass-bottomed swimming-pool as a gift for her.

A 'royal traditional wedding' was announced in March 1987 – a public, national event in the manner of the wedding of Charles and Diana. A specialist in royal pageantry was sent from England to advise on the arrangements. A date was set, and the country's main stadium was prepared.

The 'traditional royal wedding' was one example of Swazi efforts, with British help, to 'Windsorize' the monarchy, to make it 'popular'. Media events like 'walkabouts' have been introduced to make the King's face visible but his person inaccessible, to increase Desire and Fame by increasing Distance.

On the day of the wedding, an enigmatically terse story appeared in the *Times of Swaziland*: 'The royal traditional wedding of His Majesty King Mswati III, scheduled to start today, has been postponed until further notice' – in other words, cancelled permanently.

A few days after the wedding was to have taken place, about two hundred Dlamini royals met at Ludzidzini. The proceedings of the conclave were kept private, but there was no further mention of a 'royal traditional wedding'. The King married La Mngomezulu, but in private, without the foreign innovations. Then pictures began to appear of La Mngomezulu in the standardized attire of a Swazi queen, sitting in a neat row with the other queens, all as identical and conventionalized as a good hand of cards. She looked gorgeous, pouting and thwarted. La Mngomezulu had committed the offence in Swazi culture of 'pushing herself forward'. The family had pushed her back.

The King took more wives after La Mngomezulu. By the time of my visit he had seven, and an unknowable number of concubines. The Swazi King has the right, by a custom called *ukoqoma*, to claim any woman he wants for his harem. The exercise of this *droit de seigneur* is an anachronism in a modern state, but young Mswati practised it, to the irritation of monogamous Christians and modernists. At one point, gossip relates, Mswati's eye fell on a student at Waterford Kamhlaba School, a progressive international college near Mbabane at which La Mngomezulu had also been a student before being expelled. The girl anticipated a promising career as a pianist, and had no wish to be a concubine – a shortlived position with poor future prospects afterwards, especially in marriage. As soon as the palace officials arrived to collect her, the girl was sent to pack her bags and, in a bold escape from the seraglio, was whisked out the back door and taken to safety in South Africa.

When approaching the King, one crawls on one's hands and knees, and speaks of oneself in the third person, referring to oneself as a 'stick', 'dog' or other worthless thing. The Swazis say, 'The King is an animal.' He is free, awesome, beautiful, frightening. He has no surname and no master, and is restricted by no marriage taboos: he can marry whoever he likes.

His personality is said to be snappish and imperious. He spends as little time as possible on affairs of state, and loves high-tech equipment like videos and compact discs. There are rumours of missed appointments and piles of unsigned bills. He reads little and prefers oral summaries. He believes strongly in his own magical powers and that he rules by divine right and that he is richer than he actually is. Having people crawl on all fours before him influences a boy's development.

The education of the ruler must have presented particular problems. There was no tradition of written 'mirrors for princes' in Swazi culture. I therefore imagined the memoirs of a hypothetical tutor, charged with teaching the boy-king the lessons of history:

'We would meet once a week at Lozitha palace, in a miscellaneously furnished room whose principal function was obviously to store unwanted gifts from visiting dignitaries and ambassadors. I remember once trying to teach him the causes of the Russian Revolution – that the Tsar was overthrown because he made democratic reforms too late. The King never listened to anything I said. Sometimes I would give him a page of a book to read. I would hand the book to him and wait while he read it. It was the only way I could be sure of getting him to read anything. I would glance over at him as he struggled with the text, moving his lips as he read.

'At first I had high hopes for what I was doing. I wanted to do what I could for the Swazi monarchy, because it was obvious to me that the Swazis wanted a good King, especially after the disturbing period that followed the death of King Sobhuza. Because the King was young, I saw him as an empty vessel that could be filled with the essence of wise kingship. But the King wasn't taking any of it in. He seemed to think that traditional Swazi patterns of authority were enough for the government of the country, and nothing needed reforming or rethinking. A few gadgets were all that was needed for all to go swimmingly.

'I would try to argue with him, because I thought if I didn't, no one else would afterwards. But he would snarl and stand on ceremony and make the point that he was King, and his word was final. Or else he would say that such a way of doing things was "un-Swazi". It was also quite obvious to me that the King only tolerated the lessons because they were an excuse to avoid more demanding duties. Once during a lesson I remember hearing the siren of a police car, and saw the Queen Mother's Mercedes and its escort car approaching. "Oh no," he said – "my mother is coming." His mother meant hard work.

'And he was fascinated with magic. I remember he once said to me, "I have an ointment that will make you irresistible to women: you will be able to have any woman you want. Would you like me to give you some?" I said, "No, thank you!"'

I had started off this long investigation of kingship holding a principle of sceptical scientific rationalism as the basis of my understanding of the world. After four months in Africa I had abandoned this in favour of wholesale acceptance of every type of mumbo-jumbo and magic.

Magic is to Swaziland what Anglicanism is to England: the supernatural basis of the monarchy's legitimacy. The King's is the most powerful magic in the land. If a witch-doctor goes near the palace, his bag of herbs and bones loses its power. The King can make rain, turn enemy bullets into water, and transform himself into an animal.

One day as I was driving in my rented car, I asked a Swazi hitchhiker if he believed this. 'Yes, of course, I have seen him.'

'What did you see?'

'I saw a cat.'

'But how did you know it was the King?'

'Because my friend saw the same cat. It was chasing his car. He stopped the car, and when he turned around the King was opening the door and entering.'

Pascal's wager is observed in rural areas. If a person is known to be an *inyanga* – a witch-doctor or traditional healer – he is feared by all, even by those who are sceptical of magic. There is a chance that his powers might be real, so it is best to be cautious.

I was told this by a Swazi journalist called James Dlamini, who was also a chief in his home area. He scoffed at such attitudes. 'When I go back there, they ask me to make rain, because I am the chief. I have to tell them I can't make rain. I spent two years at Bible college, I am a Christian. What good is a witch-doctor? I can heal with these hands, through the power of Jesus.' If you don't believe in one kind of magic, you believe in another.

Before his dismissal, Minister of Justice Reginald Dhladhla had upset the status quo by introducing into parliament an amendment to the Witchcraft Act, 1899, a British law. Amending the act would make it easier to prosecute people for ritual murder – the practice of killing humans, usually babies purchased from overworked mothers, in order to use their body parts in the preparation of *mutis*. The 1899 act makes all traditional healing or witchcraft illegal, but places the punishment of practitioners at the discretion of the King. While outlawing it in name, in spirit the law protects witchcraft because the King stands at the apex of the hierarchy of magical power: magic is the basis of his authority, and he is unlikely to undermine that by sending *inyangas* to jail. Parliamentarians opposed the motion. One MP said that if they voted to amend the act, 'these people will bewitch us and wipe us all out.' Another said that MPs were elected through witchcraft, so they shouldn't even discuss it.

The anthropologist Hilda Kuper is the only outsider who has ever been permitted to penetrate the secrecy of Swazi society and monarchy. Her books, written over a period of nearly fifty years, are the definitive works on Swaziland. You can't study Swaziland without reading Kuper. But, as she admits herself (in the introduction to *African Aristocracy*, 1947), 'I am handicapped by not being able to publish certain data: my friendship with Sobhuza gave me important information that I bound myself not to disclose.'

Kuper's narratives occasionally turn mysterious and stony-faced at points where she knows something but is forbidden to reveal it, as in her account, published in 1986, of the struggle that surrounded the choice of Makhosetive as heir to the throne. 'Discussions of the council [of senior elders] are always private and details of what happened in the case of Sobhuza's heir must, for the present, remain confidential.' She knows, but she isn't saying. Those less privileged practise a kind of Kremlinology. A Western diplomat in Mbabane, thought to be one of the best informed, tries to follow who's in and who's out through the use of a small wooden card index with facts about prominent figures, culled from the newspapers, written on recipe cards.

Neither the newspapers nor the parliament can discuss any matters relating to the decisions of the crown. Palace politics are discussed by word of mouth only.

Moreover, the Swazis do all they can to throw the inquisitive stranger off the track. A Swazi once told Hilda Kuper, she recalls in *African Aristocracy*, 'We deceive you like anything because you are white.'

This was what was happening to me.

My fortunes improved when I met James Dlamini. He was the senior reporter on the *Times of Swaziland*, and it was he who revealed to me the Swazi saying '*Liswati Nalingisi, Zulu Nelibhunu*.' He was the only person in Swaziland who seemed to be unafraid to speak freely about the monarchy. We spent several evenings drinking together, and one night he announced, with his arm around my shoulder, 'I am going to arrange for you to see the King! I am rearranging your programme!'

He didn't take me to see the King, but one day he did take me to see one of his senior councillors, Dr John June Nquku.

Nquku was a member of the Order of King Sobhuza, a body of senior councillors who have easy access to the King because of their long and distinguished service to the nation. He was ninety-two and had been leader of the Swaziland Progressive Party before political parties were outlawed by Sobhuza II. James was my *lincusa*.

We found the old man at home, taking an afternoon nap. James woke him up.

'Is it you again, James? What do you want?'

James Dlamini is the only man in Swaziland who can rouse Swaziland's great and good from their beds with impunity. He is also the only journalist in Swaziland who dares to broach the inner workings of Swazi politics in print, in cryptic language only a Swazi can understand.

'I have someone here who wants to talk to you.'

He rose slowly. 'But I am ninety-two, and my brains are old and scrambled!' he protested, shuffling out to his sitting-room. We sat at a table and drank a cup of Milo. The house was dark and cool. Nquku's brains were well preserved in a perfectly bald dome. Although he had played a progressive role in Swazi politics once, as a councillor his views were impeccably conservative and protective of the King.

Lesotho, he said, was in South Africa's belly; it had a powerless King and was ruled by a military junta. The President of Botswana, Seretse Khama, who was the King of the Tswana, had married a white woman. Only Swaziland remained true to the principles of African kingship, and even here it was under threat.

He held up a long, straight, ancient index finger to make his point. 'The King is an Englishman. He went away to England for many years, and he learned all their customs. Now he wants to make Swaziland like England. He is also a globe-trotter, and this is wrong. The King should always stay in Swaziland, but, if he must travel, a ritual of welcoming must be performed for him when he returns.'

'Hasn't Mswati done that?'

'No!'

During the Second World War, a number of Swazis served in the British armed forces in Libya. The British suggested that Sobhuza go there to visit them, by aeroplane. The councillors – Nquku among them – said no.

'He is not a bird,' they said.

Instead, the story goes, Sobhuza sent one of his own wooden staffs as a gift to the men and as a token of himself. It travelled by air. The Swazis carried it into battle. Held aloft, it created a column of dark cloud which obscured the vision of the enemy, but which the Swazis could see through, enabling the Allied forces to carry the day.

(I read later, in Matsebula's *History*, a more prosaic account of the Swazi '91' company in Libya. They fought in Italy at the battle of Anzio. Their job was to throw smoke bombs to cover the beaches during the Allied marine landing. For this reason they were known as 'the smoke company'.)

Like any courtier, Nquku thought the King had too many advisers. 'They all sit around there and talk rubbish! They don't tell him the truth – they are all flatterers.'

One night, James and I went on a shebeen crawl. At one stage he told me to stop the car, and ran into a liquor store, emerging with something in his pocket. For the rest of the evening he drank lemonade, spiking it under the level of the counter, out of the barman's view, with gin.

As we moved from one bar to the next, he revealed to me the whole cosmology of Swazi kingship, society, politics, government: an elegant and awesome and elaborate explanation. The drunker I got, the harder it was to remember, and I wasn't taking notes. Towards the end of the evening, James wrote down a three-word summary of everything he had said. It was the key to the Swazi monarchy, the distilled essence of everything he knew as a Swazi chief and as an experienced reporter. The following morning I found it crumpled up in the back pocket of my trousers, on a square inch of white paper inscribed with ballpoint pen in loopy letters: 'Reality, Legality, Details.'

It was completely meaningless, of course. Everywhere I went in Swaziland, meaning seemed to evaporate as soon as I approached it. It glittered only from a distance, like a mirage.

But there was another king in Swaziland, and he proved easier to reach. His name was Maja II, and he was the King of the Mamba. The Mamba are an important clan in Swaziland, particularly in the reign of Mswati III.

When Makhosetive was at Sherborne, the Swazi High Commissioner in London was someone called George Mamba. The Prince would spend his school holidays with the High Commissioner and his family. Makhosetive became close friends with George Mamba's son, Ndvumiso Mamba, who was six years older. Ndvumiso was worldly, Westernized and sophisticated. He appeared at the dismissal of the regiments looking as if he'd jumped out of the pages of *GQ* magazine. George Mamba was now Foreign Minister, and Ndvumiso was legal adviser to Tibiyo, the independent national investment fund established by Sobhuza II, and one of the King's closest advisers. His office was in the Tibiyo headquarters, a wedge-shaped grey concrete slab of a building beside Lozitha Palace.

Ndvumiso Mamba was possibly the only progressive influence on the King. He was a member of the governing council of the University of Swaziland, and, after the riots at the university in 1990 that ended in several students getting shot by police, it was Ndvumiso Mamba who persuaded the King to appoint a commission of inquiry, bypassing the *Liqoqo*.

He claimed some role in persuading the King of the need for democratic reform. 'I and others spent several hours with him on this. It took some time to convince him of the wisdom of it,' he told me. Indeed, a new electoral system was announced by the end of 1991.

The Mamba clan has its own king, who has his own *incwala*, which takes place a week after the national *incwala*. Few Swazis know this. One of the conditions Hilda Kuper had to accept in return for her extraordinary access to the Swazi royal household was not to mention the Mamba king. In 1819 Maloyi, the Mamba chief, helped Sobhuza I during a decisive moment in a war against the Zulus. In gratitude, Sobhuza I gave him 'the power of his left arm', the right 'to kill his own birds' – that is, of capital punishment – and the right to hold his own *incwala*.

Until Makhosetive's period in England, the Mamba *incwala* was left out of Matsebula's official history. Because they were in some ways a state within a state, the Mamba were thought of as a kind of fifth column. When Sobhuza was a baby, there were rumours that the Mamba were preparing their regiments to march to the capital to murder him.

Inkhosi Maja II is not really a king, but he calls himself a king.

The difficulty arises over the translation of the title *Inkhosi*, which is borne by the King and by Maja, but not by the rest of the Swazi chiefs.

I resolved to go and see him. If one king wouldn't see me, the other one might.

At the junction of the Nhlangano road, I picked up a hitchhiker in blue overalls. His name was David Mamba. He was a farmer – he grew cotton and maize – and was on his way to Piet Retief in the Transvaal to meet his brother, and from there to meet someone in connection with the purchase of a tractor.

Hitchhiking is common in Swaziland. Because of the restrictive practices of a tightly knit body of bus operators, who keep the transportation business to themselves, there are not enough buses. Queuing at bus stops is scrupulously fair and disciplined and buses are always full. People from all walks and stations of life can be seen standing at the roadside waving down passing vehicles. I once brought home from work six girls in pink nylon overalls who worked at a shoe factory at the industrial estate at Matsapha. Each one wanted to get out at a different place.

I told David Mamba that I was looking for his chief. He knew him and agreed to come with me to find him. He would act as my *lincusa*.

'He might be drunk,' David warned me. 'He is a good man, but he drinks too much. When he's drunk, he's like a man from the wilderness. He goes really wild.'

'What does he drink?'

'Home brew – anything he can.' He fell silent, then turned to face me and added seriously, 'But he is a *man*, you know?'

We drove to Inkhosi Maja's homestead, a place called Engudzini, where we were told we had just missed him. If we were quick, we might catch up with him in his white pick-up.

We set off down the dirt road, and after about a kilometre we saw a stationary white pick-up at the roadside. The *Inkhosi* was at the wheel, talking to someone through the window. It began to rain heavily. David got out of the car and stood in the rain to talk to the *Inkhosi*.

Clasping his hands in front of himself, his head bowed, David put my case as we had rehearsed it hurriedly in the car. The chief stared straight ahead, looking very stern, biting down so hard I could see a tense ripple move across his cheek as he listened. Then he gave his answer, which David translated for me.

'He said to come on Wednesday, because he is very busy now.'

Afterwards, we stopped at a neighbour's homestead to drink Swazi beer, and at David's own family homestead to pick up his sister, who wanted a lift to a place near Mbabane. Her name was Miriam.

'You were lucky to find the *Inkhosi*,' Miriam said some time later, as we drove north through the noble green mountains of Swaziland.

'Why?'

'He doesn't spend much time at Engudzini these days.'

'Why not?'

'Because he was bewitched by a woman. She was jealous of him. Then she became sick. She told him about the spell when she was in the hospital, and then she died. He had a bad car accident.'

Two days later I found Inkhosi Maja II in his butcher's shop in Sitobela. Sitobela is in the low veld; the land is hot and dry. Two men were standing at the uneven zinc counter having their lunch – stew and stiff cornmeal porridge.

Inkhosi Maja was a sweet, sad man, with a humble and gentle manner. He apologized for his rusty English. His attempts to avoid an interview seemed grounded in genuine modesty. We sat facing each other on concrete blocks in the half-completed extension to his butcher's shop – the throne room of the Mamba king! – and discussed the semantics of the word *inkhosi*. He smoked constantly, and devoted much energy and motion to the manipulation of box, smoke and matches.

'There is no other way of telling it,' he diffidently insisted – '"*Inkhosi*" means "King".'

I asked him how long he'd been king/chief of the Mamba. 'I knew I was king before I was born. I am a natural born king.'

I took a photograph of him standing outside his shop, and, with a timer, another one of the two of us together. I was so grateful! Then he insisted I go and see his *Indvuna*, his Governor.

His *Indvuna* was a very old man who lived in a beautiful old homestead: a cluster of beehive huts surrounded by trees and small maize fields. A sad, old tree laden with pale-green marolo plums hung its heavy branches over the hard ground, and dropped the fruit it couldn't carry. A group of men and women passed the heat of the day dallying under a broad, shady tree, too absorbed in each other's company to pay any attention to us.

Three very formal wooden dining-chairs, covered in maroon velvet, were arranged under a sausage tree. The *Indvuna*'s earlobes were pierced with quarter-inch holes, in the old Swazi manner. His teenage son translated. The *Indvuna* ordered a small child to fetch him water to drink. The little girl brought an enamel bowl on her head. He took a long drink, then set the bowl down beside his chair.

Once we had composed ourselves, the *Indvuna* read from a large notebook, in which a text had been written in ballpoint pen in a neat, looping hand. He narrated the history of the Mamba tribe.

'The king of the Zulus, Zwide, fought against the Swazis, but the Zulus were defeated by Dlamini. Dlamini died, leaving his first-born, Makalela. And Makalela was the father of Mamba. And Mamba was the father of Maloyi. And Maloyi was the father of . . .'

'Do you want to hear all this?' the boy interrupted. The old man stopped and looked up, without raising his finger from the page, to mark where he had paused.

'Yes! Go on.' I didn't want to miss the 'begats'.

The old man continued to move his finger down the ruled lines of his book, and resumed his recitation of the genealogy of Mamba chiefs.

'Maloyi was the father of Mbatjane. Mbatjane was the father of Maja I. Maja I was the father of Bokweni.'

And Bokweni was the grandfather of the present *Inkhosi*, Maja II. Bokweni was the last powerful Mamba chief. He had stood up to the British.

I asked the *Indvuna* what kind of work he had done when he was younger. He misunderstood, and gave an answer I hadn't expected.

'He says he washed the King before the *incwala* and gave him *mutis* for kingship.' Only people from certain families can perform this ritual duty: Dlamini, Sikondze, Tfwala. He never went to the Dlamini *incwala*.

Then I asked the question again and got a different answer.

'Oh. He says he worked in the Republic of South Africa for six years.'

The old man spoke in English for the first time: 'Ninth of March, 1939!'

'He says he left the Republic of South Africa on the ninth of March, 1939.'

My final days in Swaziland were immensely depressing. Obliged to leave the comfortable house on the ridge, I moved to a thatched hut in a game park. I had eaten nothing but steak for the past five weeks. In the evenings, I would sit by the hippo pool and drink Johannesburg Riesling, hoping for the occasional glimpse of a hippo when one of them would raise its vast head out of the water. Most of the time they remained submerged. At night they came out and foraged. A hippo eats thirty-five kilograms of grass a day, and is satisfied.

What did I expect? That the King would take me to his bosom, and engage me as his dream-interpreter? Or give me a job as court astrologer?

A sign at the game reserve read:

20,000 SNARES
LIFTED FROM HLANE AND MLILWANE.
THERE ARE MORE SNARES DISPLAYED HERE
THAN THERE ARE WILD UNGULATES
IN SWAZILAND.

I was hopelessly ensnared, like an ungulate.

During these disconsolate ruminations, I decided that, as my last act in Swaziland, I would go and look for the tomb of Sobhuza II. The next day I asked one of my unreliable Swazi informants where it was.

'If you were so foolish as to attempt to go there, you would find yourself deep in a forest full of poisonous snakes and dangerous wild animals. And the tomb is on the top of a very high mountain, which you would never be able to climb. There are armed guards protecting it.' This, of course, turned out to be not entirely true.

Matsebula identifies the location in his *History*, and the map of Swaziland indicates the place with three dots marked 'royal graves'. The site was south of Nhlangano, very near the South African border. It was a very small hill with an outcrop of rock on top amid tame and picturesque countryside, off a dirt road, near a teachers' college and in view of a casino. The area was rural but densely populated, rich with cattle and small plots of maize.

It was near Shiselweni, site of the Swazi capital under Sobhuza I. Sobhuza's grandfather, Ngwane II, is also entombed here.

As I walked towards it, a pair of armed soldiers approached me at a rapid pace, radios crackling. This is where the deranged Mfanasibili had been shot trying to remove King Sobhuza's arm, in a confrontation in which he had shot dead one of the guards. Anxious, tense, but polite, they quizzed me and asked me to leave. The power of Sobhuza's bones and spirit protect the marches of his fortress kingdom, and they were protecting the bones from the likes of curious, impious wretches like me.

CHAPTER 5

Mystical Kingdom – Java

FINALLY, IN ORDER to feast my eyes on a kingdom in Asia (to put the fiasco of Swaziland behind me, and complete my survey), I proceeded through the five concentric conceptual rings of royal power in the realm of Hamengkubuwono X, Sultan of Yogyakarta, on the Indonesian island of Java.

His full name is Ngarso Dalem Sempayen-Dalem ingkeng Sinuwun Kangjeng Sultan Hamengkubuwono Senopati ing Ngalogo Abdurrahman Sayidin Panoto Gomo Khalifatullah ingkang Jumeneng Kaping Sedoso ing Ngayogyakarta Hadiningrat, *which means* Prostrate at his Royal Feet, the Most Noble Sultan, the One who Holds the Universe in his Lap, Commander-in-Chief, Servant of God the Merciful, Descendant of the Prophet, Regulator of Religion, Caliph of God, the Tenth on the Throne in the Good Country of Yogyakarta, the Prosperous Abode of Rama.

His spiritual aura is green.

In Java, kingship is a system of meaning, articulate, radiant and elaborate, in which the ruler, mankind and the cosmos fit together as parts of a single, elegant metaphysical mechanism. In Java, my journey came to an end with a loud, long oriental gong of resolution and fulfilment.

To reach the Sultan, I had to pass through five zones of experience, a movement that culminated in an intimate audience with the royal presence. My progress could be represented diagrammatically as an archery target with five rings, where the bull's-eye stands for the Sultan, and the rings around it correspond (inexactly) to the grades of the hierarchy of which he is the apex and centre. Working inward from the zone of darkness on the outer periphery, I proceeded through the kingdom, the capital and the palace, and finally reached my goal, the court. My path could be shown on this diagram as a straight arrow penetrating the five rings to the centre.

The Sultan's spiritual aura is the glow of something called *kesakten*, the supernatural energy which flows into him from God by virtue of his position, and through him in outwardly expanding rings to his family, his court, his capital, his kingdom, the world.

The social hierarchy of the sultanate of Yogyakarta resembles a Sufi brotherhood, a traditional Islamic mystical organization whose members are arranged in concentric ranks around a leader known as *quṭb*, a pole. The ranks are gradations of spiritual attainment, with the most experienced in the ring closest to the pole, and those less experienced occupying the circles of increasing size around it.

Because of his role as the channel of *kesakten*, the Sultan of Yogyakarta is the apex of this Sufi theocracy, the highest point of a hierarchy of mystical attainment, the supreme spiritual adept, the one closest to God. The higher you are in the hierarchy, the closer you are to the infinite Mind. In Yogyakarta, the ante-rooms of power are the stages of mystical attainment.

The Javanese believe that Java is the centre of the universe. Everything revolves around Java, and Java revolves around the Sultan, who is the King of the World, its nucleus. Although in this present dark age his power is in temporary eclipse, he could take over the world if he wanted to. He is the link, the pivot, between this sublunar world and the world above us. His palace is a model of the cosmos, a ceremonial mirror of the cosmic order that he imposes on earth.

At its peak, three hundred years ago, the monarchy of which the present sultanate is the successor was a model of classic Asian agricultural despotism. The land was green and fertile, the population high. Rice was produced in abundance: there was enough to feed the people and to remit a surplus to the centre. The agricultural surplus enabled the development of a refined court culture in an atmosphere of peace, order, timelessness, confidence and prosperity.

To guarantee this order, the royal administration duplicated the ruler's absolute power in franchised power bases that decreased in importance the further one travelled from the capital into the countryside. The administrative system of the ancient kingdom had the quality of light: the further away you were from the Sultan and the capital, the weaker the administrative force of the state. The state had no border, only a hypothetical zone of darkness that the light did not reach.

When central Java was subjugated by the Dutch East India Company in the seventeenth century, the monarchy was reduced to a state of decorous and resigned impotence, and its ideas of cosmic kingship were preserved through the cultivation and refinement of an elaborate court culture. The well-known products of Javanese culture – gamelan music, shadow-play, dance, all of which have fertilized twentieth-century Western art – were the indirect results of European colonial rule. Foreign force kept the monarchy prisoner, preoccupied with inwardly spiralling cycles of meaning, expressed through mysticism and art. By the time of Indonesian independence, when the sultanate's last powers were relinquished to the new state, the Sultan's rule, as traditionally conceived, was entirely mystical in nature.

But the Sultan of Yogyakarta holds something else in his lap besides the universe. He is also, in the new and separate realm of Indonesian politics, the local leader of Golkar, the party that has governed Indonesia since independence (proclaimed in 1945), and as such is the region's leading political figure. His two roles – king and politician – diverge and overlap curiously.

The reason for this duality is that his father, Sultan Hamengkubuwono IX, had been a leader in the independence movement. By backing the side that won, the sultanate adapted and survived. Hamengkubuwono IX's involvement with the independence movement guaranteed Yogyakarta's influence in the modern state of Indonesia; otherwise, the palace would today be nothing more than a museum. Indeed, although it goes against the official line to say so, one can see the political culture of the Republic of Indonesia as the direct successor to the tradition of kingship of central Java. Java is still, in practice, the centre, surrounded by a periphery of outer islands. Like a Javanese king, President Suharto has published a book of wise and mystical sayings. His predecessor, Sukarno, first President of Indonesia, was inaugurated at the spot in the palace of Yogyakarta where sultans are crowned. Yogyakarta was briefly the capital of the new republic, and Hamengkubuwono IX was its first Vice-President. The present Sultan is the heir to two traditions of power: one ancient and deeply rooted and mystical, the other modern and 'democratic'.

I asked the Cultural Attaché at the Indonesian embassy in London for advice on how to approach him.

'Think of it as peeling away the layers of the onion,' he said.

An onion made of pure light.

The first zone through which I passed – the realm of chaos – is the zone removed, by geographical distance, from the Sultan's ordering influence, a realm of disorder and darkness, without spatial orientation. It corresponded, in the path of my progress, to the tangled, strangled conurbation of Jakarta.

I arrived in darkness at an airport whose architecture evoked temples hundreds of years old, deep in the tropical jungle. The night was hot and sultry and starless.

I boarded a bus, absorbing through its sealed windows, as it speeded towards the city, my first twilit images of Indonesia from the urban wasteland on the airport road. At the bus station in central Jakarta, a cab-driver signalled numbers to me with his fingers in an incomprehensible semaphore: the amount of thousands of rupiahs he wanted to make a short journey to a hotel in a tourist ghetto.

At the hotel, I understood no one and no one understood me. The cab-driver left in fury with a quarter of the fare he'd hoped for. The desk clerk had a limited repertoire of English phrases for professional use, but pronounced them without idiom, without seeming to know why they caused me to put money on the counter.

The hotel had green walls, and its corridors were dimly lit with fluorescent tubes. The electricity supply undulated. A quartet of men in singlets played cards on a landing in the humid half-light as I ascended a staircase to my room, and the electric current rose and fell like the waves around a ship. Behind a curtain at the end of a corridor I could hear the noises of family life. In the lobby, family members lay mesmerized in front of a faded colour TV with a soiled doily and a small vase of plastic flowers on top.

Later, as I strolled out from my hotel into the night, I felt as if I was moving from Jakarta's mouth – the mechanism for engorging foreigners, with its thousands of tiny capillaries for scouring the person for money: the airport, the importunate porter, the airport minibus, the taxi, the hotel – into its throat – the hot, dark organ where the real process of absorption begins. It was a severe tropical night of ungraduated darkness. I couldn't tell what time it was, having travelled for nearly thirty hours across most of the world's time zones and the equator; I could barely tell up from down. I was plankton – eyeless, defenceless, senseless, directionless.

The night was like a bed. Traces of somnolent activity were obscurely visible. The stirrings of insomniacs and bodies restlessly tossing in their sleep rumpled the air. They lay on benches, mouths open, or hung out of car doors, half-visible, half-awake, yet present, breathing, killing time. People ate under the cloth tents of sidewalk food stalls. The pavements were cracked and puddled. The air was freighted with the smell of sewage and burning garbage.

I was attracted by the red lights of a nightclub with a beer garden in front. I crossed a ditch filled with filthy, stagnant water and passed through an ancient ornately carved gateway. A clique of prostitutes sitting at a round, white plastic patio table writhed with attention and called out to me.

The waiter in a clip-joint smirks conspiratorially: he thinks you're just ordering a drink as a cover for vice, but I honestly only wanted a drink. It's just that I had come to a brothel for it. The beer was ludicrously expensive. I looked around and drank and waved away mosquitoes, which were thick in the air. Behind me the red glow emanated from the nightclub, and a muffled disco rhythm. The night was very beautiful.

One of the prostitutes came over to my table. She was very nice. Well, nice in the sense of friendly. Well, friendly in that she had to be friendly to get what she wanted from me, which was a one-way ticket out of Jakarta. Her youth was her only asset, but it was manifestly leaking away at an alarming rate. She asked me where I was from. I gave an enigmatic answer (I told her the truth).

'Are you staying in Jalan Jaksa?' she said, referring to the tourist alley around the corner.

'Yes.'

'Which hotel?'

Nice try. In Nigeria the prostitutes bribe the desk clerks to tell them your room number. Then they ring you on the house phone. The oriental approach was more refined.

Light conversation ensued. It emerged that she longed to go to Switzerland, and was waiting for a visa – a mere formality, which could be cleared up without too much delay. Her longing was fixed in her mind as simply and as sharply defined as images on a postcard: bright red flowers under a crisp blue sky; the plume of water on Lake Geneva; Swissair planes pertly awaiting take-off from Zurich airport; diamonds; fur coat; champagne.

Switzerland represents paradise in tropical countries, just as the idea of paradise in northern climes is a tropical island.

'Is it very cold in Switzerland?'

'Yes, very cold.'

'How long is the winter?'

'About eleven months.'

'Oh . . . then I should bring a blanket?'

'It would be advisable,' I cautioned.

Satisfied that I wasn't the winning lottery ticket she was looking for in life, she made her excuses and left me alone to commune with the mosquitoes. She didn't believe me when I said I was going to see the Sultan of Yogyakarta.

At 4.00 a.m. I was awoken by a virtuoso recitation of the entire text of the Qur'an, complete with footnotes, commentary, and chorus, at rock-concert volume, from a huge loudspeaker that had been positioned directly outside my window while I was out the previous evening.

Signs in the zone of disorder always fell short of their targets: no one understood anyone else. Breakfast at the hotel was served in a domain of muted signifiers, of common incomprehension. The dining-room was an array of four tables in a corner of the lobby. A lanky young Dutchman sat at a neighbouring table. Just off the plane, stunned by the heat, and the slowness and the foreignness of everything around him, and confronted by a strange breakfast, his first in Indonesia, he was trying to fight his way out of the wet paper bag that imprisoned him by adopting the Western pose of making a fuss about it.

By now I was miles beyond this in wisdom, and observed him as one on a rock in a dark sea observes another sinking beneath the waves, calmly accepting it as cruelly inevitable. But interested all the same.

He wanted things he recognized, in vain. My breakfast was strange enough: two toasted sandwiches – one with chocolate sprinkles inside, another containing an unfamiliar marmalade – and tea in a glass. In all, it was, I recognized, a puzzled compromise with Western matutinal expectations.

Silence was observed. An old woman mopped the floor, and filled the air with the smell of sweaty ammonia. The Dutchman had to be visited by the manager, because they could tell he was angry, but no one could understand what he wanted or what he was angry about. His words emerged like bubbles from the mouth of a goldfish, as observed by other fish in the same tank. He was dissatisfied with the strange disposition of food about his plate, the sprinkles, the marmalade, the angle of the equatorial sunlight. It was ten o'clock in the morning, a bizarre time to be having breakfast anyway, and already the outside temperature was 100 degrees Fahrenheit and the air quality poor and getting worse.

After breakfast, a moment of coalescence glimmered in a phone booth when I put through a trunk call to the Kraton Yogyakarta. It was my first contact with the palace since I had received a letter from the Sultan six months earlier, welcoming my visit. (The second king in central Java, the Sunan of Solo, hadn't written back. But the light of kingship had been extinguished there, owing to the Sunan's failure to observe the due rituals that assure the harmony of the realm, so it didn't matter.) The Sultan had written

. . . it would be advisable if you could meet me in Kraton Yogyakarta after the 24th of July, except the 27th and the 28th.
Yours cordially,
Hamengkubuwono X

It was now early October. I was put through to his private secretary, Mr Suhardi.

'But I am very sorry,' he said. 'His Majesty is in Europe. He will see you when he returns.' But he would see me. It was not going to be like Swaziland, where I was virtually thrown out of the office of the King's private secretary.

I was ready to pass into the next zone, out of the realm of chaos, and into the Sultan's kingdom, which mirrored the order of the cosmos.

I took a night train from Jakarta to Yogyakarta. The slums that teem alongside the railway tracks, that I saw in darkness through my window, gave way, on my waking, to the light of sunrise over the wet rice fields, emerald green, of central Java, and the red-and-white power pylons that stand among them like feudal overseers, reflected in their mirror-like surfaces.

In Yogyakarta I posed as a tourist. Despite my efforts to distinguish myself from their jet-lagged legions (by wearing long trousers and a tie at all times for the duration of my visit), the role was forced on me. Every foreigner is a tourist in Yogyakarta. The smoggy morning I arrived, I took a *becak* – a cycle-taxi or pedicab – down the straight, wide avenue that is the spine of the town to a neighbourhood of tourist guest-houses on the southern outskirts. I sat sulkily while the driver talked and pedalled. His calf muscles were the size of rugby balls. He assumed I had come here to shop. Why else? He kept the sunshade down in spite of the burdensome sun so I could hear him as he pointed out the shops where, if I bought something, he would get, unknown to me, a commission to augment the few cents a day he earned pedalling himself into exhaustion. This is how I entered the second zone of proximity, the second layer of the mystical Yogyanese royal onion.

In fact, I had come to spend five weeks in a dark room, hanging on the periphery of an elaborate mystery, waiting for the moment in which I could bask briefly in the rays of the royal archetype, as manifested in Java. In other words, I had come to see the Sultan, but I didn't have an appointment. By now there was a dry wind blowing through my heart, an aching, anxious absence of meaning which I hoped Java would fill.

Although Yogyakarta is the cultural heart of Java, it has also become one of its main tourist attractions, the place tourists stop for a forty-eight-hour dose of culture on their way to Bali for the beach. The expectation of tourist dollars has given the town an enervating atmosphere. Giant luxury hotels now exceed in splendour the ancient temple complexes of Borobudur and Prambanan that the tourists are bused out to see. The streets teem with English-speaking hustlers steering foreigners to stalls selling shoddy handicrafts, debased batiks and shady shadow-puppets. The mystical dimension lies hidden beneath this.

I chose the cheapest guest-house I could bear, and took the first room I was shown. It was dark and had no windows, and the door gave on to an inner courtyard with a garden in which palm and mango trees kept the daytime heat at bay. I settled in to wait for the Sultan to return from Europe.

I rested for twenty-four hours, then approached the palace.

The commentary resumes.

Asian palaces do not merely convey to the beholder the wealth and power of the ruler – through the splendour of their size and design – they communicate through their architecture cosmological doctrines which establish the monarchy as an indispensable part of the universe, binding together ruler, ruled and the divine forces beyond them. In Thailand and Burma, traditional palaces are designed as models of the universe: they are circular in form, with concentric rings of construction around a centre that stands for Mount Meru, the mountain around which, in Buddhist and Hindu cosmology, the universe revolves. By duplicating the structure of the cosmos in architectural form, the state imposes the absolute order of the cosmos on earth. It establishes an analogy between earthly and cosmic order, and between the earthly and the divine rulers.

The Kraton Yogyakarta is like a huge machine for generating transcendental symbolism of this sort. Unlike the circular palaces of mainland Asia, it consists of a series of pavilions and courtyards set out in a line; its linear structure symbolizes not heaven but the virtuous individual's path through life towards spiritual fulfilment.

This line begins outside the palace, thirty-two kilometres north at the top of Mount Merapi, the volcano on the northern boundary of the Daerah Istemewa Yogyakarta, the Special Region of Yogyakarta, and ends at a beach called Parangkusumo in the south, on the Indian Ocean. When the Indonesian state of Yogyakarta was created, the sacred geography of the historical kingdom was preserved within the boundaries of the Special Region. These extremes represent the male and female principles which are united in the fulfilled soul. The palace stands at their middle point.

So if you stood in the Alun-Alun Lor, the broad square of parched grass, scuffed by the feet of football players, that stands in front of the palace, and you looked northward up the Jalan Malioboro, the road along which I made my grumpy entry into the town by cycle-taxi, you would be able to see Mount Merapi, symbol of the masculine principle, with a plume of smoke issuing from its peak, were it not for the traffic and the smog.

And if you looked southward from the back of the palace, and if you possessed miraculous vision like some ancient king of Javanese legend, you would see Parangkusumo beach, where there is a shrine to the goddess Ratu Kidul, the Queen of the South Seas, symbol of the feminine principle, to whom the Sultan performs a ritual of sacrifice once a year, and whom each new Sultan marries, at his coronation, in a secret rite of supernatural consummation.

The palace is entered not through any of the nodes or axes of this profound symmetry but through a discreet entrance tucked away at the side. From this perspective, it ceases to operate as an engine of royal symbolism and reveals itself as a kind of enormous *kampung* – a densely inhabited alley, neighbourhood or compound that is the traditional unit of Javanese living. Hundreds of people live in the palace. It would be impossible to say exactly how many, but when you approach the palace from any angle you see constantly the evidence of everyday life – children playing, laundry hanging out to dry, someone washing a car, TV aerials – in glimpses behind the high whitewashed walls.

The first time I tried to pass through the gate that leads into the Sultan's quarters I was turned away by the gatekeeper, who thought I was a tourist who had strayed off the permitted path. It was my first encounter with an *abdidalem*, a traditional palace servant: he wore a tight-fitting tunic of indigo blue with conservative black pinstripes, a loose skirt and a stylized turban-like cap of batik cloth. He sweetly waved me away. I bowed gratefully. Tactically retreating outside the wall, I resorted to a cheap Indonesian/English dictionary I had bought in the market the night before and which was to let me down constantly throughout my sojourn in Java, and managed to extract from it a string of words that formed a comprehensible, if oafishly blunt, Indonesian sentence. I returned to the gatekeeper and parroted this string of words and then forgot it an instant later: '*Saya mencari Tuan Suhardi*' – 'I am looking for Mr Suhardi.' This was the Sultan's private secretary, with whom I had spoken from a telephone booth in Jakarta approximately two days earlier.

As a result of the efficacy of these words, I was suffered to pass through to the next level of security, which was of a military character, with uniforms and pistols, desks and telephones. The *abdidalems* drinking tea on their mat were just window-dressing.

From the military post, I was admitted to the Sultan's antechamber, the office of his private secretary. I must have come here a dozen times subsequently to go through the courtier's motions of supplication.

A path led to the offices through an open maze of whitewashed walls, shaded with trees. The cages of the Sultan's songbirds hung in the branches; his horses snorted in their stables. A silent, barefoot *abdidalem* escorted me. I wore shoes, socks, a suit, a tie and a hat.

I passed through a gateway, under the monogram of Hamengkubuwono VII, who had built this part of the palace in the early part of this century. The office of Mr Suhardi was in a room in the Sultan's residence, a spacious pavilion surrounded by a garden in which peacocks and bantams roamed about, with rooms giving on to a broad porch. Mr Suhardi was my *friend at court*.

He was a kindly, old, retired English-teacher, with a domed bald head and solemn, exquisitely slow Javanese manners. He had been appointed by the new Sultan to deal with Anglophone visitors. He offered me a glass of sweet, pink fizzy liquid to drink, served on a silver tray brought in by a servant. I didn't touch the drink until bidden, following Javanese etiquette. Javanese etiquette also determines that you should point at things with your thumb, that you speak elliptically rather than directly, and that you should address senior persons as '*bapak*', meaning 'father'.

Bearing these things in mind, I stated my case.

After rattling off a list of subjects, I said I was interested in the spiritual dimension of Javanese kingship, in its functioning as a Sufi theocracy, and that I wanted to attend traditional religious ceremonies inside the palace. This was the heart of the matter, and I had mentioned it immediately. He looked at me in a puzzled, calm, polite way and smiled and said nothing for a moment.

He advised me to see a lecturer at the university who had a reputation as an expert in such matters, a specialist in the 'paranorm-AL', he said, emphasizing the last syllable. It was clearly a subject in which the Javanese took a good deal of interest.

He also advised me to wait.

Unlike the other tourists, I was here to stay put. I wasn't interested in shopping or in tours. I didn't even visit Borobudur, the magnificent Buddhist temple complex – the rival of Angkor Wat – forty kilometres north-west of Yogyakarta. Instead, to kill time, I opened my copy of *War and Peace* and began to read it. It had 1,412 pages, including the Introduction. I bought a packet of clove-flavoured Indonesian cigarettes and smoked them in the evenings one by one. They crackled and spewed out sparks, like little volcanoes. I would sit in the dim fluorescent light of the hotel courtyard and read Tolstoy and wave away mosquitoes. The hotel staff would bring me a thermos of tea and a piece of cake at about nine o'clock, and I would throw bits of cake to the lizards, testing their appetites and carrying-skills with morsels of increasing size. The other guests came and went after an average stay of two nights. I never exchanged a word with any of them.

By day, the tourists floated around the town half-naked, in loose pastel-coloured garments, carrying thousands of dollars worth of sophisticated consumer electronics. Compared to the petite Javanese, they were big-boned giants. I was interested in transcendental kingship. With them it was just *Bali*, *Bali*, *Bali*.

After a while I became a conspicuous presence in the town. I never bought anything. The *becak*-drivers and wide boys came to recognize me, and gave up trying to get money out of me.

I looked at a cheaper room in a grimy hotel where no one spoke English. The room was unsafe, noisy and had a sticker of Saddam Hussein on the wall.

I ate late at night in the lowest dives, sitting shoulder to shoulder with *becak*-drivers on a noodle-vendor's sagging wooden bench, eating head-down in the glow of a kerosene lamp.

The traffic swirled around the palace. I endured the constant irritation of voices clamouring for attention and money, the false smiles, the cries of 'Where are you from? Where you go?' Walking through the town was like wading through a tank of warm water, so I rented a bicycle and joined the flow of traffic that hurtled around the Kraton. By day and by night I circumbicycled the Sultan's palace.

Eventually he returned from Europe.

I put a call through to my friend at court. Trying to make a call from a payphone in Yogyakarta's tropical smog was slow and difficult. The coins were sticky, and their denominations hard to master. My friend at court advised me to continue to wait.

I paid a typist to type a letter to the lecturer in Javanese spirituality Mr Suhardi had mentioned: Dr Suparjar, specialist in the paranorm-AL. She worked in a little office that opened on to the street and had caught my eye as I was passing.

Everything in Yogyakarta is a symbol of something. The town itself is a diagram of mystical reality. At the top of the Jalan Malioboro stands an ornate monument festooned with light-bulbs, commemorating Sultan Hamengkubuwono VIII's attainment of mystical union with God. It is columnar in shape because a vertical stroke is the same as the Arabic letter A, Alif, written as a downward stroke of the pen. Alif is the first letter of the name of God, Allah, and its sound, *aaaaaah*, is also the sound of your mortal breath, demonstrating that God and your continued earthly existence are the same thing. The monument stands at a busy intersection, and there are traffic-lights built into its four sides. It once had a ball on top, symbolizing decisiveness, but it fell off in an earthquake.

The line from this monument to the palace (the same line that extends to Mount Merapi in the north and to Parangkusumo in the south) is cut by the railway line. The railway was built by the Dutch colonialists. The meaning of this is that technology and foreign values interfere with spiritual progress.

Mr Suhardi told me that in order to achieve perfection one must free oneself from worldly temptations. This principle, he said, is represented by the Kepatihan Building, an office building off the Jalan Malioboro. Jalan Tikora, where there are numerous food stalls, stands for the need to master desire. And the market represents the obligation to free oneself from the tyranny of material possessions.

Over the centuries, Hindu, Buddhist and Islamic eras in succession have left their imprint on the culture of Java, but, beneath them, an older, deeper Javanese tradition has persisted. It is a cult of kings, built on the notion that the souls of the great rulers of Javanese history possess an eternal supernatural power which is a continuation of the spirituality and charisma they demonstrated in life. Traditionally minded Javanese make humble pilgrimages to their tombs, to petition these royal saints and to offer sacrifices. This is the indigenous religion of Java, combining a belief in the maraboutic powers of charismatic individuals with the pious veneration of an enduring Javanese historical identity.

The nearest of these sacred sites was Kota Gede, the fortress-capital of the Mataram dynasty, which by now has been absorbed into the urban sprawl of Yogyakarta. To reach it, I walked through the villages on the semi-agricultural outskirts of the city, where junked cars and piles of worn-out tyres alternate with wet rice fields.

What remains of Kota Gede is a hamlet in an antique maze of lichen-covered brickwork gateways and pavilions, embellished in a curious zigzagging style, shaded by gigantic mango trees. Its name means 'great city', but the place is nothing more than a cemetery now. Here is entombed Senopati, a sixteenth-century king who founded the Mataram dynasty, the predecessor of the present line of sultans.

Inside the complex there are two large cisterns, deep stone tanks with wooden roofs. At one of them, I saw an elderly woman throwing pink-and-white flower petals on to the water, saying 'Eat! Eat!' to some albino catfish.

There is a legend about these catfish, which I reconstruct from the various broken-English versions I heard.

One night Senopati was entertaining one of the nine *walis* who had brought Islam to Java, Sunan Kalijogo. Senopati's wife served them catfish, cooked in curry. Kalijogo liked it, and asked what it was. Senopati told him, and with a kingly flourish said that, as a sign of his gratitude, Kalijogo and his descendants could eat as many as they liked for as long as Islam remained in Java. He told Kalijogo to throw the bones down from the balcony into the cistern. When he did so the flesh instantly grew back on to the bones, and the fish came back to life. The fish took on immortality, but also a white colour, which still distinguishes them.

These sacred immortal albino catfish (that eat flower petals) have the power to grant wishes. I wished that I might see the Sultan as soon as possible.

The royal cult's most important site is Imo Giri, twelve kilometres south of Yogyakarta, the sacred mountain at the summit of which almost all the kings of Java since the middle of the seventeenth century have been buried. It was founded by Sultan Agung (r. 1613–45), the hero-king of Javanese history and mythology, in order to establish the *keramat* – sainthood – of the rulers buried there, in spite of the fact that he was a Muslim and that there was nothing Islamic about putting royal graves at the top of a mountain. But he was Javanese.

In his *History of Java* (1817), Stamford Raffles records the following inscription in ancient Javanese on a stone found near Surabaya. It is advice to an unknown king: 'if you ever wish to fortify your soul, go to the summit of a mountain, which is the place for earnest supplication in silence, awaken your firm and sincere heart, let there not be any dregs of your nature; but let the soul assume non-existence and pray.' At the top of a mountain, one's soul is as close to God and as far away from the earth as it is possible to be. It is a matter of elementary spiritual geography. It is where Moses went to receive the tablets of divine law. It is where the kings of Buddhist scripture went to consult enlightened hermits.

Sultan Agung was a master of the spiritual exercises recommended in this inscription. They enabled him to attain mystical union with God for ten minutes at a time and, as a result, to accumulate and retain tremendous power. He is the greatest saint-king of all, and the model of Javanese kingship.

I climbed the 375 steps to the tombs. In amber candlelight in a low-ceilinged stone chamber, I sprinkled a fistful of pink-and-white flower petals over the sarcophagus of Sultan Agung, and prayed to the God of the Christians. An elderly *abdidalem* sitting beside it nodded and touched his bowl. I put in 500 rupiah.

These meditations were to prepare me for my encounter with the Sultan.

In every one of the kingdoms I had visited up to now I had seen the hand of the British at work, shaping, altering or inventing the institution of kingship and its history. I had come to Java hoping to find just one kingdom where this hadn't happened. But, as the result of obscure political manœuvrings in Europe in connection with the Napoleonic wars, the Dutch temporarily ceded Indonesia to the British, and for five years (1811–16) Indonesia was a British dominion. It was long enough, I discovered, for them to leave the mark I had come so far to escape.

In Yogyakarta, the most conspicuous evidence of British throne-craft is the Pakualaman, the principality ruled by the Pakualam (the Axle of the World), a subordinate state carved out of the kingdom of Yogyakarta to establish a political counterweight to the power of the sultanate. The author of this textbook application of the principle of divide and rule was Sir Thomas Stamford Raffles (d. 1826), the famous colonial administrator, naturalist and founder of Singapore, who was the first British Lieutenant-Governor (i.e. ruler, in this case) of Java and its dependencies.

The principality is nothing more than a quarter of the city of Yogyakarta with its own small and unremarkable palace. But, because of a deal brokered during the independence struggle between Hamengkubuwono IX and the Pakualam to cement relations between the two royal houses, the Pakualam and not the present Sultan is the Governor of the Special Region of Yogyakarta (population 2 million). The agreement was that Hamengkubuwono IX would be governor and the Pakualam Vice-Governor, with the Pakualam inheriting the position of Governor on the death of the old Sultan. It is one of the odd disjunctions of modern Indonesian politics that this junior prince should have the highest position in the region's government. It goes completely against the grain of expectations. Everyone in Yogyakarta thinks the new Sultan should be Governor.

The Pakualaman was created by the British, and as a result it has absolutely no metaphysical significance. Raffles gave the first Pakualam a state coach in 1814, a year after the principality was founded. It was Raffles's own personal coach; there wasn't time to order one from Britain. The Javanese did their best to turn it into a sacred royal object, and gave it the name The Honourable Lord Brilliant Black Pupil, but the regalia of the Pakualam are nothing compared with those of the Sultan.

When I visited, foam sofas were being unloaded from a truck outside the Gate of the Flowers Denoting Wisdom, for a 'shopping ceremony' to be held in the square in front of the palace that weekend.

There was also the matter of Solo, the second extant kingdom of central Java, whose king, the Sunan of Solo, Pakubuwono VIII, had not answered my letter. His name means 'The Pivot of the Universe'. The modern kingdom of Solo was created after the fall of Mataram in 1755, when the dynasty (which was based at Solo) split into two branches. One branch established itself at Yogyakarta, and the other at Solo (also known as Surakarta) sixty-five kilometres north-east of Yogyakarta, each separate kingdom considering itself superior to the other.

The forces of history have favoured Yogyakarta, particularly since independence. Solo's culture was always more conservative than Yogyakarta's, and the Sunan, believing the independence struggle to be a dark cloud that would pass in time, took the side of the Dutch, the guarantor of the court's peaceful introspection. The Dutch were defeated, Indonesia became independent, and Solo lost its remaining political influence.

There is a problem with cosmic harmony in Solo, as that act of poor political judgement demonstrated. The pivot of the universe is notoriously wobbly. In 1984 the palace burned down. In Java, why something happened is more important than how it happened. Some say the reason for the fire was that the *pusaka*, the sacred heirlooms, which normally protect the palace from fire, flood and earthquake, had lost their efficacy because they had not been looked after properly. Others say that the Sunan's spurned mistresses flew over the palace dropping fire on it. The Sunan had to make amends for his carelessness with a purification ceremony in the palace grounds; a bull's head was sacrificed, a ceremony that hadn't been performed for hundreds of years.

The Sunan spends little time in Solo, preferring to attend to private business interests in Jakarta. In Solo I was told that he maintains invisibility in order to enhance his prestige, but nobody believes that in Jakarta.

Nothing worked in Solo. Everything I attempted there came to naught, clear evidence of a deficiency of Harmony. In particular: (i) An American academic I was hoping to see there turned out to have left several months ago to start a teaching job in Chicago. (ii) My room in a guest-house had a wall that didn't reach the ceiling, and on the other side of the partition a pair of German hypochondriacs muttered and wheezed all night, and refused to turn out their light, despite my testy demand that they do so. (iii) The palace had been rebuilt and redecorated in a vulgar, fake manner, with a central pavilion encircled by kitschy garden-centre statues of Greek divinities 'to symbolize Christianity'! (iv) A palace official I had been recommended to see was also unavailable. When I got to his house there were wreaths outside, and groups of mourners coming out, bearing a coffin to a waiting hearse. I had just missed him.

By this time it was clear that I had exhausted this particular zone, and was ready to pass into the next zone of proximity. The most obviously visible of the boundaries set between the Sultan and the world was the wall that surrounded the royal city situated in the heart of Yogyakarta. The purpose of the wall, one kilometre square, was to prevent the Sultan's power from diffusing endlessly throughout the universe, to contain it. To pass through it was the next stage of my progress.

This thick, sloping, whitewashed rampart, discoloured by rain, fumes and fungus, with ornate turrets at each corner and a broad, cracked, concrete walkway along the top where children go to practise graffiti, and with in places a fetid ditch at its base, has been woven into the fabric of the town. Fruit-vendors, lottery-ticket-sellers, barbers, booksellers and motorcycle mechanics have built their shops against it. Patches of waste ground under it shelter beggars at night. The graceful arches of its elaborate gateways have been notched and gashed by the barging entry of trucks that have tried to squeeze through despite being too big. Decaying flybills pasted against it at eye level transmit broken signals about ephemeral events. It is festooned with telephone cables, and camouflaged by the trees and buildings that have grown up inside and outside it. In places it is completely invisible.

Besides keeping the Sultan's power in, the wall was intended to keep invaders out, of course. But this latter function has long ceased to be of any significance. In modern Yogyakarta, the wall is the *container* of the supernatural power that descends from God directly into the Sultan and spreads from him in concentric rings outward – to the *abdidalems*, their families, the population of the capital, and the kingdom as a whole – through ritual. On Thursday nights, the eve of the Muslim day of congregational prayer, residents of the town circumambulate the palace walls, hoping to accumulate some of the spiritual power radiating from the royal beacon within, an activity obviously analogous to the circumambulation of the Ka'ba at Mecca, the House of God, which like the Kraton is also considered the centre of the world.

Later I managed to meet up with a Kraton guide who was willing to share these mysteries with me, in more or less comprehensible English. Her name was Agustina, and she became my great guide and friend. One day I asked her about the custom of walking around the palace walls. 'It is true,' she said. 'I do it myself sometimes, even though I am Catholic. People in Jakarta say, "I need money, so I get a job." Here, if maybe I need clothes for my children, I walk around the palace walls and tomorrow my sister comes with some clothes and says, "Do you need these?" '

The area inside the palace walls, the *beteng*, was formerly exclusively inhabited by palace servants and officials. Because they live in this zone of proximity to the Sultan, the *abdidalems* are considered to possess a supernatural advantage that those living outside do not have. It was the most beautiful part of the city. I was longing to stay inside this area, not in the tourist ghetto I was occupying. Tourists are forbidden from staying here, but a few academic researchers had managed it, and I envied them. The umbrella of sky over my part of the town was brown with smog and the air roared with the ceaseless racket of motorcycle engines; here at night you could see the stars through the palm branches and the air was filled with birdsong. I would wander around the *beteng*, glimpsing the interiors of houses, with their glowing aquariums (pink and green) and televisions (blue-grey).

One night, as I was watching (over the blurring pages of *War and Peace*) the tropical fish in the illuminated tank in the Cirebon Restaurant sinking and floating in their stream of air bubbles, I struck up a conversation with one of the English-speaking youths who make a living as tourist guides. His name was Widinogroho. He said he lived inside the *beteng* and, after a while, invited me to come the following evening to visit him in his *kampung*. I was dying for an invitation to a home in the *beteng*: it meant I was penetrating the next layer of the onion.

The following evening, inside his studenty lodgings, Widinogroho gave me rambutans (a dark-red spiny fruit closely related to the lychee), freshly purchased from the market and still in their paper bag, and Java coffee, and I gave him a xeroxed copy of an ethnomusicological work about the court gamelan of Yogyakarta.

At one point in our conversation an old woman drifted past the doorway. Spying a visitor, she stopped at the door, and the youth got up to admit her. Her mouth was stained with betel-nut; she was ninety years old, and had only recently retired from her work as a masseuse. She said she had lived through the Japanese occupation, and spoke only Javanese, not Indonesian. She nodded proudly when Widinogroho translated these distinctions to me. She wore a woollen cardigan, a sarong, and worn plastic sandals. Her eyes were milky; I appeared before her as a mute, foreign blur.

'Do you eat rice in your country?' she asked me.

'No, we eat bread.'

'What crops do you grow?'

I had been asked this question before, in Swaziland, and was just as unable then to give a satisfactory answer. The only crop that came to mind was oil-seed rape, the tall synthetic-yellow plant that has disfigured the English countryside in recent years. Then I tried to focus my memory on the rudiments of the 'set-aside' programme of the European Common Agricultural Policy.

'Hay,' I said, at a loss. 'Apples.'

'What about strawberries?' her grandson said, springing to my aid.

'Oh yes, strawberries.'

He told her that I was interested in learning about past Sultans. She promptly slapped her knee and began to bawl out her favourite old anecdotes. She was particularly fond of Hamengkubuwono VIII, because her husband (long dead) had been a cook in the palace kitchen during his reign, and he used to be allowed to bring home huge quantities of food.

'Hamengkubuwono VII had four elephants. They used to bellow on important occasions. You should have heard them bellow at his funeral!' She slapped her knee. Elephants are beasts of war.

Then she began a half-hour monologue consisting of four stories about previous Sultans, three of them about Hamengkubuwono VIII and one about Hamengkubuwono IX, all of them variations on the theme of the king going among his people unrecognized.

Hamengkubuwono VIII loved the people, and he liked to check on the work of the *abdidalems*. To do this, he would occasionally go out disguised as an ordinary person. One day he issued a decree – his word was final – to the effect that no one should leave the city between the hours of the sunset and the night prayers. We don't ask why. To see that his word was being obeyed, he went out during the hours of curfew, dressed in humble clothes, wheeling a poor man's bicycle, like a poor man. As he passed the palace gates, a guard stopped him and said, 'Don't you know the king has said that no one may go out at this hour? Don't you respect the Sultan?' Not recognizing him, the guard took the disguised Sultan to the police station. But at the police station he was recognized. The guard was shocked, and went very pale.

Hamengkubuwono VIII owned a sugar-cane plantation, and he wanted to make sure that those in charge of the plantation were looking after it properly. So he went in disguise to the plantation and tried to steal sugar cane. A guard stopped him and reprimanded him, and he was sent to the same police station. The police chief recognized the Sultan, and the plantation guard was shocked.

A few months later, both guards – from the palace and from the plantation – were summoned to the palace. They both felt guilty for what they had done, and expected to be punished.

The Sultan said, 'You have carried out your jobs very well. I do not punish you but give you a reward instead.'

She slapped her knee and told another one.

Hamengkubuwono IX used to drive his own car from Jakarta (where he spent most of his time, serving as Defence Minister and Vice-President of Indonesia) to Yogyakarta. One day a vegetable-vendor was on her way from her village into town to sell her produce. The Sultan's car passed, and she flagged it down and asked the driver to take her to Kranggan Pasar, the main market in Yogyakarta. The driver helped her to load her goods into the car. At the market, the vendor offered to pay the driver, but he refused the money. She said, 'I will give you 1,000 rupiah. The normal fare is 500. Why don't you take it? Are you crazy?' Everyone in the market recognized the Sultan but didn't say anything. The Sultan helped the woman unload her vegetables, and then drove away. When he was gone, the other traders told the woman who the man was who had driven her into town. She was so shocked she died.

Other sources say 'fainted'.

Eventually I was given some likely days for an interview, then one day, then a precise hour. I was to present my questions in advance, written. 'His Majesty will answer some of them, but he may not answer all of them,' Suhardi said.

There was something he didn't want me to ask about, but at this stage I wasn't sure what it was.

I would go to sleep every night with the enigmatic broken English of Javanese explanations rattling around my head, while a pink gecko upside down on the ceiling scanned the menu in the dark.

But now I was effectively inside the palace.

The Kraton Yogyakarta has nine gates, which symbolize the nine orifices of the human body, which in the highest state of meditation are all closed. Each of the palace's squares and pavilions, which are set out in line, represents a stage in the spiritual development of a human being in the course of his life: conception, birth, adulthood, marriage and maturity. Therefore the palace represents the act of meditation on the progress of the virtuous individual through life. The abode of the Sultan is the last stage, the heart of the palace. The Sultan is the soul of the body politic, and the symbol of the individual soul in a state of fulfilment.

I bought a book called *The Royal Palace (Kraton) of Yogyakarta: its Architecture and its Meaning*, by a prince named K. P. H. Brongtodiningrat, which goes into this matter in detail. In it, he points out that the linear symbolism of the palace also represents the evolution of the human soul from a divine spark, passing through the influences of the four elements, to conception in the womb, to the development of head, heart and sex, to the development of the five potencies of spirit, feeling, soul, passion and mind.

K. P. H. Brongtodiningrat writes of the Kraton's metaphysical symmetries (in a chapter headed 'The Psycho-Genetical Meaning of the Architecture of the Kraton'); 'The enchanting beauty of the spot makes us feel serene and the darkness of our humour seems to leave us.'

But the front view of the palace was interrupted by two giant, rusting metal pylons, which illuminated the football pitch on the Alun-Alun Lor, the square which represents 'the image of the ocean of our mind which seems borderless and endless'. And across the square, cinemas showed violent oriental movies: the huge countenances of Bruce Lee and Charles Bronson, bleeding, furious, their heads wreathed in emblematic images of sadistic triumph and destruction, loomed over it from their billboards like malevolent deities. I missed one film called *Tricky Brains*, which looked good. I really wanted to see *Romantic Blood*, but didn't, and I never made it to *Bullet in the Head* (the image of the ocean of our mind).

When I told Mr Suhardi, soon after my arrival in Yogyakarta, that I wanted to investigate the sultanate's mystical dimension, I had naturally received an evasive response. While the container of kingship (the palace and everything connected with its outward show) was plainly visible to me, and radiated meaning, what it contained (its inner mysteries, the Sufi cult in operation) belonged to an invisible realm, reserved for its adepts, which I would never penetrate. Nevertheless, I was attracted, like a moth, to the glimmers of light that shone through the chinks in the closed door of that esoteric world of knowledge. After I had been in Yogyakarta for a few weeks, a bright glimmer occurred. It would soon be the Sultan's birthday.

In Java, one's birthday takes place every thirty-five days, owing to the use of a traditional calendar employing concurrently a five-day and a seven-day week. Any given day has two names, one from each cycle. The Sultan was born on Monday-Pon, and

Monday and Pon coincide once every thirty-five days thereafter. That conjunction – *selapan* – is one's birthday in the Javanese system.

Prayers offered on the eve of one's *selapan* are thought to be particularly effective, particularly the Sultan's prayers. On the eve of his *selapan* the Sultan is believed to attain mystical union, which draws down supernatural power from God which then radiates from him throughout the kingdom. He stays in ritual seclusion, fasting, accumulating power. To encourage him in this spiritual undertaking, he is given an offering of three kinds of rice gruel – plain, plain mixed with brown, and brown, representing Brahma, Vishnu and Shiva: the Hindu triad of birth, life and death.

I knew this, and soon after I arrived I asked Mr Suhardi when the *selapan* was. I was bound to be there when one took place.

'November the eleventh,' was his reply.

'Will I be able to attend it?'

'Yes.'

November the eleventh was Monday-Pon. In addition to private palace rituals, there was to be a concert of traditional gamelan music at the palace, broadcast live over Radio Republik Indonesia.

At the beginning of November I mentioned the *selapan* again. 'Will I be allowed to attend the *selapan* ceremony?'

'What ceremony?' he said.

I told him: the *selapan*. He seemed puzzled.

'We've been talking about it. We've spoken about it at least twice.' He acted as if he hadn't the faintest idea what I was talking about; it was like a mirage in my journey of waiting that evaporated as soon as I thought myself approaching it.

But Java unfolds its secrets like a ripe satsuma its segments: I could tell that I was being kept away from the reactor's core, so to speak: the Sultan in divine communion on the night of his *selapan*. Mr Suhardi thought I wanted to witness the intimate palace ritual, which of course I did, but I was willing to settle for the gamelan concert, and once that became clear Harmony prevailed. Mr Suhardi was properly acting as the Sultan's veil, seeking to protect the uninitiated (with no place in the theocratic hierarchy) from the bright blinding fire of the royal spirituality.

★

I have already mentioned Agustina, my guide. Mr Suhardi had kindly introduced me to her. She was one of the uniformed guides that escort tourists through the Kraton, pointing out and explaining its points of interest. She was small and serious, and spoke shattered English at a furious rate, a stream of speech fragments of such mind-boggling fancy (as she enthusiastically explained particularly recondite Javanese notions) that by the time one idea had settled down in my mind, in all its marvellousness, new ones were on the wing and I was missing them. Her father was a senior *abdidalem* – he lived in the palace precincts, while she lived just outside – and she had inherited his love of Javanese culture. With her help, I obtained a typed and officially stamped document from Krida Mardawa, the Kraton's office of music, permitting me to attend the broadcast concert in the palace on the night of the *selapan*. Thanks to Agustina, I was *inside* on the night of power.

I met her outside the Kraton on the evening of the concert. Inside, the transfigured, magical atmosphere which is the Kraton's intended state (i.e. before the indignity of tourism) had bloomed in the coolness of the night. I saw then that the ghosts of the tourists leave the palace promptly at the end of the day, but those of the past Sultans remain and come to life. A group of princesses, neatly coiffed, predominantly azure in costume, obscure fruit of the wide-spreading royal family tree, appeared through the foliage as we entered, standing in a trim row, accepting the greetings of guests. The wives and daughters and other unplaceable kinfolk of Hamengkubuwono IX, they lived discreetly in the cluster of cottages in the Kraton's heart, around the Sultan's residence.

As we passed through the courtyards of the Kraton, I saw a palace priest in white robes sitting under a pavilion in front of a charcoal-burner, surrounded by a circle of seated *abdidalems*, offering, Agustina told me, prayers and incense to the souls of dead Sultans.

We sat together on a mat on the polished tile platform of the gamelan pavilion. The musicians sat at their antique instruments. Apart from the radio engineers who sat beside the musicians, we were the only audience. As we waited for the concert to begin, we read from the *Kitab Betaljemur*, the Javanese manual of divination.

I wanted to see what the forecast was for my interview with the Sultan, which was scheduled for two days after the *selapan*.

The *Kitab Betaljemur* gives advice on all matters: where and when to dig a well, the character of new-born babies, which semiprecious stones to wear, talismans for keeping away evil spirits, what it means when you hear a ringing in your left ear early in the morning (you will be visited by a relative) – everything. It includes a thieves' horoscope, advising thieves on what to steal, the best hour to steal something, and in which direction to run after stealing it. This makes it easy to catch thieves, as thieves consult it and follow its recommendations exactly, and this makes their movements easy to predict.

In my case, the manual counselled against undertakings between the hours of six and eight in the morning on that particular day, and between twelve to two in the afternoon. As my interview was scheduled for 8.00 a.m., this was auspicious.

The concert began with the leader's rap on a hollow wooden block, setting in motion the gamelan's slow, elegant music. The concert lasted about three hours, with long pauses on the hour so that the radio station could broadcast the news.

Gamelan music is a crucial expression of Javanese royal ideology: its peaceful, regular sound – like a benign celestial clockwork – is a reflection of the ordered universe of which the court is the centre and the Sultan the invisible prime mover. Javanese court gamelan music employs longer, slower rhythmic phrases than the more frenetic, faster Balinese version: in Java the royal tradition is stronger than in Bali, and its music must reflect a universe that operates on vast scales of time and movement. The bigger the universe seems through its slow, stately musical representation, the more powerful appears the one who holds it in his lap.

It also supports the Sultan's role as an exemplar of traditional spirituality. It is peaceful, meditative music, demonstrating that the kingdom is not only the model of an ordered cosmos, it is the outward realization of inner tranquillity as well. Pythagoras believed that we love music because it reminds us of the celestial harmonies we heard before conception, before our souls descended to the earthly realm to be incarnated or incarcerated in our heavy, fleshly bodies. In Yogyakarta, you can hear that sound without waiting for the soul's liberation: in Stockhausen's words, 'The main thing is that we create sounds so pure that they are a vessel for the cosmic forces – let's say *the* cosmic force that runs through everything.'

The gamelan, which means the orchestra of mainly tuned percussion instruments, looks very easy to play. The musicians, many of whom are old men who have been playing it for most of their lives, are so familiar with the music that a performance is a distinctly casual affair: most players have a small glass of tea and a cigarette beside them as they play. With celestial mechanics this reliable, it's not necessary for musicians to exert themselves.

A gamelan piece has no written score, only an unwritten, understood, underlying melody in the minds of the performers: what they play only alludes to this original abstract melody.

The way this music is rehearsed reflects its harmonious, decorous philosophy. The musicians take their places at the beginning of a rehearsal with the minimum of discussion. Each is aware of his own rank and musical ability, and his position in relation to the rank and ability of others. A piece is performed from start to finish, without interruption, regardless of mistakes. There is none of the Western practice of stopping a piece and correcting an individual performer's error. When the piece is finished, they play it again from the beginning, and in this way the mistakes are gradually ironed out, but without causing embarrassment to anyone, and preserving the social harmony of the ensemble.

The musicians play elaborate ornate instruments with personal names like Lord Sweet Thunder, Fierce Fighting Dragon and Lord Flowing Honey.

I made several hours of tapes, that night and thereafter. Audible throughout the recordings is the high-pitched squeaky chattering of a large community of bats that inhabited the pagoda-like roof of the pavilion in which the orchestra played. When I mentioned the noise to one of the *abdidalems*, he said that, although the bats were a problem, it was pointless to drive them out as they returned immediately afterwards. They were the squeaky wheels in the celestial mechanism.

Kawindrasutikna, the head of Krida Mardawa, the Kraton's department of music, wore a large purple stone on a ring on the index finger of his right hand, and a large yellow stone on a ring on the index finger of his left hand, to balance the vital forces in his body. We sat on mats at a low table on the porch outside his office. Agustina translated. Before he attained his present position his name was Raden Rio Endradipura.

He said he had entered palace service as a dancer when he was sixteen. His father was a soldier, his grandfather was a monk, and his son is a pop musician. He had been an *abdidalem* for sixty-two years.

Under Hamengkubuwono X, there had been an increase in music in the Kraton, he said, in gamelan and *wayang wong* (the traditional dance drama). *Wayang wong* educates the character.

'You know that the present Sultan danced in the *wayang* as Arjuna,' he said – Arjuna being the warrior-prince-hero of the *Bhagavadgita*. (Like the young Louis XIV playing Apollo in court dramas.)

'Was he a good dancer?' I asked.

'Automatically.' Meaning, he was automatically a good dancer because he was a prince.

Kawindrasutikna's seniority, and his consequent position in one of the innermost rings of mystical proximity, owed less to his musical experience than to his length of service. He had been orbiting past and present Sultans for so long that he had accumulated a lot of radiated *kesakten*. The palace is not a meritocracy. One of the most senior *abdidalems* I met had been making tea (in a large iron pot) in the palace for the past fifty years. His work was superfluous. When large volumes of tea were needed, outside caterers were brought in. The important thing was that he behaved like an *abdidalem*: still and composed, reflecting the unchanging order over which the Sultan presides. *Abdidalems* are not expected to show initiative, for that belongs to the Sultan alone.

An elaborate etiquette is observed to regulate the relations between people of different grades in the hierarchy, from the Sultan at the top to junior *abdidalems* at the base of the pyramid.

The Javanese language is so formal in this respect that there are nine different ways of saying 'you', depending on the social status of the person you are talking to, and your status in relation to him.

Kawindrasutikna said, 'This job is not dynamic, it's not energetic. It looks like we have nothing to do. But we have the benefit of blessing from the Sultan. It's something you can't see, but it's possessed by the *pusaka* [the Sultan's sacred heirlooms]. I don't understand it exactly, but if I go to a sacred place – to the tomb of Sultan Agung – and meditate, I get blessing from it – a piece of the cake – so I will become better.'

So the motionless *abdidalems*, sitting decorously for hours on the shady porches of the royal pavilions, awaiting orders that never come – alert, aware, correct, calm – are not doing nothing: they are basking in the invisible rays that emanate from the Sultan.

The *pusaka*, the Sultan's crown jewels so to speak, also absorb this power because they have been handled by past Sultans. They have personal names, like Kangjeng Kyai Ageng Plered, a spear, or Kyai Ageng Kopek, a kris, or dagger. These sacred heirlooms are ritually cleaned once a year. Failure to look after them properly can upset the harmony of the realm, as in Solo. The *pusaka* give off a green glow, Suhardi told me. 'Her Majesty has experienced that. She told me personally. The strange thing is, one person might see it, and another who is present at the same time does not see it. That's why it's very difficult to prove.'

The palace swarms with the spirits of dead Sultans, and the *abdidalems* and those familiar with the palace can see them. Later I met the Keeper of the Yellow Pavilion. He told me that shortly after he began to work at the palace he saw a snake emerge from underneath the Yellow Pavilion. He knew it was the soul of a former Sultan, coming out for a breath of fresh air. Knowing it was the soul of a former Sultan, he did nothing to disturb it. Only persons who fast regularly have experiences of this sort, he said.

'Things happen in the palace that aren't logical,' Agustina said. That January, a dance performance had been put on at the Kraton for some American visitors. One of the dancers was wearing a mask of Garuda (the mythical bird ridden by Vishnu). All through the dance he kept hearing a voice behind him say, 'Give me a banana, give me a banana.' Afterwards he said, 'Who was that following me around the stage asking for a banana?' No one. So they made a sacrifice of bananas and incense, and the voice fell silent: it was a spirit that was hungry for a banana. 'Western people can't see any of this. It's like paper and metal: a magnet can pick up metal, but not paper.'

Suhardi too was affected by this. One day he said to me, 'Do you mind if I tell you this story? Shortly after I started working here, I needed a picture of Hamengkubuwono IX. I knew I had one, but, although I looked everywhere for it, I just couldn't find it. Then I said the words "Ngarso Dalem" [the first words of the Sultan's title, which have a magical force]. The next day, I saw the photograph right there on my desk. I can't explain it!'

Even the Dutch believed Hamengkubuwono IX could be in ten places at once.

One day I met an *abdidalem* who was acting as a guide in the Kraton. His name was Aris Soeyanto, and his palace name was Mas Bekel Joyowiruno. He showed me the coronation pavilion, then invited me back to his home for tea. He lived in a tiny house in what had obviously once been the royal stables, around the carriage museum. The stables had been turned into a *kampung*, with washing drying on lines and chickens running about.

His wife brought us jasmine tea, then lay on a wooden bed in the next room, quietly singing a pop song. She had short hair, wore a big white T-shirt, and was young and beautiful.

I asked him why he worked as an *abdidalem*. His eyes fell back deep, and became warm and dark, knowing and mysterious.

'We work here to become rich, but rich in the heart, not in money. I earn 3,750 rupiah a month. If I work twenty-four hours on guard duty, the pay is not enough to buy two packs of cigarettes. We gamble, but just as a game, to keep ourselves awake, for fifteen, twenty-five rupiah.'

He became an *abdidalem* of the lowest rank in 1975, and was promoted to *bekel* four years later. He is now a *bekel* of the third degree.

I told him that I was hoping to see the Sultan, and that I had been waiting for him to return from Europe. 'The Sultan was in London,' he said knowingly, 'attending a secret conference of kings and crown princes on the paranorm-AL.' Then he added, with a twinge of fear, 'But don't tell him I told you that.'

He had seen the spirit of the late Sultan. One night, three years before, he and some other *abdidalems* were keeping the night watch at the Kraton gatehouse. They were playing cards, gambling for small sums, to keep themselves awake. At this time, the late Sultan, Hamengkubuwono IX, was in a hospital in America, being treated for what was to be his last illness. At the hour of his death in America, the watchmen saw the figure of the Sultan pass through the gate and enter the palace.

Then the *bekel* fetched his kris – his ceremonial dagger – to show me, his sign of rank.

A kris can make you invulnerable to weapons. It can stand on its point, and can fight with other weapons. When taking it out of its sheath, you must move the blade slowly, meditating on the symbolism: the Sultan is the blade and the people are the sheath. The blade is the mystical knowledge; the sheath is the religious law that contains it in everyday life. The sheath is the walls that surround the palace; the blade is the Sultan's spiritual power contained in it.

The most powerful ones are made of meteorite iron, the miraculous metal that falls from heaven. The Ka'ba at Mecca has at its heart a rock of the same substance, a meteorite that was worshipped by the pagan Arabs before Islam claimed it for the Abrahamic tradition.

The oldest and most potent krises were made by men who had attained the highest levels of spiritual concentration. They could focus so much power through themselves that they could shape the iron of the blade with their thumbs. A kris transfers to its owner the spiritual condition of its maker, the mood he was in when he made it. If he was in love at the time, the owner will find it easy to fall in love. If he was thinking murderous thoughts, the blade will eventually be used to kill someone.

There was still the matter of 'mirrors for princes' to consider. This was a particularly rich field in Yogyakarta. Unlike the Emir of Kano, the Sultan of Yogyakarta had kept his library more or less intact. With the exception of the cheap calendar on the wall, and the tea in the glasses of the elderly *abdidalems* who looked after the place, nothing seemed to have changed in the Kraton library for eighty years. The librarians sat cross-legged at low wooden desks, nodding off amidst the timeless murmuring of the volumes of invented genealogies, usually going back to Adam, and mythological histories that defend past Sultans' claims to *wahyu*, the luminous aura of dynastic legitimacy that passes from one sultan to the next.

Agustina and I opened the richly illuminated *Babad Baratayuda* – a *wayang* (shadow-play) text based on the Hindu *Mahabharata* – to an illustration of two opposing armies, one led by a prince: a Javanese ruler in the role of Arjuna. The human figures looked like *wayang* puppets, stylized, thin warriors, hailing arrows at each other. The text's subject was legendary wars between ancient Javanese princely heroes, elevated and adorned to the level of scripture.

Traditional Javanese historiography is based on the premise that prophecy is the source that contains the richest ore of truth. We think that if a thing is made up it isn't true. For the Javanese, a thing is true *only* if it is made up. The intuitive inner meaning of history is far more important than a meaningless and disorderly array of facts. There is history of the past and history of the future. Both are equally valid as history. This approach allows the violent transfer of kingship from one scheming, murdering usurper to the next to be represented as the orderly, fated, divinely decreed transition of *wahyu* from one legitimate dynasty to the next. In 1705, for example, the Solonese Prince Pangeran Puger, with Dutch help, seized power from his nephew, Amangkurat III, becoming Pakubuwono I. In the *Babad Tanah Jawi*, the usurpation is transformed into an astonishing supernatural event:

The story was told that the king's [Amangkurat III's] manhood stood erect and on top of it was a glittering light the size of a grain of pepper. But nobody observed it. Only Pangeran Puger saw it. Pangeran Puger quickly sipped up the light . . . and the manhood ceased to stand erect. It was God's will that Pangeran Puger should succeed to the throne.

I longed to be able to read these books. My only clue to their contents was an English catalogue of the library's holdings, giving brief, tantalizing synopses of each volume. For example:

Serat Nitik Mataram, 1935: 'An examination of the reign of Sultan Agung, beginning with lessons on statecraft, moral education, divine worship, death and deliverance, followed by stories of the supernatural power of Sultan Agung.'

Serat Suryaraja Danureja VI, 1847: 'An extract of the allegorical pseudo-history describing the political views, background and reign of Hamengkubuwono II, from his appointment as Crown Prince up to his last years as Sultan. With instructions to his son, Panembahan Anangkurat on military strategy, statecraft and mysticism. Original manuscript by Hamengkubuwono II, presented as a *pusaka*.'

Serat Makutharaja, 1846: 'A manuscript on statecraft, beginning with guidance for kings on how to rule, followed by a brief account of such kings as Sultan Seda Krapyak, Sultan Agung, Amungkarat I, II, and III, Pakubuwono I, Amungkarat IV, Hamengkubuwono I, II, III and IV, ending with a mystical treatise on the human essence as the basis of the soul . . .'

All year, the Sultan saves his fingernail, toenail and hair clippings, and once a year he sacrifices them to Ratu Kidul, the Queen of the South Seas. Ratu Kidul is a kind of female Neptune: in the Javanese imagination she is green-skinned, coiffed in seashells, adorned with seaweed, and attended by finny courtiers. 'Ratu' is Austronesian for 'chief', and is still used in Fiji as a title.

One of the ceremonies attending the Sultan's coronation is his supernatural marriage to Ratu Kidul. The act represents the union of masculine and feminine principles in his person. In Javanese philosophy, the union of these two opposing, complementary principles signifies spiritual fulfilment; the act of sexual intercourse is consequently considered a kind of communion with God. This union of opposites in himself is one of the Sultan's most potent attributes.

The imagery of fulfilment through the union of the male and female principles has been adopted by traditions of kingship all over Asia, as if they were all drawing from the same imaginative well. Ancient Vietnamese kings styled themselves the Great Father and Mother King. The Aga Khan, leader of the Isma'ili sect, a figure who embodies many of the attributes of divine kingship, says when addressing his followers, 'I give to each of you . . . my most affectionate paternal maternal loving blessings.' On the straight path of human development represented by the architecture of the Kraton, the Sultan's throne on the raised platform called Siti Hinggil, the Kraton's most exalted spot, represents the stage of sexual intercourse, the union between male and female.

In *Psychology and Alchemy*, Jung analysed the symbolism of medieval treatises on alchemy. Alchemy's object was the attainment of gold, a pure metal. The alchemists believed that making it involved a process of refinement, of purging matter of its impure elements. Jung believed that the alchemists' conception of this process, as expressed in their otherwise opaque literature, was an analogy of the progress of the human soul towards fulfilment. He pointed out that one of the higher stages of this alchemical-spiritual progress is the Marriage of the King and Queen, the resolution of duality into oneness. For traditions of kingship to have adopted this beautiful conception leads one to the conclusion that kingship is ultimately a living symbol of the human self in its highest state. This is the ultimate meaning and purpose of kingship: as a symbol of the self in its highest state of fulfilment.

The annual rite of sacrifice to Ratu Kidul takes place at a village called Parangtritis, on the beach called Parangkusumo, twenty kilometres south of Yogyakarta. In addition to the shrine of Ratu Kidul, there are saints' tombs in the mountains overlooking the village, and Indonesia's generals come here from time to time to meditate in the caves. Known to tourists as Meningitis, Parangtritis itself has all the charm of Tijuana, a dead-end town addicted to excitement, but endlessly thwarted in its expectation of the big time.

There I sat at a table on the porch of a cheap hotel. The air was sticky and salt. There were flies everywhere. Two bored, sunburned Swedish girls turned up their eyes when I sat down. I ate a fried fish served in a swarm of flies. The landlady eyed me greedily (I suffered from walking-dollar-bill syndrome in Java), and asked me if I planned to stay the night at her hotel. When I said no and asked her what time the ceremony started, she mendaciously told me it started at ten o'clock, so that if I stayed till then I'd be compelled to stay in her hotel. But I knew that it was a sunset ritual.

After dinner, I looked at the shrine. It was a modest affair: a small altar in a walled enclosure with a floor of sand. With the help of a priest, dressed like a palace *abdidalem*, an old woman was burning offerings to Ratu Kidul. By the time she was finished it was dark.

The name Parangtritis means 'where the flower blooms at midnight'.

Finally the time came to enter the zone of intimate knowledge.

Like white light split into its component parts by a prism, *kesakten* divides into forces with different qualities once it is brought down into the sublunar realm. One of the colours, or wavelengths, into which *kesakten* divides is *keramat* (maraboutic sainthood). Another is *wahyu*, divinely given royal legitimacy, which is said to be greenish-blue in colour. *Wahyu* is the Arabic word for revelation or divine inspiration: the same word is used to describe the revelation of the Qur'an to the Prophet Muhammad. In Javanese tradition, it descends like a fireball from heaven into the person of the legitimate ruler. Bapak Sugiri, the Keeper of the Yellow Pavilion, said he had seen it one night in his garden, descending from the clouds and disappearing into the treetops.

By the time of Hamengkubuwono X's coronation in 1989, the people of Yogyakarta weren't sure that the *wahyu* had been transferred from the late Sultan, Hamengkubuwono IX, to the Crown Prince. Rumours abounded. According to one, there had been inadequate ceremony in the passing on from father to son of the important sacred dagger Kyai Jokopitur. This dagger, from which the Sultan must never be separated (like the US President's sacred briefcase containing the nuclear codes, the key to the annihilation of the world), must be passed personally from one Sultan to the next, to ensure an unbroken chain of spiritual succession. Hamengkubuwono X merely inherited it.

The kris was passed from Hamengkubuwono VIII to Hamengkubuwono IX in the most dramatic fashion. Ill and dying, the elderly Sultan abruptly summoned his young son home from his studies in the Netherlands, at the University of Leiden. It was 1939, and the Second World War was about to begin: 'the storm clouds were brewing.' The metaphor is apt in the light of what follows. The Crown Prince arrived home in October, and was met by his father at the port of Jakarta, then still called by its Dutch name, Batavia. As they rode together in the train to Yogyakarta, the old Sultan handed the sacred dagger to his son. Before the train reached Yogyakarta, the old Sultan lost consciousness. The train arrived, the Crown Prince disembarked and the Sultan was carried to hospital. Although it was the dry season and the sky was clear and sunny, the moment of royal disembarkation was accompanied by a peal of thunder. The Sultan died a few hours later. A few weeks later, Germany invaded the Netherlands. If the Crown Prince had stayed to complete his degree, the succession in Yogyakarta would have been broken.

The death of the king is always attended by omens and portents, to signify the world wobbling on its pivot. For example, *The Glass Palace Chronicle*, a chronicle of the ancient kings of Burma, records that on the death of King Rampaung in 301 BC, 'two suns appeared and fought till noon'; when Rakhan died in 220 BC, 'stars appeared in the daytime'; while on the day of the death of Hkanlaung (182 BC) 'a great shellfish dropped from the sky.' The thunder that signalled the transition from Hamengkubuwono VIII to Hamengkubuwono IX also marked a shift in historical eras: from an era of colonial dependency to an era of the Second World War, the Japanese occupation and the struggle for independence.

At his coronation, Hamengkubuwono X sat bolt upright on a backless stool, to demonstrate stiffness of spine, resolution. In his belt was the sacred dagger Kangjeng Kyai Slamet. During the ceremony he contemplated the verses of the Qur'anic sura 'Ikhlas', which means 'Sincerity of Heart in the Service of God' – the inner Islam, which no one can see, as opposed to the outer Islam of the law:

> Say, 'He is God, the One and Only;
> God, the Eternal, Absolute.
> He begetteth not, nor is He begotten;
> And there is none like Him.'

His face was a mask of hieratic calm. Hamengkubuwono's peaceful, steady gaze signified publicly that its power was unchanging and eternal. It showed that his spirit burned with a laminar flame, unruffled by temporal emotion. In his official portrait, his head is surrounded by an ethereal, golden glow. In this representation, the aura of *wahyu* resembled the Persian *farr*, the halo of flame traditionally shown around the head of a king in paintings.

His demeanour was *halus*: controlled, elegant, quiet. A serene composure represents the mastery of supernatural forces. It is the outward sign of intense spiritual discipline.

The Sultan is master of mysticism, master of meditation. The sign of his power is his ability to concentrate, to absorb supernatural power and to focus it through himself. Sitting under a tree, Sunan Kalijogo practised ascetic meditation with such firmness that the roots of the tree grew over him, and no one could find him. His meditation was so powerful that he could transport himself to Mecca to perform Friday prayers.

The Javanese also believe that power should not be seen to be exerted; that a ruler should not be seen to conquer his enemies: it should have happened already.

Hamengkubuwono X's coronation address was entitled 'The Momentum of Assured Resolution', and subtitled (less esoterically) 'A Throne Dedicated to the Welfare of People's Social and Cultural Life'. In it, he was careful to emphasize the role of the sultanate as a cultural institution dedicated to the principles of *Pancasila*, the ideology of the Republic of Indonesia. He noted that most of the people of Yogyakarta lived in poverty and ignorance, and announced his 'sincere devotion to uplift their dignity'. He promised to act in the best spirit of the sultanate's tradition of 'patrimonial leadership', and 'to endeavour to acquire the soul of the meaningful title of Hamengkubuwono, not merely inherit a throne'.

Even so, because of his inexperience and the disconcerting manner in which he had acquired the sacred dagger, there were some who weren't sure that the *wahyu* had been transferred to the new Sultan. But after a while people noticed a change in him: his face had become 'bright', they said. This was taken as evidence that the *wahyu* had come to rest with the new Sultan after all.

The feeling among the palace servants is that Hamengkubuwono X is still young in his spirituality, as he has only been Sultan for three years, and no miracles are expected of him yet.

The morning of my audience arrived. I was told to be fifteen minutes early, so I came half an hour early. I wore my usual ritual attire: the suit, tie, etc.

My interview with the one who holds the universe in his lap was a very formal encounter, although it was intended to convey informality. There were three of us, speaking three languages. I posed my questions (which had been submitted in writing a few days previously) in English; Mr Suhardi translated them into high Javanese, addressing the Sultan as 'Ngarso Dalem'; and the Sultan answered in Indonesian. If he spoke Javanese, he would have to use the highest speech level, the one reserved for the Sultan, and speak down to me and Mr Suhardi. As a leading Golkar politician, and an Indonesian, a republican and a democrat, he had to avoid this.

In fact I was amazed by the extent to which the Sultan tried to appear humble. He received us in a modest, homey sitting-room decorated with knick-knacks, some of which were splendid and fittingly awe-inspiring (a stuffed tiger), others sentimental and kitschy (a model of a geisha girl in a glass box, a model of the Prambanan temple in silver, a miniature koto on a stand). A door was open on to a garden that was still fresh with dew. Outside, there was a tennis-court, and a noisy caged bird that constantly interrupted our interview. I sat on a small sofa; he sat on a hard chair on a worn, fluffy pink cushion, leaning forward.

The Sultan wore slippers, a long-sleeved patterned shirt, black trousers, and rings with huge stones. He had a serious, sincere face, and a small black mole on his right cheek.

As a preliminary, I presented the gift I had brought him from London: a copy of *Sultans in Splendour*, a book of photographs of the Ottoman court. I was surprised to see him open the package and study the book attentively for several minutes, leafing through the pages, noting the author's biographical details on the flyleaf, making a careful show of appreciation. I had thought that Javanese etiquette determined that the Sultan would not acknowledge the gift at all (as the King of Tonga had not). Afterwards I mentioned this to Suhardi, and he told me that the Sultan was being 'democratic' in visibly appreciating my gift in my presence.

I began to work through my list of questions. The Sultan smoked American cigarettes while Mr Suhardi translated, nodding approvingly as the secretary spoke. Suhardi was there not just as an interpreter but in a role like that of the Tongan *matapule*, the king's speaker, the one who mediates between king and commoner. The Sultan understood English; the arrangement of having an interpreter preserved a formal distance between us, attempts at being 'democratic' notwithstanding.

I asked about *wahyu*. The Sultan spoke, and Suhardi nodded, and then turned to me and spoke. His answer was a traditional evocation of Javanese kingship, but it could easily have been a Sufi's description of progress along the path of mysticism to enlightenment: the ruler's union with the people here is analogous to God's union with the person.

'In Javanese philosophy, a leader must pass through stages. This is what is meant by *wahyu*. First he must pass through the stage of *laku*, which is the performance of good deeds for the people. This is a process that takes a long time. When a leader has practised *laku*, that means that he is supported by the people. When the people trust him, we say he has passed the stage of *sawiji*, which literally means 'being one'. It implies an intimate relationship between leader and subjects. After a leader has passed the stage of *sawiji*, then he receives *wahyu* from God Almighty. The people should then accept him as leader: there should not be any doubt, because he has passed the stages of *laku* and *sawiji* to *wahyu*. A leader should not think only of himself – this is the big difference from the Western political view.

'The philosophical meaning of the coronation itself is the vertical relationship between the king and God. But after the coronation there is another ceremony, a procession along the town walls, which is a symbolization of the horizontal relationship. There is a vertical relationship between the king and God, and a horizontal relationship between the king and the people.'

Having been obsessed for so long by the idea of 'mirrors for princes', I was interested to know how the Sultan perceived the matter of his own special education as Sultan.

'There isn't any special education for the Sultan, since he is living in a republican country. This is quite different from his predecessors, who were living under Dutch colonialism. But the late Sultan, his father, taught him to join social and political organizations, to talk to people, to give speeches and lectures, to form a close relationship with society.

'At present, as we know from palace traditions, the king or Sultan is the decision-maker. Everything is decided by the Sultan, but at the same time the Sultan is in the political movement in Yogyakarta, and is the head of Golkar, an organization in which democracy is important. There seems to be a dilemma for the Sultan, so he combines both systems. While in the palace, the Sultan is the decision-maker; in the organization, he considers the opinions of other officials.'

That was the gist of it.

A female servant came in with a tray of tea and cakes which she placed on the low table between my chair and the Sultan's. Traditional court etiquette compelled her to waddle on her haunches while moving in the presence of the Presence. Having put the tray down (with commendable steadiness of hand), she then held her hands to her face in the conventional attitude of prayer, her two thumbs parallel and pointing upward and held under her nose, in token of respect. Then she waddled out. I lost track of what the Sultan was saying while this display of contortionism was going on.

Agustina had said to me that, like most Yogyakarta people, she thought the Sultan should be the Governor of the state some day. I asked him if he wanted to be Governor. It would, after all, be natural. It was only according to a deal made at the time of independence that the present Pakualam is now Governor.

The Sultan himself dealt with the question with the skill of a politician who is also a good tennis-player. He answered, then sat back and savoured his smoke as Suhardi translated. He nodded in support of Suhardi's choice of words, regarding me serenely.

'His Majesty never thinks of it, because it depends on the central government in Jakarta. As you know, as soon as the Sultan begins to think of a political role, that implies ambition, and that would be in contradiction to his status as the Sultan of Yogyakarta, and betraying the ancestors' code.'

As we worked our way down the list of questions, I was approaching the one that would penetrate the final layer of the onion. It was question number seven, concerning his spiritual role. I wanted to know what a living Sultan thought about his role as the conduit of divine power. As if sensing my increasing tension as the moment drew near, Suhardi broached the matter first.

'His Majesty says, with regard to question seven, that everything he has to say on the matter can be read in his coronation speech, a copy of which I will give you, in English translation.'

My first attempt to grasp the key of power had failed. I read the speech later. It said nothing about meditation.

Then the Sultan very modestly excused himself to receive the Chief of Police in the Yellow Pavilion.

'His Majesty has very tight schedules,' Suhardi said in explanation, smiling sycophantically. Tick tock.

Rather than waste time while the Sultan was away, I asked if I could see the inside of a room I'd passed on my way into the room in which our interview was taking place; it seemed much grander and more interesting than the one we were in.

'Can I look in that room there?'

'No! You can look in, but you cannot go inside.' He was very firm about this.

I stood at the threshhold of the Sultan's bedchamber. The focal point was an enormous bed, with two statues of seated figures, male and female, in wedding costume, on either side of it. This was the bed on which the fertility of the realm would be ensured. There was a little cocktail bar with wheels, stocked with bottles of aperitifs.

Like most kings, the Sultans of Yogyakarta had numerous wives and countless children – in the Javanese case, to demonstrate possession of *kesakten*. Hamengkubuwono IX had five wives, fifteen sons and sixteen daughters, but Hamengkubuwono X has only one wife and five daughters. (I asked a guide why the Sultan only had one wife. The answer was Indonesian rather than Javanese: 'family planning'. The Sultan was showing a good example of population control in the fourth most populous country in the world.)

He returned from his meeting. In my second attempt at asking him about his spiritual role, I put the question in terms of the external forms of religion, rather than the inner form. I saw again that Suhardi was trying to avert my curiosity from the mystic centre: the hidden must remain hidden, while the stranger, in Java on a tourist visa subject to expiration, must make do with the visible.

'As you know, one of his royal titles is "Khalifatullah", and His Majesty himself is a *hajji*: he has made the pilgrimage to Mecca. He very often is in communication with people from other religious groups . . . There were fifteen ulema at his coronation . . . Very often His Majesty is invited to open a new church . . .'

On the third attempt, I got an answer: 'Speaking of the meditation, His Majesty still observes it, but, since the society is changing from traditional to modern, His Majesty would not like to expose that kind of thing. That is, he would rather refrain from talking about that to society, because it might elicit some contradictions, opinions and so on. This is a very personal matter which he observes in his own way. The important thing is that, by meditating, he will be given some warning to be faithful to his mission.'

In other words, as a politician, he doesn't want to say, Vote for me, I can make the sea boil.

Finally, the Sultan proudly showed me his enormous royal bed, and suavely smoked a Marlboro as I stood and admired it.

Three times during my stay in Yogyakarta I would cycle up to the northern part of the city, over the river on whose steep banks the rickety wooden houses of the poor perched precariously, beyond the Gadjah Mada University, past the students' food stalls, to see Dr Suparjar, a mystic, and a lecturer at the university, and he would explain to me the mystical significance of things. His commentaries touched on everything, including the meaning of life itself.[1]

I went to see him the day after my interview with the Sultan. The previous night, I had had a dream in which the Sultan had invited me, and a group of other Westerners, to dinner at the Kraton. There were about thirty of us altogether, and we travelled part of the way to the Kraton by helicopter, over water.

I dreamed that we sat in groups in a large reception room, and I met the Sultan's wife, who (in my dream) turned out to be American, with red hair. A little girl, their daughter, amused us with impressions of different types of furniture. At one point she stood on a *chaise longue* and upset a cup of coffee which I had placed on it, spilling coffee on to the upholstery. The Sultan was very agitated by this, and told me to wash the covering immediately, so that it wouldn't stain. I pulled it off. As it was attached with Velcro, the Sultan thought I was tearing the fabric,

[1] In Javanese philosophy, the meaning of life lies in the spirit of the moment in which you were conceived. To lead a fulfilling life, recollect the moment of your conception and live in the spirit of it.

Why? Because within this moment the union of the male and female principles takes place, which is the basis of the fulfilled self and in human beings is an analogue of union with the divine.

The enduring puzzle of the 'meaning of life' is based on a prior assumption that life is fulfilled through meaning: that human life is a meaningful text that is fulfilled only through being read and understood. An animal can lead a fulfilled life without feeling the need for meaning in it.

which alarmed him further, and so on. A variation of the common anxiety dream.

When I arrived at Dr Suparjar's house, he said to me, 'Are you having dinner with the Sultan tonight? He has invited a group of foreigners to dine with him.'

I said I hadn't been so favoured, while inwardly noting that Dr Suparjar's reputation for expertise in the 'paranorm-AL' was indeed well earned.

A pantheon of divine beings danced in his imagination: Jesus, Vishnu, Muhammad, Ali and Bima (a character in the Javanese shadow-play). 'But the Prophet Khidr is the most powerful of all,' he believed.

He described the scene that had eluded me, the non-existent core of the onion: the meaning and end of kingship. It was the end of the journey.

'It is to be found when the Sultan is on his throne, and the *abdidalems* are sitting around him calmly, together seeing the Alif. That's real meditation, real power. It comes from him not as a man but as one who sits at the feet of God. Hamengkubuwono represents the concentricity of inner space and outer space: that is, cosmic consciousness.'

The day before I left Yogyakarta, I watched the Sultan playing in a football match between Golkar and local government officials.

The rainy season had started. The streets were flooded, and the alleys grey with mud. Outside the stadium, the noodle-vendors had set up their stalls under improvised awnings. Inside, the Sultan and the other politicos sat in their VIP tent. The Sultan had stepped out of his mystical aura; he wore a purple warm-up suit, smoked a big cigar, and bantered broadly, with his arm over the back of his neighbour's chair – body language that would have become an American politician of the good ol' boy school, rather than the refined prince Arjuna he used to play in palace dramas. Loud Indonesian pop music blared over the PA system.

The rain came down heavily. We waited for it to subside, but it didn't, so the teams decided to go on to the field and start the game in spite of it, which showed a gung-ho spirit becoming in the governing party.

I beheld two dozen paunchy, desk-bound men in their forties playing football in a tropical downpour but making the best of it. The commentary was lively and loud. The Sultan, playing full back, acquitted himself honourably. Whenever he got hold of the ball, the commentator enthusiastically referred to him as 'Sri Sultan' or, when he had time, by the title 'Sultan Hamengkubuwono X'. The Sultan played a very *halus* game, exemplifying power-retentive Javanese kingship. Like Arjuna on the battlefield remaining still and unmoved in the presence of his enemies, he didn't try to score, or attempt anything flashy, unlike his distinguished team-mates, who thought the key to victory and success lay in heading the ball over the longest possible distance. Everyone but Sultan Hamengkubuwono X was gambling vaingloriously with serious neck injury. The meaning of his game was twofold. Its exterior meaning was, I am a team player. Its interior meaning was, I retain power.

After the match, the Sultan gave out the prizes. The teams lined up in a row, and he handed out soccer balls from a plastic sack, and jerseys that by now were soaking wet from the rain.

God alone is omniscient.

Select Bibliography

TONGA

Sione Latukefu, *Church and State in Tonga*, Canberra: Australian National University Press, 1974.

John Martin M.D., *Tonga Islands: William Mariner's Account*, Tonga: Vava'u Press, 1981.

J. C. Beaglehole, *The Journals of Captain Cook on his Voyages of Discovery*, Cambridge: Cambridge University Press, 4 vols., 1955–67.

Noel Rutherford, ed., *The Friendly Islands: a History of Tonga*, Melbourne: Oxford University Press, 1977.

OMAN

John Wilkinson, *The Imamate Tradition in Oman*, Cambridge: Cambridge University Press, 1987.

Wendell Phillips, *Oman: a History*, London: Longmans, 1967.

Frederik Barth, *Sohar*, Baltimore: Johns Hopkins University Press, 1985.

John Townsend, *Oman: The Making of a Modern State*, London: Croom Helm, 1977.

J. E. Peterson, *Oman in the Twentieth Century: Political Foundations of an Emerging State*, Croom Helm/Barnes & Noble: London/New York, 1978.

NIGERIA

William Bascom, *The Yoruba of Southwestern Nigeria*, Illinois: Waveland Press, 1984.

Robert Smith, *Kingdoms of the Yoruba*, London: James Currey, 1988.
Sir Alan Burns, *History of Nigeria*, London: George Allen and Unwin, 1972.
The Revd Samuel Johnson, *The History of the Yorubas*, London: Routledge, 1921, and Lagos: CSS Bookshops.
Hugh Clapperton, *Journal of a Second Expedition into the Interior of Africa*, London: John Murray, 1829.
Richard Lander, *Records of Captain Clapperton's Last Expedition to Africa*, London: Cass, 2 vols., 1967.

SWAZILAND

J. S. M. Matsebula, *A History of Swaziland*, 3rd edn, Cape Town: Longman, 1988.
Hilda Kuper, *The Swazi: a South African Kingdom*, 2nd edn, New York: Holt, Rinehart and Winston, 1986.
Hilda Kuper, *Sobhuza II: Ngwenyama and King of Swaziland*, London: Duckworth, 1978.
Philip Bonner, *Kings, Commoners and Concessionaires: The Evolution and Dissolution of the Nineteenth-Century Swazi State*, Cambridge: Cambridge University Press, 1982.
A. R. Booth, *Swaziland: Tradition and Change in a Southern African Kingdom*, Boulder: Westview, 1983.

JAVA

Koji Miyakazi, *The King and the People: the Conceptual Structure of a Javanese Kingdom*, University of Leiden dissertation, 1988.
R. Heine-Geldern, 'Conceptions of State and Kingship in Southeast Asia', *Far Eastern Quarterly* 12 (1942), 15–30.
M. C. Ricklefs, *A History of Modern Indonesia*, London: Macmillan, 1981.
Mark R. Woodward, *Islam in Java: Normative Piety and Mysticism in the Sultanate of Yogyakarta*, Tucson: University of Arizona Press, 1989.
Roger Vetter, *Music for the Lap of the World: Gamelan Performance, Performers and Repertoire in the Kraton Yogyakarta*, PhD dissertation, University of Wisconsin: Madison, 1986.

Benedict R. O'G. Anderson, 'The Idea of Power in Javanese Culture', in *Culture and Politics in Indonesia*, ed. C. Holt, Ithaca: Cornell University Press, 1972.

KINGSHIP

David Cannadine and Simon Price, eds, *Rituals of Royalty: Power and Ceremonial in Traditional Societies*, Cambridge: Cambridge University Press, 1987.

Clifford Geertz, 'Centers, Kings and Charisma: Reflections on the Symbolics of Power', in *Local Knowledge: Further Essays in Interpretive Anthropology*, New York: Basic Books, 1983.

Norbert Elias, *The Court Society*, New York: Pantheon, 1983.

Louis Marin, *Portrait of the King*, Minneapolis: University of Minnesota Press, 1988.

MIRRORS FOR PRINCES

Wisdom of Royal Glory (*Kutadqu Biliq*), *A Turko-Islamic Mirror for Princes*, tr. Robert Dankoff, Chicago: University of Chicago Press, 1983.

T. H. Baldwin, *The Obligations of Princes* (translation of al-Maghili's *Taj al-Muluk*), Beirut, 1932.

Kai Ka'us b. Iskandar, Prince of Gurgan, *A Mirror for Princes: The Qabus Nama*, tr. Reuben Levy, London: Cresset Press, 1951.

An English translation of 'The Book of the Secret of Secrets', falsely ascribed to Aristotle, appeared in Steele's edition of the Latin *Secretum*, Fasc. V (1920), *Opera hactenus inedita Rogeri Baconi*, Oxford: Oxford University Press, 1909–40.

al-Ghazali, *Book of Counsel for Kings* (*Nasihat al-Muluk*), tr. F. R. C. Bagley, Oxford: Oxford University Press, 1964.

Index